Using Key Passages to Understand Literature, Theory and Criticism

Using Key Passages to Understand Literature, Theory and Criticism is a completely fresh and innovative approach to teaching and learning literary theory: using short passages of theory to make sense of literary and cultural texts. It focuses on the key concepts that help readers understand literature and cultural events in new and provocative ways. Covering a wide variety of iconic and contemporary theorists, the book offers a broad chronological and global overview, including thirty passages from theorists such as Viktor Shklovsky, Roland Barthes, Judith Butler, Diana Fuss, Jean Baudrillard, Kwame Anthony Appiah, Michel Foucault, Monique Wittig, and Eve Sedgwick.

Built on the premise that scholars use theory pragmatically, *Using Key Passages to Understand Literature, Theory and Criticism* identifies problems, puzzles, and questions readers may encounter when they read a story, watch a film, or look at artwork. It explains, in detail, thirty concepts that help readers make sense of these works and invites students to apply the concepts to a range of writing and research projects. The textbook concludes by helping students read theory with an eye on finding productive passages and writing their own "theory chapter," signaling a shift from student as critic to student as theorist.

Used as a main text in introductory theory courses or as a supplement to any literature, film, theater, or art course, this book helps students read closely and think critically.

Barry Laga is a Professor of English and the Department Head of Languages, Literature, and Mass Communication at Colorado Mesa University, USA. He teaches literary theory, American literature, film, and composition, and publishes on American literature, film, and cultural studies. He was a Fulbright Scholar at Universiteit Antwerpen, Belgium, and Universität Leipzig, Germany.

Using Key Passages to Understand Literature, Theory and Criticism

Barry Laga

Routledge
Taylor & Francis Group

LONDON AND NEW YORK

First published 2019
by Routledge
2 Park Square, Milton Park, Abingdon, Oxon OX14 4RN

and by Routledge
711 Third Avenue, New York, NY 10017

Routledge is an imprint of the Taylor & Francis Group, an informa business

© 2019 Barry Laga

The right of Barry Laga to be identified as author of this work has been asserted by him in accordance with sections 77 and 78 of the Copyright, Designs and Patents Act 1988.

All rights reserved. No part of this book may be reprinted or reproduced or utilised in any form or by any electronic, mechanical, or other means, now known or hereafter invented, including photocopying and recording, or in any information storage or retrieval system, without permission in writing from the publishers.

Trademark notice: Product or corporate names may be trademarks or registered trademarks, and are used only for identification and explanation without intent to infringe.

British Library Cataloguing-in-Publication Data
A catalogue record for this book is available from the British Library

Library of Congress Cataloging-in-Publication Data
Names: Laga, Barry, author.
Title: An introduction to theory and criticism: using key passages to understand literature and culture / Barry Laga.
Description: Abingdon, Oxon; New York, NY: Routledge, 2019. | Includes bibliographical references and index.
Identifiers: LCCN 2018022046 | ISBN 9781138561953 (hardback; alk. paper) | ISBN 9781138561977 (pbk.; alk. paper) | ISBN 9781351357487 (web pdf) | ISBN 9781351357463 (mobikindle)
Subjects: LCSH: Literature—History and criticism—Theory, etc. | Criticism.
Classification: LCC PN81.L34 2019 | DDC 801/.95—dc23
LC record available at https://lccn.loc.gov/2018022046

ISBN: 978-1-138-56195-3 (hbk)
ISBN: 978-1-138-56197-7 (pbk)
ISBN: 978-0-203-71017-3 (ebk)

Typeset in Bembo
by codeMantra

Contents

	Acknowledgments	vii
	Introduction: joining the community	1
1	Becoming a subject	14
2	Scripting identity	22
3	Doing not describing	29
4	Enjoying the carnivalesque	38
5	Reading as writing	46
6	Simulating the real	53
7	Creating a space between	61
8	Performing gender	70
9	Locating trauma	77
10	Intersecting identities	84
11	Locating alterity	93
12	Poaching texts	101

13	Cultivating rhizomes	108
14	Reconciling double consciousness	117
15	Shocking readers	123
16	Joining power and knowledge	130
17	Revealing the uncanny	137
18	Questioning human/nonhuman boundaries	144
19	Historicizing and contextualizing	152
20	Signifying through time	160
21	Thinking ecologically	166
22	Recognizing conceptual metaphors	174
23	Representing disability	181
24	Losing and recovering our sovereignty	189
25	Resisting the dominant culture	196
26	Adapting and appropriating	204
27	Describing homosocial relationships	213
28	Defamiliarizing the familiar	221
29	Questioning gender binaries	229
30	Building on another's work: identifying key concepts	237
	Index	243

Acknowledgments

Fingerprints cover this textbook, from my professors at Purdue University and Brigham Young University who laid a solid foundation to my students at Colorado Mesa University who reminded me to keep learning, from Becky Bernal and other CMU library support staff to my administrative assistant Angela Kimmel and student assistant Jordann Morgan who completed endless favors. I am particularly grateful for my colleagues Colin Carman, Robin Calland, Kurt Haas, Julie Barak, William Wright, Kristen Hague, and Eric Lackey. They responded to ideas, offered advice, supplied examples, read chapters, and expressed enthusiasm for the project. I am grateful for my children Ian, Hillary, and Conrad who read chapters or at least nodded approvingly. I owe much to the readers who vetted my proposal and voiced their approval. I am especially thankful for Polly Dodson, Ruth Hilsdon, Zoë Meyer, and Emma-Leigh Craig at Routledge who believed in the project's potential and labored to improve my work. I thank as well Paige Force and her editorial and publishing team at codeMantra. Above all, I am indebted to my wife Caprice, a diligent and close reader, who saved me from many embarrassing errors. She is my most enthusiastic supporter and collaborator.

Introduction

Joining the community

> We stand, above all, for sharing the powers and pleasures of this language with one another and with all those who seek our guidance in attaining those powers and pleasures.
>
> (Robert Scholes *Rise* 72)

WHAT DO CRITICS AND THEORISTS DO?

When we read George Saunders' *Lincoln in the Bardo* (2017), view Yorgos Lanthimos' *The Lobster* (2015), look at Pablo Picasso's *Les Demoiselles d'Avignon* (1907), watch August Wilson's *The Piano Lesson* (1987), or stare at Marina Abramović in the Museum of Modern Art, we can take at least two paths: critique or theorize. Criticism and theory invite us to pose different kinds of questions, ask us to engage with what we read and watch in different ways. Criticism and theory give us something to *do* when we read, watch, listen, and participate.

Critics interpret

What does it mean to "interpret" a text? Most conventionally, interpretation means to "expound the meaning of," "to render (words, writings, an author, etc.) clear or explicit," and "to elucidate; to explain" ("Interpret" 1131). In his analysis of T. S. Eliot's "The Waste Land" (1922), Lawrence Rainey adds that when we are "confronted with inexplicable patterns and mazes of contradiction, we seek a hidden shapeliness that will enable us to accommodate them" (124). Interpreting, then, is the act of integrating the new and unfamiliar into a meaningful network. We make the unfamiliar familiar. Finally, Steven Mailloux reminds us that "to interpret" finds its roots in the Latin *interpretatio*, suggesting "to expound" and "to explain," but also "to translate." He adds that "in its etymology, then, 'interpretation' conveys the sense of a translation pointed in two directions simultaneously: *toward* a text to be interpreted and *for* an audience in need of the interpretation" (121). Therefore, when we ponder a poem, read a story, watch a film, or view art, we make the obscure known, the indirect straightforward, and the ambiguous explicit. We clarify the parts we don't understand, explain how elements work together, recognize underlying patterns, and translate the literal and the figurative, all in an effort to construct meaning, identify significance, discern a purpose or effect, and connect with others.

Critics judge and evaluate

We certainly care about the quality of our art, and as a result, we evaluate or judge a work's merit, value, and craft. We assess how well a text measures up to a standard. For example, in his review of the film *Annihilation* (2018), Christopher Orr asserts that

> Leigh's Ventress is deliberately enigmatic but, once revealed, her secret is utterly inconsequential. And while Portman's grief and guilt—explained in part by a painfully unnecessary backstory—are meant to be a primary engine of the film, they never quite coalesce into anything moving or meaningful.

Katy Waldman reviews Kate Braverman's collection of short fiction *A Good Day for Seppuku* (2018), and she concludes that "Braverman excels at flooding readers in images that throb with menace or pleasure, as if descriptive language were a vein into which our most primal fears and desires could be injected." Note that Waldman and Orr are passing judgment, assessing how well the film and short stories do what they do. Phrases like "inconsequential," "painfully unnecessary backstory," "never quite coalesce," and "excels" focus our attention on quality of execution instead of deciphering, elucidating, or translating the work for us.

In short, as critics, we make two critical moves: we judge a text's value and quality, and we make a text meaningful and intelligible. Or as Robert Scholes suggests, we read centrifugally, embracing "the life of a text as occurring along its circumference, which is constantly expanding, encompassing new possibilities of meaning" (*Protocols*, 8).

If a critic makes sense of a text and judges its worth, what does a theorist do?

Theorists generate and question standards and criteria

Theorists generate and interrogate the very standards we use to evaluate or judge a text. If a critic says, "The novel is well written," the theorist asks, "How do you define 'well written'?" If the critic declares that Shakespeare's *Hamlet* transcends its time, then the theorist may question whether it is possible for any work to "transcend its time." And criteria surround us, from ancient Rome's Horace who declares that "Poets aim either to benefit or to please, or to combine the giving of pleasure with some useful precepts for life" (107) to Richard Rorty's "If it is to have inspirational value, a work must be allowed to recontexualize much of what you previously thought you knew" (133). Matthew Arnold is a theorist when he declares that "the best poetry will be found to have a power of forming, sustaining, and delighting us" (430), and Harold Bloom theorizes when he asserts that "The strongest poetry is cognitively and imaginatively too difficult to be read deeply by more than a relative few of any social class, gender, race, or ethnic origin" (520). In other words, theorists establish or define standards and criteria and argue with other people's criteria or definitions of quality.

Theorists define and redefine

We theorize the moment we define a word, concept, or category, just as Karen Armstrong is a theorist when she asserts that "mythology is an art form that points beyond history to what is timeless in human existence, helping us to get behind the chaotic flux of random events, and glimpse the core of reality" (7), and David Bartholomae theorizes when he claims that "strong readers ... remake what they have read to serve their own ends" ("Introduction" 15). Ross Murfin and Supryia M. Ray are theorists when they define a lyric poem as "a brief imaginative and melodic poem characterized by the fervent but structured expression of the personal thoughts and emotions of a single, first-person speaker" (276). Mary Louise Pratt theorizes when she writes that "autoethnographic texts are representations that the so-defined others construct *in response to* or in dialogue with those texts" (35). In sum, this kind of theorist describes or questions the nature, scope, and qualities of words, concepts, and categories.

Theorists describe methods

Theorists explain *how* to do something; they offer a methodology. The moment I tell you *how* to read or write poetry, I am a theorist. Robert Scholes theorizes when he asserts that reading requires us to "uncover the implications of the opposition by exploring all the relationships of similarity and difference" (*Textual Power* 33). Paul Bové offers us a methodology when he writes, "We might ask such things as, How does language work to produce knowledge? How is language organized into disciplines?" (62). Jacques Derrida clarifies a methodology when he insists that "Deconstruction does not consist in moving from one concept to another, but in reversing and displacing a conceptual order as well as the nonconceptual order with which it is articulated" (21). Scholes, Bové, and Derrida theorize when they describe a strategy, technique, or *way* to understand and make sense of what we read and watch.

Theorists describe general principles and explain phenomena

To describe the final role theorists play, it may help to first think about science. Writing for *National Geographic*, David Quammen reminds us that theory is "not a dreamy and unreliable speculation, but an explanatory statement that fits the evidence." The *Oxford English Dictionary* echoes this definition by noting that a theory is a "scheme or system of ideas or statements held as an explanation or account of a group of facts or phenomena" ("Theory" 902). Both definitions convey the same function: a theory provides a framework for understanding what we experience and observe.

Literary and cultural theorists are engaged in the same activity, but instead of focusing on natural phenomena like gravity, evolution, and atoms, they concentrate on cultural practices, representations, and language. To borrow from the language the *OED* employs, literary and cultural theorists describe a scheme or system of ideas or statements held as an explanation or account of what texts are and what they do, how they do what they do, and how we produce them, their effect on us, and what we do with them. They propose general principles (not just an explanation of a particular poem or novel) and explain literary phenomena. Or, as Rita Felski summarizes, "theory simply is the process of reflecting on the underlying frameworks, principles, and assumptions that shape our individual acts of interpretation" (2). For example, what is literature? What characterizes the "literary"? What is the purpose of literature? What is the relationship between the author, reader, context, and the text? What is the connection between historical contexts, literature, and literary practices? Why do writers write and readers read? What is the relationship between the reader and writer and racial, sexual, geographic, class, or gender identities? What is the source of creativity? What is the role of the reader and the writer? Notice that all those questions address ambitious foundational issues. They address principles and categories. They investigate literary and cultural phenomena. The answers to these questions apply, not to particular texts, but to entire categories of texts, readers, writers, and situations.

Theorists and critics work together

We discuss theorists and critics as though they never cross paths. However, not only do critics and theorists need each other, sometimes our argument requires us to both theorize and critique. We may define a concept and apply it, generate a standard, then use it, describe a method, then test it, or gather eclectic examples and propose a scheme to make sense of them. Gilberto Perez sums up the relationship between theory and criticism rather well:

> We need theory to organize our observations and make sense of our experience. But, in its turn, theory needs the test of experience. We must check a theory against the evidence, and we must be prepared to revise or rethink the theory in active give and take with what we observe. Theory hand in hand with experiment, sometimes theory leading the way, sometimes experiment: That is how theory works in science.... In the study of the arts, what takes the place of scientific experiment is what we call criticism. Criticism is the eye that perceives, the mind that apprehends, the sensibility that takes in the actual work of art.

We aspire to this double role. We learn to move back and forth between theory and criticism. An established theory helps us understand a difficult text that confuses or perplexes us. A concept may help us understand a work in a new way. On the other hand, sometimes a poem, story, image, or film resists the concepts and theories we use to understand it, and as a result, the text prompts us to generate a new explanation, interpretive system, or theory. In short, as Perez declares, "Theory hand in hand with experiment, sometimes theory leading the way, sometimes experiment."

HOW DO WE WORK LIKE A SCHOLAR?

This textbook differs from other introductions to literary and cultural theory in two ways. First, rather than encountering a theorist's complete essay, book chapter, or book, you will only read a few key passages. Second, rather than focusing on schools of criticism like formalism, structuralism, post-structuralism, Marxism, gender criticism, ethnic criticism, and so forth, you will encounter specific concepts like homosocial desire, attunement, defamiliarization, performativity, or the writerly text. What merits a change in method?

While primary source anthologies and schools of criticism have their advantages, these approaches do not mirror what most professional scholars actually do. Admittedly, when prompted, a scholar may recognize that she is working within particular intellectual frameworks or traditions, but few scholars choose a text and think, "I'll read this poem from a post-structuralist perspective, and I'll read that novel using a historicist lens." Scholars do not think in terms of "schools" when they undertake projects. So how *do* professional scholars work?

Scholars identify problems, puzzles, and questions

Scholars begin with a problem, puzzle, or question. Something sparks their curiosity, ignites their desire to figure things out. This process can begin for a number of reasons. We cannot catalog all the ways a short story, film, painting, or cultural practice piques the interest of a scholar, but the following situations illustrate a few reasons to research and write:

- The particular way a writer, filmmaker, or artist employs textual elements may invite our attention, and these features may include a work's structure, setting, character, language, rhyme, meter, figures of speech, imagery, point of view, editing, cinematography, sound, *mise-en-scene*, color, texture, line, composition, etc.
- A text may be difficult to understand, perhaps due to its unfamiliar form, subject matter, language, or context.
- A misguided or incomplete interpretation requires a response. We may find that another reader's insights are problematic, limited, incorrect, or unconvincing.
- Authors often write about their own work or comment on literature and art in general, and these observations often generate questions or provoke a response.
- A text may be in the news, or it may be particularly important, relevant, or significant at this moment in time. The text or author

may be celebrating an anniversary, or someone may be sponsoring a retrospective of an artist's work. A new adaptation may prompt us to revisit the original.

In sum, scholars have to create a context for their contribution. They have to justify the existence of their argument, and they make room for their insights by identifying problems, puzzles, or questions that they must solve and answer.

Scholars join a community

When we travel, we sometimes bump into people who speak differently than we do. Sometimes it is a matter of a few words: "metro" instead of "subway" or "tube," "lorry" instead of "truck," "berm" instead of "mound." We might be confused for a moment, but we adapt easily enough. When we encounter those who speak an entirely different language, we often hope that they will accommodate us and speak our language so we can buy a bus ticket, order a latte, or ask for directions. We soon recognize, however, that we can get only so far in a new country if we do not speak the language. And the process takes time because it is not just a matter of learning vocabulary and syntax, but values, customs, and practices. But once we engage, we can participate in a meaningful way.

Joining an academic community follows the same process. David Bartholomae reminds us that the student "has to learn to speak our language, to speak as we do, to try on the peculiar ways of knowing, selecting, evaluating, reporting, concluding, and arguing that define the discourse of our community" ("Inventing" 4). Asserting that a student "has to learn to speak our language, to speak as we do" may make us flinch. The demand to give up our own voice and imitate another rubs against our desire to be independent and authentic. But Bartholomae is drawing attention to the fact that different communities have different ways of speaking and thinking. Literary scholars and professors may speak English, but they often sound like they are speaking another language. Words like *aporia, decentering, heteroglossia, interpellation, discourse,* and *signifier* can make us feel like we do not belong. And just as a language involves more than new vocabulary, learning to be a scholar requires learning to think like one as well. Academic communities have particular value systems, practices, and conventions. Admittedly, this "discourse," these "ways of knowing, selecting, evaluating, reporting, concluding, and arguing" constrain and limit us, but they also empower us if we learn these ways of thinking and speaking. In other words, it may help to think of a university, a discipline, even a particular course as a foreign country that invites you to learn new ways of thinking, writing, and even being. As Joseph Harris phrases it, "to become a lawyer, a historian, a biologist, or a social worker, you need to learn to think and talk like a lawyer, a historian, a biologist, or a social worker" (35). And as with learning French, Spanish, Swahili, Arabic, Hebrew, Latin, Mandarin, or Hindi, you do not lose your original language. Instead, what will probably happen is that your "native" language, your particular voice and values, will color the new language. You may speak with an accent at first, signaling that you are learning the language. That is fine. I speak French and German with an accent, but I am able to communicate and express my ideas when I am in Paris or Berlin. In fact, my accent contributes to my particular voice. Studying at a university, then, provides us with opportunities to develop a form of academic polylingualism, an ability to participate in multiple disciplines and discourses.

Scholars contribute to the conversation

Related to our foreign language metaphor is the very familiar idea of thinking of a discipline as a conversation. We learn what others have said so that we can enter the discussion. One phrase that has helped me understand my role as a scholar and student, more than any other, is the demand to "respond to or build upon" what others think. That little phrase gives purpose to everything I write and say, and it is the engine that moves all scholarly work. Research, from a five-page essay to a 500-page tome, is based on the idea that we first learn what others have said and then we respond. We extend an idea, perhaps completing a thought, just as we do in a conversation. What we say and write grows out of a larger discussion. And the goal? Harris describes the benefits of thinking of writing as a dialogue:

> It suggests that the goal of such writing is not to have the final word on the subject, to bring the discussion to a close, but to push it forward, to say something new, something that seems to call for further talk and writing. ... A dialogue is not a debate. you don't win a conversation, you add to it, push it ahead, keep it going, 'put your oar in,' and maybe even sometimes redirect or divert the flow of talk.
>
> (35–36)

To join that community, we have to speak the language, and that involves, in our case, emulating how literary scholars and cultural critics think and write about literature, film, art, performance, and practices.

We can respond to and build upon what others have said in a variety of ways, but the rhetorical strategies this book embraces most often ask you to borrow and extend theoretical concepts.

Scholars use concepts

Once scholars find a reason to write by identifying a problem, puzzle, or question that others are working on, they pursue their answers and solutions in different ways. When we examine scholarly articles and books, we notice that writers often choose a key concept from a theory-oriented work which they then clarify by contextualizing the passage and unpacking its implications. Then, they apply that concept to a text, cultural event, representation, or cultural artifact. In other words, they make sense of a work by using someone else's language, ideas, and methods. They inhabit another's intellectual system or framework in order to say something new and interesting.

Plus, scholars use a variety of concepts in the same discussion to solve problems and answer questions. In the process of crafting an argument, scholars may combine a collection of concepts. This practice of building on theorists who may be asking different, even competing questions, prevents us from placing these scholarly projects neatly under the same intellectual umbrella. Instead, we notice a constant "responding to and building upon" key concepts that serve a scholar's critical interests at different points in her article or chapter, and these passages often come from a wide range of disciplines and approaches. For example, in her introduction to *Between Men: English Literature and Male Homosocial Desire* (1985), Eve Sedgwick builds on the work of, among others, Gayle Rubin, Louis Crompton, K. J. Dover, Kathleen Barry, Catherine MacKinnon, and Karl Marx. Later, she works with Claude Lévi-Strauss, Michel Foucault, René Girard, Jacques Lacan, and Sigmund Freud. These theorists hail from disciplines and approaches we might characterize as feminism, anthropology, structuralism, deconstruction, history, economics, intellectual history, philosophy, and psychoanalysis. We usually say that *Between Men* contributes to queer theory, but the work is far more complex than that simple category suggests. Each concept serves a different purpose. Consider as well Rita Felski's *Uses of Literature* (2008). In her chapter on shock, Felski builds on Leo Bersani to make a point about the "contemporaneity of shock," Sigmund Freud to introduce the idea of *Nachträglichkeit*, Elisabeth Ladenson to clarify the idea of "chronological chauvinism," and Georg Simmel to discuss the role of shock in modern life. Each concept serves a specific purpose as she develops her argument, and the different parts contribute to a larger discussion about reading for shock.

One goal of this textbook, then, is to encourage you to think less in terms of "schools of criticism" and singular approaches and embrace instead a more varied approach, all in an effort to engage in a larger conversation about those problems, puzzles, and questions that pique the curiosity of literary and cultural critics. Following the lead of professional scholars, you will learn to generate insightful observations with a few rich and portable ideas, and you will find ways to combine concepts to develop an extended argument. To echo a Renaissance goal popularized by Desiderius Erasmus, you will develop *copia*, or an abundant and ready supply of language and strategies.

Scholars speak multiple languages

Admittedly, literary scholars speak differently than, say, mathematicians, biologists, and psychologists, but even literary scholars differ from each other. Every chapter of this textbook asks you to learn and speak a new language. As I tell my students, you need to "speak Shklovsky," "speak Butler," "speak Barthes," and "speak Caruth." Adopt their language. Employ their terms. But it is not a mere matter of vocabulary. The specialized terms give us different ways to understand literature, film, art, or any other kind of cultural representation. Consider ways to discuss an Emily Dickinson poem:

> "Faith" is a fine invention
> When Gentlemen can *see*—
> But *Microscopes* are prudent
> In an Emergency.

Following Viktor Shklovsky, we might talk about the way this poem *estranges* or *defamiliarizes* the idea of faith. Stephen Greenblatt may encourage us to discuss the poem in terms of *mobility and constraint* and *technologies of control*. We talk about the poem as a *writerly* or *readerly* text when we use Roland Barthes. In every case, we understand her poem differently, and the process enriches the reading experience.

We might be tempted to think that these terms are mere academic jargon, fancy words to talk about a simple poem. However, as Cass R. Sunstein explains, "What might seem to be unintelligible gibberish, or jargon, often has precision, shorthand, and nuance that cannot be captured in ordinary language." What is more, that unfamiliar vocabulary offers us a new way of understanding a work because those terms contain different ways of talking about a text's beauty, relationships, significance, meaning, and function.

Consider another reason for inventing new terms. In *Cultural Criticism, Literary Theory, Poststructuralism*, Vincent Leitch coins a new phrase, "regimes of reason," instead of using a more familiar term like "ideology."

> If only because the word and concept *ideology* have come in recent times to possess contradictory significations connected with contending political allegiances, I prefer to use regime of reason/ unreason to do some of the work of ideology. More important, the notion of regime of reason does not entail commitments to certain problematical Marxian ideas: to the questionable base/ superstructure model of social and cultural formation; to the belief that resistance and revolution are uncoded activities; to the vexing view that most socially sanctioned thinking is false consciousness; and to the millenarian certainty about the ultimate direction and victor of history.
>
> (3)

In other words, competing connotations and problematic associations weigh down "ideology" with so much heavy baggage that it becomes necessary to invent a new word or phrase so that we can think about cultural criticism in a new way. Using the phrase "regimes of reason" allows Leitch to assign his own connotations rather than redefine the word "ideology," explaining what he wants to preserve or reject in the more familiar term.

Of course, before we use specialized terms, and keeping with our foreign language metaphor, we need to translate them, and that act of moving from one language to another, from theoretical to ordinary language and back again, is what this textbook is all about. In short, thinking and writing like a scholar require us to learn a new language so we can join a larger conversation about what we read, watch, and experience. This new language allows us to *respond to* and *build upon* what others have said, and in the process, we invite others to the conversation.

THINK LIKE A BELIEVER

Related to speaking like a theorist is what Peter Elbow calls "the believing game," a pedagogical tool he introduced in *Writing Without Teachers* (1973), a book on teaching composition. He picks up the topic in a conference essay in 2008 where he reminds us that the *"doubting game* represents the kind of thinking most widely honored and taught in our culture. It's sometimes called 'critical thinking.' It's the disciplined practice of trying to be as skeptical and analytic as possible with every idea we encounter" (1). Thanks to the doubting game, "we can discover hidden contradictions, bad reasoning, or other weaknesses in them" (1). We like playing this game, and we should keep playing because being a thoughtful person requires that kind of enlightened skepticism.

He contrasts the "doubting game" with the "believing game," a

> disciplined practice of trying to be as welcoming or accepting as possible to every idea we encounter: not just listening to views different from our own and holding back from arguing with them; not just trying to restate them without bias; but actually *trying* to believe them.
>
> (1)

We should momentarily "believe" because believing allows us to "scrutinize and test" (1). Yes, we should question popular and appealing ideas and concepts for flaws and cracks, but we should also test theories and concepts by trying them on. As Elbow explains, "often we cannot see what's good in someone else's idea (or in our own!) till we work at believing it" (2).

Using Key Passages to Understand Literature, Theory and Criticism invites you to *believe* in this sense. Every chapter invites you to believe, at least momentarily, in the truthfulness, accuracy, and value of the concept, all in the name of testing its explanatory power. This ability to doubt and believe, embrace and question, is yet another intellectual skill we hope to develop as we study literary and cultural theory.

WORKS CITED

Armstrong, Karen. *A Short History of Myth*. Canongate, 2005.
Arnold, Matthew. "The Study of Poetry." *The Critical Tradition*, 3rd ed., edited by David H. Richter, Bedford/St. Martin's, 2007, pp. 429–434.
Bartholomae, David. "Inventing the University." *Journal of Basic Writing*, vol. 5, no. 1, 1986, pp. 4–23.
———. "Introduction." *Ways of Reading: An Anthology for Writers*, 9th ed., edited by David Bartholomae and Anthony Petrosky, Bedford/St. Martin's, 2011, pp. 1–21.

Bloom, Harold. *The Western Canon*. Houghton, 2014.

Bové, Paul A. "Discourse." *Critical Terms for Literary Studies*, 2nd ed., edited by Frank Lentricchia and Thomas McLaughlin, U of Chicago P, 1995, pp. 50–65.

Derrida, Jacques. *Limited Inc*, edited by Gerald Graff, Northwestern UP, 1990.

Dickinson, Emily. "'Faith' Is a Fine Invention." *Final Harvest: Emily Dickinson's Poems*, edited by Thomas H. Johnson, Little, 1961, p. 20.

Elbow, Peter. "The Believing Game—Methodological Believing." Conference Essay, *Conference on College Composition and Communication*, 2008, works.bepress.com/peter_elbow/20.

Felski, Rita. *Uses of Literature*. Blackwell, 2008.

Harris, Joseph. *Rewriting: How to Do Things with Texts*. Utah State UP, 2006.

Horace. "The Art of Poetry." *Classical Literary Criticism*. Translated by Penelope Murray and T. S. Dorsch, Penguin, 2000.

"Interpret." *Oxford English Dictionary*. vol. 7, 2nd ed., Clarendon, 1989.

Leitch, Vincent B. *Cultural Criticism, Literary Theory, Poststructuralism*. Columbia UP, 1992.

Mailloux, Steven. "Interpretation." *Critical Terms for Literary Studies*, 2nd ed., edited by Frank Lentricchia and Thomas McLaughlin, U of Chicago P, 1995, pp. 121–134.

Murfin, Ross and Supryia M. Ray. *The Bedford Glossary of Critical and Literary Terms*. 3rd ed., Bedford/St. Martin's, 2009.

Orr, Christopher. "*Annihilation*: A Beautiful Heap of Nonsense." *The Atlantic*, www.theatlantic.com/entertainment/archive/2018/02/annihilation-review/554006. Accessed 25 February 2018.

Perez, Gilberto. "In the Study of Film, Theory Must Work Hand in Hand with Criticism." *The Chronicle Review*, 6 November 1998. www.chronicle.com/article/In-the-Study-of-Film-Theory/26679.

Pratt, Mary Louise. "Arts of the Contact Zone." *Profession*, 1991, pp. 33–40.

Quammen, David. "Was Darwin Wrong?" *National Geographic Magazine*, ngm.nationalgeographic.com/ngm/0411/feature1/fulltext.html.

Rainey, Lawrence. *Revisiting 'The Waste Land.'* Yale UP, 2008.

Rorty, Richard. *Achieving Our Country: Leftist Thought in Twentieth-Century America*. Harvard UP, 1998.

Scholes, Robert. *Protocols of Reading*. Yale UP, 1989.

———. *The Rise and Fall of English*. Yale UP, 1998.

———. *Textual Power*. Yale UP, 1985.

Sunstein, Cass R. "In Praise of Jargon." *The Chronicle Review*. 14 February 2016, chronicle.com/article/In-Praise-of-Jargon/235266.

"Theory." *Oxford English Dictionary*, vol. 17, 2nd ed., Clarendon, 1989.

Waldman, Kate. "The Alien Richness of Kate Braverman's Short Stories." *The New Yorker*, www.newyorker.com/books/page-turner/alien-richness-kate-braverman-short-stories. Accessed 25 February 2018.

CHAPTER 1

Becoming a subject

> All ideology hails or interpellates concrete individuals as concrete subjects.
> (Louis Althusser 117)

PROBLEMS, PUZZLES, AND QUESTIONS

Many read poems to glean a message. What do literary texts convey about, say, relationships? Billy Collins' short poem "Divorce" (2008) describes a marriage gone awry:

> Once, two spoons in bed,
> now tined forks
>
> across a granite table
> and the knives they have hired.

In this case, Collins' poem uses figurative language to portray divorce as an unpleasant and violent business. But what goes unsaid in this poem? What does Collins assume about what marriage *ought* to be? What is taken for granted when we talk about marriage? And why is asking about what the poem *does not* say instead of focusing on what it *does* say a useful tack to take?

In 2004, art historian Linda Nochlin delivered a series of lectures at Harvard University that focused on Renoir's *Great Bathers*, and the lectures led to *Bathers, Bodies, Beauty: The Visceral Eye* (2006). She reminds us of the need to understand these paintings in context, for the images are the "result of certain kinds practices, the product of a particular shifting structure of cultural institutions at a particular moment of history" (52). At one point, she describes the formation of particular market forces and positioning of the artist as specialist and genius, and she asserts that "certain positions and formations gradually emerge which call into being subjects who will fill them" (41). Notice the reversal of cause and effect. Instead of saying that artists become specialists and geniuses who then shape the market, Nochlin claims that a particular socioeconomic order and new notions of the artist create new identities. How does that process work? How can, or in what sense, do cultural institutions "call into being subjects who will fill them"?

Herman Melville's short story "Bartleby, the Scrivener: A Story of Wall Street" (1853) describes a clerk named Bartleby who copies legal documents. Although very silent and mechanical, Bartleby completes his work. However, after a few days pass, the lawyer who hired Bartleby asks him to proofread a document, and Bartleby replies with "I would prefer not to" (502). Repeatedly, the lawyer asks Bartleby to obey: "You are decided, then, not to comply with my request—a request made according to common usage and common sense?" (503). Bartleby indicates that he prefers not to complete the task. Bartleby performs fewer and fewer assignments until he does nothing at all. After the lawyer fails in various ways to help Bartleby, the police place Bartleby in prison where he dies of starvation. He prefers not to eat. How do we make sense of Bartleby's refusal to comply? Is Bartleby heroically resisting social expectations and demands? Is he asserting his agency in the face of corporate culture? Is he subverting "common usage and common sense"? Or, is he trading one identity for another? Instead of assuming his role as legal copyist, is Bartleby taking on the role of sacrificial victim? Is there another way to make sense of Bartleby's defiance?

These examples share a preoccupation with the role our social arrangements play in constructing identity and our relationships with others. Do we create social relationships, or do these relationships construct us? Does society impose values and hierarchies upon us, or do we willingly embrace them? Can we escape the social system?

KEY PASSAGES

Before Louis Althusser, many Marxist scholars asserted that ideology refers to "false consciousness," or the idea that ideology serves the dominant classes by hiding the truth about how our economic system exploits subordinate and marginalized groups. According to this view, people comply with the socioeconomic system because they do not know any better. They embrace a fake version of reality. Althusser revises our understanding of how ideology works in "Ideology and Ideological State Apparatuses (Notes towards an Investigation)" (1970). By combining psychoanalytic concepts with structuralist and Marxist socioeconomic theories, Althusser offers a useful way to discuss how culture encourages us to embrace certain social hierarchies, roles, values, attitudes, and identities, but not others. Althusser's ideas matter to us because cultural representations—literature, film, art, performances, etc.—serve an ideological function. Along with institutions like religion, education, government, political parties, and family, what we read and watch shapes our identity and relationships with others in subtle ways.

Admittedly, Althusser's vocabulary intimidates. However, once we explore the terms and concepts, we will see that Althusser helps us better understand the conditions of our social life, and he reminds us that what we think is natural and nonnegotiable is, perhaps, socially constructed and changeable.

> I say: the category of the subject is constitutive of all ideology, but at the same time and immediately I add that *the category of the subject is only constitutive of all ideology insofar as all ideology has the function (which defines it) of "constituting" concrete individuals as subjects*. In the interaction of this double constitution exists the functioning of all ideology, ideology being nothing but its functioning in the material forms of existence of that functioning.
>
> (116)
>
> As a first formulation I shall say: *all ideology hails or interpellates concrete individuals as concrete subjects*, by the functioning of the category of the subject.
>
> (117)
>
> This is a proposition which entails that we distinguish for the moment between concrete individuals on the one hand and concrete subjects on the other, although at this level, concrete subjects only exist insofar as they are supported by a concrete individual.
>
> (118)

> I shall then suggest that ideology "acts" or "functions" in such a way that it "recruits" subjects among the individuals (it recruits them all), or "transforms" the individuals into subjects (it transforms them all) by that very precise operation which I have called *interpellation* or hailing, and which can be imagined along the lines of the most commonplace everyday police (or other) hailing: "Hey, you there!"
>
> (118)
>
> Assuming that the theoretical scene I have imagined takes place in the street, the hailed individual will turn round. By this mere one-hundred-and-eighty-degree physical conversion, he becomes a *subject*. Why? Because he has recognized that the hail was "really" addressed to him, and that "it was *really him* who was hailed" (and not someone else).
>
> (118)
>
> Ideology has always-already interpellated individuals as subjects, which amounts to making it clear that individuals are always-already interpellated by ideology as subjects, which necessarily leads us to one last proposition: *individuals are always-already subjects*. Hence, individuals are "abstract" with respect to the subjects which they always already are.
>
> (119)

DISCUSSION

A few concepts will help us make sense of those key passages. We will identify, then connect the dots.

First, *individuals* differ from *subjects*. When Althusser refers to *individuals*, he is talking about unique people who live in the world and whose qualities and attributes differ from other individuals. Individuals are "concrete" in the same sense that a particular red poppy in my backyard differs from the abstraction "flowers." A *subject* has at least two connotations. On the one hand, a *subject* is more abstract and impersonal. For example, when we discuss "the subject" in a sentence, we refer to the grammatical place in that sentence. The subject is defined by its location in relation to other parts of the sentence, not by a particular person, place, or thing. Therefore, when we discuss "subjects" or "subject positions," we are referring to impersonal roles or positions within an organization or system. For example, my subject position, at any given moment, might be teacher, father, citizen, or administrator, but at other times I am a student, son, tourist, or faculty member. The context and the relationship I have with others define my identity or subject position.

On the other hand, *subject* also suggests "subject to" in the sense that one is under another's control or jurisdiction. We are *subject to* a monarch. We are *subject to* laws, policies, and procedures. We are also *subject to* preexisting social codes, categories, roles, and definitions. For example, the moment we are born, we are *subject to* preexisting ideas about gender, race, class, nationality, sexuality, etc. We do not define ourselves as much as we have to respond to a social framework that exists before we even arrive on the scene. Consider this analogy: when we play chess, we feel as though we are in control. We are free to move a pawn here or a knight there. However, we are *subject to* the rules that govern chess. We do not determine the layout of the board, the ability of individual pieces, or the goal or aim. Instead, we play within the framework we call "chess." To act otherwise is to play another game.

Second, *hailing* or *interpellating* refers to the specific act of inviting someone to respond, to be recognized. Interpellating "recruits" someone in the sense of asking him to voluntarily enroll or enlist. Interpellation is complete when the person responds: "By this mere one-hundred-and-eighty-degree physical conversion, he becomes a *subject*. Why? Because he has recognized that the hail was 'really' addressed to him, and that 'it was *really him* who was hailed' (and not someone else)" (118). In other words, an *individual* becomes a *subject* in two ways. First, by willingly turning and responding, the individual voluntarily places himself in relation to the one who is hailing him. Second, he takes on the identity that was offered, and he *subjects* himself *to* the one who is calling him.

How do the dots connect? What do individuals, subjects, hailing, and interpellating have to do with ideology? Note that ideology is less a noun than a verb: "*ideology has the function (which defines it) of 'constituting' concrete individuals as subjects*" (116). In other words, ideology's task is to hail, interpellate, or invite us to become *subject to* particular assumptions, social categories, values, attitudes, and roles. Responding to those invitations transforms us into *subjects*, for we willingly acknowledge the call or invitation, and we recognize that the call is for us. We willingly become part of the social system.

But what does Althusser mean by "always-already interpellated individuals as subjects" (119)? Althusser admits that he describes the process "in the form of a temporal succession" (118), but he clarifies by saying that "but in reality these things happen without any succession. The existence of ideology and the hailing or interpellation of individuals as subjects are one and the same thing" (118). In other words, we never really enjoy a time when we are "individuals" who are free of ideology, free of a social system that constantly invites us to respond to specific values, social arrangements, and categories. Instead, we are born into a social system. We inherit, so to speak, particular attitudes and ideas about what it means to be male, female, Black, gay, Chicana, Scot, Muslim, working class, Catholic, etc. Social hierarchies, divisions, and definitions exist long before we are born. To return to the chess example, we are, in a sense, born into the game. There was never a moment when we were not playing chess, never a moment when there were no rules and identities.

But are we not free to choose? Are we not free agents? Do not people resist socially constructed categories of race, class, gender, nationality, sexuality, etc. all the time? Yes. However, those acts of rebellion still take place within the game, and resistance is always *in response to* preexisting social codes. And even if we are wildly successful in our effort to redesign the game or system, we have merely replaced one social system with another. A different set of values, hierarchies, and social order will continue to call or interpellate us. We are inevitably *subject to* social codes and identities. While saying that we cannot escape ideology's ability to transform us into subjects may make us feel powerless, Althusser's theory of ideology is, in a sense, neutral. The process of encouraging us to assume that some values and social arrangements are natural and obvious applies to all values and hierarchies, ones that we may even champion and celebrate.

POTENTIAL PROJECTS

We may not be able to escape ideology or be outside of ideology's ability to transform us into subjects, but we can, perhaps, recognize the subject positions ideology asks us to embrace and identify the strategies texts use to interpellate us. Our task, then, requires us to explore how language and images naturalize and normalize socially constructed values, relationships, and identities.

Identify the invitation

Use as your operating assumption the idea that literature, film, art, and institutions are ideological in that they hail, interpellate, or invite us to become *subject to* particular social categories, values, attitudes, roles, and identities. More specifically, examine, say, how a novel invites readers to believe that specific hierarchies, social roles, and identity attributes are natural, normal, and commonsensical.

As for method, we are used to looking at the *content* of images and language. For example, the *Batman* franchise reinforces the importance of overcoming childhood fears in order to restore law and order. Wordsworth portrays daffodils, and the memory of daffodils is a source of pleasure and joy. Or as we saw with "Bartleby, the Scrivener," by portraying the effects of mindlessly copying documents, Melville may be critiquing the numbing world of law and commerce. In short, we often read literature like philosophy in narrative form.

However, what Althusser is asking us to do is more subtle. Instead of looking at what is said, focus on what is assumed. What does the text take for granted? How does the text perpetuate assumptions? As I asked earlier when I discussed Billy Collins' poem, what does Collins assume about what marriage *ought* to be? What is taken for granted when he talks about marriage and divorce? Importantly, how does his use of metaphor—spoons, forks, and knives—reproduce those assumptions?

Or, let us examine the first line of the "Gettysburg Address" (1863): "Four score and seven years ago our fathers brought forth, upon this continent, a new nation, conceived in liberty, and dedicated to the proposition that all men are created equal." The phrase "our fathers" hails us as children and as brothers and sisters, governed together under patriarchy. The use of "fathers" also constructs men as initiators, innovators, and creators, yet Lincoln excludes women from the conception and even birthing process. The phrase "all men are created equal" perpetuates the notion of men as universal. The "conception" metaphor also transforms political philosophy into a natural, even inevitable process, and it goes without saying that we should celebrate a social order conceived in liberty. Portraying the "new nation" as offspring anthropomorphizes a political state, and the word "dedicated" suggests this political child has a singular purpose. Lincoln casts the founding of the United States, not in terms of revolution, but a birth that excludes women from the creative process. In short, with a bevy of rhetorical tools, Lincoln legitimizes and naturalizes political revolution and patriarchy. He asks us to respond to his plea for unity.

Notice the interpretive moves: Discuss your text in terms of how it hails and interpellates readers or viewers. Talk in terms of how it constructs identity, perpetuates specific assumptions, and portrays people, places, things, and actions in such a way that we embrace a social order and a specific set of values as normal, natural, and obvious. How does the work's diction invite us to identify with one identity instead of another? How does language legitimize some hierarchies, social roles, and values, but not others? How does the portrayal of particular identities, institutions, groups, and practices invite us to align ourselves with some, but not others? How do cause-effect relationships encourage us to adopt certain subject positions instead of others? How does point of view encourage us to recognize ourselves in some characters, but not others? In short, make claims about how the text recruits and constructs a social identity for us, naturalizes a particular social system, and legitimizes specific hierarchies and values.

Identify the power and limitations of parody

Literature, film, and art often provide ideological analysis for us. Parody is an especially effective tool. *Saturday Night Live* skits, for example, expose unspoken assumptions and mock "truths" we take for granted. Films like *Shaun of the Dead* (2004), *Austin Powers* (1997), and *Monty Python and the Holy Grail* (1975) draw attention to genre conventions and the values they perpetuate. Annie Finch's "Coy Mistress" (1997) exposes and questions the sexist assumptions in Andrew Marvell's "To His Coy Mistress" (1681) and Anne Sexton's "Cinderella" (1971) mocks romance narratives. On the other hand, Althusser reminds us that there is no escaping ideological process. Parodies, however critical of the status quo, still function ideologically.

Your task: choose a form of parody and make two critical moves. First, explain how the parody performs the work of an ideological critic. How does the work draw attention to unspoken assumptions, question the normal, natural, and commonsensical, and disrupt the process of hailing individuals. Second, turn your critical eye to the parody itself. How does the parody interpellate the reader or viewer? How does the parody try to naturalize or normalize a particular set of values, attitudes, hierarchies, and social arrangements? In short, how does the parody offer its own ideology that "goes without saying"?

WORKS CITED

Althusser, Louis. "Ideology and Ideological State Apparatus (Notes Towards an Investigation)." *Lenin and Philosophy and Other Essays*. 1970. Translated by Ben Brewster, Monthly Review, 2001, pp. 85–126.
Collins, Billy. "Divorce." *Ballistics*. Random, 2008, pp. 98.
Lincoln, Abraham. "The Gettysburg Address." *Our Documents*, www.ourdocuments.gov/doc.php?flash=false&doc=36&page=transcript. Accessed 11 January 2018.
Melville, Herman. "Bartleby, the Scrivener: A Story of Wall Street." 1853. *The Norton Introduction to Literature*, 12th ed., edited by Kelly J. Mays, Norton, 2017, pp. 496–522.
Nochlin, Linda. *Bathers, Bodies, Beauty: The Visceral Eye*. Harvard UP, 2006.

CHAPTER 2

Scripting identity

> Collective identities, in short, provide what we might call scripts: narratives that people can use in shaping their projects and in telling their life stories.
>
> (Kwame Anthony Appiah 22)

PROBLEMS, PUZZLES, AND QUESTIONS

In the *Republic* (circa 380 BCE), Plato expresses his anxiety about the value of poetry. Among the many reasons he cites—poetry merely imitates, poetry is a few degrees removed from the truth, and poetry "nourishes and waters [the passions] when they ought to be dried up" (54)—he also draws attention to a narrative's ability to shape identity:

> For, my dear Adeimantus, if our young men were to listen seriously to such unworthy utterances instead of laughing at them, it would be difficult for them, being mere mortals, to think themselves above such behaviour, and to rebuke themselves if it occurred to them to speak or act in this way; without shame or restraint they would break out into dirges and laments at the slightest occurrence.
>
> (27)

For Plato, poetry's ability to portray the gods in less than ideal ways encourages Athenian youth to behave in a similar way. The portrayals of frenzied gods who weep and wail legitimize bad behavior. Plato is certainly right that narratives may shape how we act and establish social norms, but is that power always harmful? Can fictional representations shape our identity and our understanding of ourselves? If so, how so?

Hannah Webster Foster's epistolary novel and cautionary tale *The Coquette* (1797) describes the dating dilemmas and tragic life of Eliza Wharton. In a curious passage, Eliza recalls a moment when the stately Mrs. Richman accuses her of keeping company with a "seducer." Eliza replies, "I hope, madam, you do not think me an object of seduction!" Mrs. Richman replies,

> I do not think you seducible; nor was Richardson's Clarissa, till she made herself the victim, by her own indiscretion. Pardon me, Eliza, this is a second Lovelace. I am alarmed by his artful intrusions. His insinuating attention to you are characteristic of the man.
>
> (38)

Mrs. Richman is referring to Samuel Richardson's novel *Clarissa* (1748) which describes the seduction and ruin of the heroine. Notice how Mrs. Richman uses Richardson's novel as a way to make sense of Eliza's behavior by using the character names Clarissa and Lovelace to describe *kinds* of people. In what sense can characters become examples or models for us to follow or avoid?

In the film *Stranger than Fiction* (2006), the character Harold Crick begins to hear a woman's voice omnisciently narrating his actions. Harold learns that the voice belongs to a critically acclaimed author living in town. He tries to intervene to save his own life, for the events the author composes on her typewriter occur to Harold in real life. The author allows Harold to read a draft of the final chapter, and he accepts what appears to be a tragic ending. The narrative encourages us to ask, what is the relationship between fictional narratives and our own lives? In what sense do narratives shape our lives and endow them with meaning and significance?

KEY PASSAGES

Kwame Anthony Appiah wrote *The Ethics of Identity* (2005) in response to larger debates about how we treat those who differ from ourselves, for as Appiah explains, "in the end, everything that matters morally, matters because of its impact on individuals" (ix). Appiah connects ethics to identity by asserting that "identities make ethical claims because … we make our lives *as* men and *as* women, *as* gay and *as* straight people, *as* Ghanians and *as* Americas, *as* blacks and *as* whites" (xiv). In other words, when, say, Martin Luther King Jr. advocated for civil rights, he advocated *as* a black man. When Gloria Anzaldua argued for recognition and rights, she wrote *as* a woman, *as* a Chicana, and *as* a gay woman. Appiah reminds us that "when we are asked—and ask ourselves—*who* we are, we are being asked *what* we are as well" (xiv). We have personal identities, but also public and collective identities. Connecting ethics with identity prompts Appiah to ask, among other questions, "Do identities represent a curb on autonomy, or do they provide its contours?" (xiv). That question could be rephrased in more general terms: Do identities limit or enable us? What role do they play? What is the source of our identities? Appiah suggests some useful answers that guide how we read:

> In constructing an identity, one draws, among other things, on the kinds of person available in one's society. Of course, there is not just *one* way that gay or straight people or blacks or whites or men or women are to behave, but there are ideas around (contested, many of them, but all sides in these contests shape our options) about how gay, straight, black, white, male, or female people ought to conduct themselves. These notions provide loose norms or models, which play a role in shaping our plans of life. Collective identities, in short, provide what we might call scripts: narratives that people can use in shaping their projects and in telling their life stories.
>
> (21–22)
>
> So we should acknowledge how much our personal histories, the stories we tell of where we have been and where we are going, are constructed, like novels and movies, short stories and folktales, within narrative conventions. Indeed, one of the things that popular narratives (whether filmed or televised, spoken or written) do for us is to provide models for telling our lives. At the same time, part of the function of our collective identities—of the whole repertory of them that a society makes available to its members—is to structure possible narratives of the individual self.
>
> (22)
>
> It is not just that, say, gender identities give shape to one's life; it is also that ethnic and national identities fit a personal narrative into a larger narrative. For modern

> people, the narrative form entails seeing one's life as having a certain arc, as making sense through a life story that expresses who one is through one's own project of self-making. That narrative arc is yet another way in which an individual's life depends deeply on something socially created and transmitted.
>
> (23)

These passages are particularly valuable for those of us who study literature and film, but some details require explanation: What does Appiah mean by "constructing" an identity? What does he mean by "norms or models"? What does "collective identity" mean? What is a life script? How might life scripts serve our interests?

DISCUSSION

Where do our identities come from? Some assert that our identity is biological or fixed in some way that we have little control over who or what we are. According to this view, as time passes and we reflect on our life, we *discover* who we are. Others assert that we are completely autonomous and free of constraint, thus able to craft our own identities as we wish. We *create* ourselves. Appiah critiques these choices by arguing that the first view "suggests that there is no role for creativity in making a self" (17) and the second view misleads us because it maintains that "there is *only* creativity, that there is nothing for us to respond to" (18). Appiah seeks a reasonable middle ground.

When Appiah writes, "in constructing an identity," it sounds like he believes that we create ourselves, but he goes on to say that we define who we are by responding to and building upon "the kinds of person available in one's society" (21). These competing versions of what it means to be, say, gay, straight, black, white, Asian, Hispanic, male, or female provide us with preexisting models or examples that shape how we define ourselves. In other words, constructing an identity is a form of negotiation and dialogue with an array of choices presented before us: "to create a life is to create a life out of the materials that history has given you" (19). We have, one could say, limited freedom to construct our identity.

This social dimension of our identity is what Appiah refers to when he uses the phrase, "collective identity." When Appiah talks about identity categories like male, female, American, British, Korean, Jew, or Latino, he is talking about "collective identities" or labels developed over time in specific social and historical contexts, long before we arrive on the scene. They are "social not just because they involve others, but because they are constituted in part by socially transmitted conceptions of how a person of that identity properly behaves" (21). For example, the collective identity "working class" is a product of years of discussions, images, and narratives. To be "working class" is to identify with the social codes that define that group. By claiming a collective identity, we connect ourselves to other people. It is a kind of shorthand way to say, "I belong with them."

To return to a question Appiah poses, "Do identities represent a curb on autonomy, or do they provide its contours?" (xiv), we can safely say, "both." Socially constructed collective identities constrain us because historical processes have already limited what it means to be black or white, male or female, gay or straight. A collective identity is an inheritance foisted upon us. On the other hand, these identities provide the building blocks for our identity. And just as choosing to be a particular character in a play may limit who we are, taking on that role also gives us an identity. We become someone others recognize, and that identity also creates "forms of solidarity: if I think of myself as an X, then, sometimes, the mere fact that somebody else is an X, too, may incline me to do something with or for them" (24). An identity, therefore, simultaneously enables and constrains.

Comparing identities to roles in a play helps us understand Appiah when he concludes that "Collective identities, in short, provide what we might call scripts: narratives that people can use in shaping their projects and in telling their life stories" (22). He reminds us that literature and film "provide models for telling our lives" (22). Stories are important because they not only establish possible characters and settings, but the narrative arcs also provide an array of choices and map cause–effect relationships. For example, Appiah reminds us that "gay identities may organize lives around the narrative of coming out; Pentecostalists are born again; and black identities in America often engage oppositional narratives of self-construction in the face of racism" (23). And by making our story part of a larger story, our personal experiences gain value and significance. Seemingly, random events become meaningful and coherent, or we exclude irrelevant details from our narrative. In other words, scripts structure our experiences in meaningful patterns.

Note that Appiah insists that "only the collective identities have scripts" (23). Why? When Appiah discusses "collective identities," he is referring to "kinds of person available in one's society" (21). The word "kinds" is important, for "kinds" refers to a group or category. "There is," he explains,

> a logical category but no social category of the witty, or the clever, or the charming, or the greedy. People who share these properties do not constitute a social group. In the relevant sense, they are not a kind of person.
>
> (23)

Therefore, there is no life script for "the wit," but there is for collective identities like white, black, Native American, Latina, queer, French, Yankee, etc. because they describe a socially constructed "kind" of person, a group that one can identify with and claim.

POTENTIAL PROJECTS

Remember that Appiah argues that we both inherit and create our identities, and we have discussed how a society, in the form of narratives we read and watch, offers us a "whole repertory" of collective identities that we can use to give our lives meaning and a coherent structure. Our focus is less on how individuals have actually used those models and examples, and more on the "repertory" itself. In other words, we explore the *source* of the narratives, the specific "novels and movies, short stories and folktales" (22), that help define our collective identities. Note, too, that different kinds of narratives compete when it comes to defining those identities. For example, Mary Antin's *The Promised Land* (1912), Julia Alvarez' *How the Garcia Girls Lost Their Accents* (1991), Bessie Head's *A Question of Power* (1973), and Lan Cao's *Monkey Bridge* (1997) offer a variety of narrative arcs that define the collective identity we call "an immigrant." We are not asking which version is more true, accurate, or even useful than another. Instead, all are worthy of discussion because they are part of the repertory of identities our society makes available to us.

Identify models and scripts

Following Appiah's lead, embrace for a moment the idea that literary narratives and films "provide models for telling our lives" (22). More specifically, explore how stories and images define collective identities. According to these narratives, what does it mean to be gay, straight, black, white, male, or female, etc.? What qualities do "these kinds of people" have? What do they value? How do they behave? Based on cause-effect relationships, the narrative establishes what options do we have if we belong to that group? How do we respond to others? For example, Jane Austen's *Emma* (1815) narrates the life of a young, beautiful, rich, and genteel young woman. What collective identity does Emma represent? How does the narrative arc "provide models for telling our lives" (22)? How does Emma's story help us fit our personal narrative into a larger narrative? On the other hand, Sophie Caco narrates her own story in Edwidge Danticat's novel *Breath, Eyes, Memory* (1994). According to this novel, what does it mean to be a Haitian woman? What does it mean to be a rape victim? What "loose norms or models" (22) does the story offer for immigrants and women? These two examples remind us that narratives are transforming characters—Emma and Sophie—into "the kinds of person available in one's society" (21), and because we are looking at collective identities, the narratives offer different models for making sense of our own lives.

Link narrative arcs and collective identities

A related project is to identify particular narrative arcs that collective identities use to structure and make sense of their experiences. Identifying a "narrative arc" means we look for common and conventional kinds of stories. A *Bildungsroman* or coming of age narrative, for example, traces a young person's intellectual and emotional development from childhood to adulthood and offers a pattern that gives his or her experiences a plot and structure. This narrative arc suggests that we become an "adult," "man," or "woman" when we learn something essential that grants us that identity. In stories and songs, American slaves often used an emancipation narrative as described in the Hebrew Bible to shape what they experienced in the American South into a coherent story that offers meaning and hope. Appiah reminds us that "gay identities may organize lives around the narrative of coming out" and "Pentecostalists are born again." In short, what common plot structures organize a group's experience? What kinds of narrative arcs "fit a personal narrative into a larger narrative" (23)? What does a group gain by using that particular narrative?

WORKS CITED

Appiah, Kwame Anthony. *The Ethics of Identity*. Princeton UP, 2005.
Foster, Hannah Webster. *The Coquette; or, The History of Eliza Wharton*. 1797. Oxford UP, 1986.
Plato. *Classical Literary Criticism*. Translated by Penelope Murray, Penguin, 2000.

CHAPTER 3

Doing not describing

> The performative should be doing something as opposed to just saying something.
> (J. L. Austin 132)

PROBLEMS, PUZZLES, AND QUESTIONS

Consider part of a key sentence in the final paragraph of "The Declaration of Independence" (1776), the founding document of the United States:

> We, therefore, the Representatives of the united States of America, in General Congress, Assembled, appealing to the Supreme Judge of the world for the rectitude of our intentions, do, in the Name, and by Authority of the good People of these Colonies, solemnly publish and declare, That these United Colonies are, and of Right ought to be Free and Independent States.

What is significant about the phrase "We ... do ... solemnly publish and declare, That these United Colonies are, and of Right ought to be Free and Independent States"? Does this declaration describe a revolutionary act or *is* it revolutionary? Does the declaration *state* or *produce* independence? Or, as Jacques Derrida asks,

> Is it that the good people have already freed themselves in fact and are only stating the fact of this emancipation in [*par*] the Declaration? Or is it rather that they free themselves at the instant of and by [*par*] the signature of this Declaration?
> (Derrida 9)

The "introduction" to Kurt Schwitters' "Ursonate" (1932), an experimental poetic work whose structure is similar to that of a classical sonata, challenges readers and listeners:

Fümms bö wö tää zää Uu,
            pögiff,
                      kwii Ee.
Oooooooooooooooooooooooooooooooo,
dll rrrrrrr beeeee bö
dll rrrrrrr beeeee bö fümms bö,
  rrrrrrr beeeee bö fümms bö wö,
      beeeee bö fümms bö wö tää,
         bö fümms bö wö tää zää,
            fümms bö wö tää zää Uu.

(qtd. Motherwell 371)

Traditional interpretive tools encourage us to ask, "What is Schwitters suggesting? What is Schwitters trying to say? Or more specifically, what do the words "bö, fümms, tää" mean or refer to?" But are those the right questions to ask? Is there another way to make sense of "Ursonate"?

A line from Gertrude Stein's "Susie Asado" (1912) seems more comprehensible, but actually stumps most readers: "A lean on the shoe this means slips slips hers." Susie Asado was a flamenco dancer, and the imagery of the slipping shoe makes sense to a degree, but that hold gives way when we encounter the rest of the stanza:

> When the ancient light grey is clean it is yellow, it is a silver seller. / This is a please this is a please there are the saids to jelly. / These are the wets these say the sets to leave a crown to Incy.

(549)

Ultimately, deciphering the poem line by line and word by word ends in frustration. But if the poem is not "saying" anything, then how do we understand it? How can we make sense of the poem while still resisting the urge to translate the figurative into the literal?

This is an odd assortment of texts: a declaration of political independence, an experiment in sound, and a seemingly nonsensical poem. What do they have in common? In what sense might they depend on the same linguistic structure or rhetorical operation?

KEY PASSAGES

Harvard University invited moral philosopher J. L. Austin to deliver the William James Lectures in 1955. The collected lectures were published as *How to Do Things with Words* in 1962. Austin contributes to a larger debate about language as a system of structures or a group of practices. That is, does language merely *describe* the world, or does it *accomplish* something? Austin is especially interested in statements that are not true or false, but *felicitous*. Consider the following examples Austin provides:

> 'I do ...' —as uttered in the course of the marriage ceremony
> 'I name this ship the *Queen Elizabeth*'—as uttered when smashing the bottle against the stem.
> 'I give and bequeath my watch to my brother'—as occurring in a will.
> 'I bet you sixpence it will rain tomorrow.'
>
> (5)

How do these statements differ from sentences like "I live in Berlin. She ate catfish last night. We will read books in New York in May"? For Austin, the first set of examples are "performative," while the second set are "constative." As we will see below, understanding the difference between these two kinds of language acts helps us make sense of particular kinds of texts and prepares us for some arguments we encounter in recent discussions of gender, postmodernism, deconstruction, and the avant-garde.

> To utter [a performative] sentence (in, of course, the appropriate circumstances) is not to *describe* my doing of what I should be said in so uttering to be doing or to state that I am doing it: it is to do it. None of the utterances cited is either true or false.
>
> (6)
>
> The performative should be doing something as opposed to just saying something, and the performative is happy or unhappy as opposed to true or false.
>
> (132)

> But nevertheless, the type of performative upon which we drew for our first examples, which has a verb in the first person singular present indicative active, seems to deserve our favor: at least, if issuing the utterance is doing something, the "I" and the "active" and the "present" seem appropriate.
>
> (67)

While these passages represent only a part of Austin's larger work on speech acts, his contrasting of constative and performative utterances and his reframing of successful performatives as "happy or unhappy as opposed to true or false" (132) merit explanation.

DISCUSSION

The first passage contains three claims that require unpacking. First, Austin asserts that phrases like "I do, I name, I give and bequeath, I bet" do not describe an action; they are performing the action. In other words, saying "I do, I name, I give and bequeath, I bet" are the acts of agreeing to marry, christening a boat, giving one's possessions away, and making a wager. Words are practices or events. Or, as Austin phrases it, "Here we should say that in saying these words we are *doing* something—namely, marrying, rather than *reporting* something, namely *that* we are marrying" (13). Expressed yet another way, these particular phrases, along with others like promise, apologize, pledge, vow, declare, resign, etc. do not describe events; they *are* the event. Note, too, that the choice of verbs has nothing to do with performatives. For example, the sentences "I said 'I do'," "I christened the boat The Queen Elizabeth," "I gave and bequeathed my possessions," and "Yesterday I bet you five dollars" do not perform any actions; they are merely past tense, and as a result, they describe what happened. Austin calls these kinds of sentences *constative* utterances because they declare or describe, and they are subject to verification.

Second, what does Austin mean by "in, of course, the appropriate circumstances" (6)? Context matters. For example, saying the phrase "I do" during a play on stage has no effect. Recalling an event, as in, "At the altar, my friend said, 'I do'," does not perform the action. Saying words outside the context of an actual marriage ceremony has no effect. Also, Austin notes that an "appropriate" or effective performance has "a verb in the first person singular present indicative active" (67). This stipulation makes sense as well. Declaring "He does... She names... They give and bequeath... You bet..." describes actions instead of performing them, as does a shift to past or future tense. However, Austin recognizes exceptions: while "first person singular" seems appropriate, we can easily see that phrases like "We christen thee... We promise... We bet... We bequeath..." are perfectly acceptable performatives, as are some second-person constructions like "You are hereby authorized to pay..." (57). Plus, Austin offers a non-exhaustive list of necessary conditions: He notes that there must be "an accepted conventional procedure" that includes "the uttering of certain words by certain persons in certain circumstances" (14). He also notes that "the particular persons and circumstances in a given case must be appropriate for the invocation of the particular procedure invoked" (15), the speaker must complete the correct procedure, and, for lack of a better phrase, the speaker must be aware of what she is doing. Importantly, performatives done in bad faith are still performatives. For example, I may not have any intention of keeping my promise, but I am, in fact, committing myself when I say the words, "I promise." Or, I may not have money to pay you, but I did make a bet when I said, "I bet you five dollars."

Third, because this particular language act *performs* an action, we do not talk about performatives in terms of being true or false. In response to someone saying "I do" at a Christian wedding, we cannot say, "That is untrue. That is a false statement" in the same way we can dispute assertions like "The River Thames flows into Lake Superior" or "Charlotte Brontë was born in New York." Declaring a christening of a boat, a wager, or a promise "false" or "untrue" does not make sense either. And that is why Austin talks about *felicity*, or the "smooth or 'happy' functioning of a performative" (14). The effect of these performatives is felicitous or infelicitous because they perform their action well or poorly; they succeed or fail. *Validity* is another way to understand felicity. For example, if I do not have the proper authority, my naming of a boat is not valid and has no effect.

Although Austin's theory of performatives seems limited to particular kinds of sentences, especially statements that are not true or false but valid or felicitous, his insights into how language works have profound and useful applications when we read literary texts, watch films, and experience art. Austin never departs from a close attention to sentences and speech acts, but the basic principles he uncovers serve us well when we discuss language and texts as a set of practices.

POTENTIAL PROJECTS

Austin's simple concept reframes language as a set of acts, but how does the notion of performative utterances encourage us to think differently about literary texts, films, art, cultural practices, and other representations? Jonathan Culler reminds us that Austin's notion of performatives may define literary discourse: "Like the performative, the literary utterance does not refer to a prior state of affairs and is not true or false. The literary utterance too *creates* the state of affairs to which it refers" (96). How so? As Culler explains, literary works bring "into being characters and their actions" and they "bring into being ideas, concepts, which they deploy" (96). In short, the notion of literature as performative "contributes to a defense of literature: literature is not frivolous pseudo-statements but takes its place among the acts of language that transform the world, bringing into being the things that they name" (96). The idea that literature and art bring worlds into being speaks to the power of language on a grand scale, but the notion of performatives also helps us make sense of particular works that resist our desire to reduce them to *constative* utterances, mere descriptions of the world or statements about the world. The projects below reframe the way we read a wide range of literary and cultural representations.

Ask what a work is doing not saying

Building on the idea that language performs an action, that language is a practice or event, helps us make sense of texts that seem more interested in *doing* something rather than *saying* something. Think of entire works or parts of works as performative utterances. To make sense of the examples cited in the PPQ section, consider what Stein, Schwitters, and the Declaration of Independence are performing. Stein and Schwitters vex us until we stop asking what their works mean and ask instead, what are they doing? In both cases, we may conclude that they are using language as musical notes. Stein herself explains that

> what I may call the early Spanish and Geography and Play period finally resulted in things like Susie Asado and Preciosilla etc. in an extraordinary melody of words and a melody of excitement in knowing that I had done this thing.
>
> ("Lectures," 306–307)

More importantly, it is only in the act of reciting aloud "Susie Asado" and "Ursonate" that we experience the work, just as a musical score is an event the moment we hear it. The result is not true or false but *felicitous*. Our "interpretation" is less an explanation of what a work "means" or says, but an account or description of how well the work performs its task. Discuss how the work is "doing something as opposed to just saying something" and explain how the performative effect is "happy or unhappy as opposed to true or false" (132). Finally, as always, explain *how* the text does what it does.

Identify texts that embody, enact, and act

Another way to think about performatives is to recall that the work enacts or embodies its own argument. We have already drawn attention to Susan Howe, Julia Kristeva, and Jonathan Safran Foer's work in other chapters, but we can understand them in yet another way when we think of them as performatives. For example, not only does Howe's "Incloser" (1993) suggest that female American writers have broken patriarchal enclosures to express themselves, but Howe herself escapes enclosures by creating an unconventional collage of textual fragments. Kristeva writes in "Stabat Mater" (1977) that "First there is division, which precedes the pregnancy but is revealed by it, irrevocably imposed. ... Then another abyss opens between this body and the body that was inside it: the abyss that separates mother and child" (145). Her essay, divided as it is into two columns and marked by competing discourses, embodies and enacts that division. In Foer's *Tree of Codes* (2010), a boy describes a colorless sky as "a screen placed to hide the true meaning of things, a facade behind which there was an overintense coloring" (90–91), and what we hold in our hands are die-cut pages that give us only a glimpse of what is to come, a kind of screen that hides the meaning of things. John Barth's story "Lost in the Funhouse" (1968) draws attention to the conventions of storytelling as he narrates the story, and this self-reflexive technique enacts Barth's conviction that "Artistic conventions are liable to be retired, subverted, transcended, transformed, or even deployed against themselves to generate new and lively work" (205). Or consider two visual examples. Norman Rockwell's image on the cover of the February 13, 1960, issue of *The Saturday Evening Post*, "Triple Self Portrait," not only produces a self-portrait, but the painting comments on portraiture as a genre by drawing attention to the process of producing a portrait. Spike Jonze's film *Adaptation* (2002) performs the act of ruminating on the process of adaptation as we watch the film which adapts Susan Orlean's *The Orchid Thief* (1998). In short, your task is to use Austin's concept of performatives to clarify the logic and craft of texts that embody or enact the argument of the text itself. You need to explain that these kinds of works do not just portray or describe events, but they *are* the events themselves. Their form *is* the argument. They do what they say they are doing. Following Austin, the question, then, is not whether or not the representation is accurate or true, but "felicitous." Do these works perform their action well or poorly? Do they succeed or fail in their performance of their argument?

Reread Austin

Austin's theory of performatives and his larger discussion of "illocutionary acts" (utterances classified by content and their force or effect) sparked the interest of Jacques Derrida, and we can follow this discussion in *Limited Inc* (1988) which contains several documents. First, originally a conference paper, Derrida's "Signature Event Context" (1971) opens the volume and addresses the question of context: Can context guarantee correct or accurate meanings? Can context limit *undecidability*? Is there a difference between serious and non-serious language? Second, Gerald Graff, the editor of the collection, summarizes John R. Searle's "Reiterating the Differences: A Reply to Derrida" (1977), a critique of Derrida's reading of Austin. Searle questions four aspects of Derrida's argument, and he concentrates on language's capacity to convey intent. Third, Derrida replies to Searle in "Limited Inc a b c …" (1977). Finally, "Afterword: Toward an Ethic of Discussion" (1988) is written by Derrida in the form of a letter to the editor Gerald Graff.

As you read Austin, Derrida, and Searle, trace the various arguments about meaning, context, intention, and communication. Are there limits to a context's ability to constrain meaning? In what sense does writing convey an author's intention? In what ways does language (mis)communicate what we are thinking or (mis)understand what others are trying to say? And more specifically, does our ability to repeat, cite, and graft language undermine our ability to convey what we intend?

WORKS CITED

Austin, John Langshaw. *How to Do Things with Words*. 1962. Oxford UP, 1965.
Barth, John. "The Literature of Replenishment." *The Friday Book*, Putnam, 1984, pp. 193–206.

Culler, Jonathan. *Literary Theory: A Very Short Introduction.* Oxford UP, 2000.
"The Declaration of Independence." *National Archives,* www.archives.gov/founding-docs/declaration-transcript. Accessed 27 February 2018.
Derrida, Jacques. "Declarations of independence." *New Political Science,* vol. 7, no. 1, 1986, pp. 7–15.
———. *Limited Inc.* 1988, edited by Gerald Graff, Northwestern UP, 1990.
Foer, Jonathan Safran. *Tree of Codes.* 2010. Visual Editions, 2011.
Kristeva, Julia. "Stabat Mater." *Poetics Today,* vol. 6, no. 1/2, 1985, pp. 133–152.
Rockwell, Norman. "Triple Self Portrait." *The Saturday Evening Post,* 13 February 1960.
Schwitters, Kurt. "Ursonate." *The Dada Painters and Poets: An Anthology,* edited by Robert Motherwell, Belknap, 1989, p. 371.
Stein, Gertrude. "Lectures in America." *Gertrude Stein: Writings 1932–1946,* edited by Catharine R. Stimpson and Harriet Chessman, Library of America, 1998, pp. 191–336.
———. "Susie Asado." *Selected Writings of Gertrude Stein,* edited by Carl Van Vechten, Vintage, 1990, p. 549.

CHAPTER 4

Enjoying the carnivalesque

> Carnival celebrated temporary liberation from the prevailing truth and from the established order.
>
> (Mikhail Bakhtin 10)

PROBLEMS, PUZZLES, AND QUESTIONS

If you were in the Stux Gallery in New York in 1987, you would have encountered a Cibachrome print that portrays a crucifix seemingly bathed in amber. The crucifix itself is a deep luminescent yellow, submerged in a red-yellow liquid. Random bubbles seem to float here and there. Officially titled *Immersion (Piss Christ)*, Andreas Serrano's print spawned controversy that lasted for years. What makes viewers pause, but only after some research, is the source of that rosy glow: blood and urine. How do we make sense of such a print? Is it, as some argue, blasphemous sacrilege? Is the image, on the other hand, a beautifully composed and reverential portrayal of Jesus on the cross? Our conclusion, perhaps, depends on a series of questions: How do we feel about blood and urine? What is our attitude toward the body and bodily functions? What degrades, and what dignifies?

Nathaniel Hawthorne's "Young Goodman Brown" (1835) describes a young husband who takes leave of his wife Faith and travels deep into the woods where he meets nearly every community member he knows, from Goody Cloyse who taught him his catechism to the voice of the minister he heard every Sunday. All gather in the middle of the forest where they meet a dark figure who declares, "'Welcome, my children,' ... 'to the communion of your race'" (73). Goodman Brown cries out and tries to resist baptism, and a moment later he finds himself alone in the dark. He returns to the village, "a stern, a sad, a darkly meditative, a distrustful, if not a desperate, man" (75). Why does Goodman Brown turn away from the people he knows? Why does he distance himself, scowl, and frown? How do we make sense of the ritual in the woods? What does his reaction have to do with refusing communion with his race? What is the relationship between sacred covenants and the profane collective human race?

Burning Man is an event that invites thousands of people to Nevada's Black Rock Desert to create Black Rock City, a "temporary metropolis dedicated to community, art, self-expression, and self-reliance. In this crucible of creativity, all are welcome." Guided by "10 Principles" that range from "radical inclusion," "gifting," and "decommodification" to "communal effort," "civic responsibility," and "immediacy," and supported by tickets that cost over $900, Burning Man offers a space for free expression of all kinds, from art, intellectual ruminations, and social networking to new age spirituality, drugs, and sex. It is part pagan ritual, spiritual awakening, creative atelier, and entrepreneurial incubator. As co-founder Larry Harvey explains,

> Uniquely expressive acts get transformed and elaborated into social rites, and through participation they accrue a breadth and depth of meaning which can only be produced in a communal setting. It is the primal process by which culture is created.

Beyond committing criminal acts and trying to adhere to the 10 Principles, designers offer Burning Man as an uninhibited space, free of most social rules and conventions. Is Burning Man an unofficial event, home to normally prohibited activities, or does the festival exemplify sanctioned freedom, contained anarchy, and pseudo-liberation? Does it matter so long as participants enjoy each other's company, express their freedom, and indulge in new relationships?

A photograph of a crucifix, an allegory about Puritans, and a weeklong festival in the Nevada desert make odd company, but the examples invite us to question the fundamental connections we experience with our physical body, the relationships we form with others, and the social rules and practices we live by. Often taught to value mind over body, the spiritual over the material, we struggle to find value in the earthy and tangible. So how are we to make sense of representations that direct our attention to and even celebrate the body? And when does celebrating our body and bodily life become a political act? What is the relationship between freedom and community?

KEY PASSAGES

The profane, crude, and fleshy caught the attention of Soviet scholar Mikhail Bakhtin who wrote *Rabelais and His World* (1965), a treatise that developed the concept of the "carnivalesque" as expressed by medieval common folk culture. *Carnival* has Latin roots meaning "removal or putting away of meat." However, carnival celebrations actually indulge in meat and all kinds of food and festivities prior to Lent, a forty-day period of abstinence that prepares believers for Easter. Note, too, that carnival is linked to other raucous festivals, particularly the "Feast of Fools" which often took place in January. These "unofficial feasts" appealed to Bakhtin because they renewed the "collective ancestral body" (19) and indulged in a utopian ideal. As an exemplary case of the carnivalesque, Rabelais' goal, according to Bakhtin,

> was to destroy the official picture of events. He strove to take a new look at them, to interpret the tragedy or comedy they represented from the point of view of the laughing chorus of the marketplace. He summoned all the resources of sober popular imagery in order to break up official lies and the narrow seriousness dictated by the ruling classes.
>
> (439)

The carnival has revolutionary potential by rebelling against the establishment and socially constructed hierarchies, values, norms, and rules, and as a result, the concept offers us a way to make sense of works and practices that question ruling ideologies and offer alternatives to the prevailing social order.

> As opposed to the official feast, one might say that carnival celebrated temporary liberation from the prevailing truth and from the established order; it marked the suspension of all hierarchical rank, privileges, norms, and prohibitions. Carnival was the true feast of time, the feast of becoming, change, and renewal. It was hostile to all that was immortalized and completed.
>
> (10)
>
> In grotesque realism, therefore, the bodily element is deeply positive. It is presented not in a private, egotistic form, severed from the other spheres of life, but as

something universal, representing all the people. As such it is opposed to severance from the material and bodily roots of the world; it makes no pretense to renunciation of the earthy, or independence of the earth and the body. We repeat: the body and bodily life have here a cosmic and at the same time an all-people's character; this is not the body and its physiology in the modern sense of these words, because it is not individualized. The material bodily principle is contained not in the biological individual, not in the bourgeois ego, but in the people, a people who are continually growing and renewed. This is why all that is bodily becomes grandiose, exaggerated, immeasurable.

(19)

Degradation here means coming down to earth, the contact with earth as an element that swallows up and gives birth at the same time. To degrade is to bury, to sow, and to kill simultaneously, in order to bring forth something more and better. To degrade also means to concern oneself with the lower stratum of the body, the life of the belly and the reproductive organs; it therefore relates to acts of defecation and copulation, conception, pregnancy, and birth. Degradation digs a bodily grave for a new birth; it has not only a destructive, negative aspect, but also a regenerating one. To degrade an object does not imply merely hurling it into the void of nonexistence, into absolute destruction, but to hurl it down to the reproductive lower stratum, the zone in which conception and a new birth take place. Grotesque realism knows no other lower level; it is the fruitful earth and the womb. It is always conceiving.

(21)

It is based on the conception of the world as eternally unfinished: a world dying and being born at the same time, possessing as it were two bodies. The dual image combining praise and abuse seeks to grasp the very moment of this change, the transfer from the old to the new, from death to life. Such an image crowns and uncrowns at the same moment. In the development of class society, such a conception of the world can only be expressed in unofficial culture. There is no place for it in the culture of the ruling classes; here praise and abuse are

> clearly divided and static, for official culture is founded on the principle of an immovable and unchanging hierarchy in which the higher and the lower never merge.
>
> (166)

Like many of his Soviet colleagues, Bakhtin is interested in formal elements that characterize literary language, but he also draws attention to literature's social and ideological implications. One way to make sense of these passages is to focus on key juxtapositions and role reversals which mark differences not only in aesthetics but also in power and values.

DISCUSSION

Bakhtin discusses the carnivalesque in the context of François Rabelais' multivolume work *Gargantua and Pantagruel* and French medieval culture. By foregrounding Rabelais' satiric edge, Bakhtin helps us understand how folk culture responds to the "official and serious tone of medieval ecclesiastical and feudal culture" (4). This attention to a work's social function opens the door to the particular way that carnival humor critiques ideology, or the system of values and practices that ruling groups want to present as natural, normal, and commonsensical.

As the key passages reveal, Bakhtin defines the carnivalesque in the form of oppositions: official/unofficial, prevailing truth/emerging truth, ranked/equal, prohibited/free, spectator/participant, severed/together, heaven/earth, limited/abundant, static/fluid, masculine/feminine, immortal/mortal, complete/becoming, dead/alive, nonexistence/existence, laughter/seriousness, cerebral/genital, and mind/body. That is, Bakhtin juxtaposes the official, authoritative, and spiritual order with the unofficial, transgressive, and material life of common people, and by doing so, he links authority with sterility and the lowly with fertility and growth. The carnivalesque provides opportunities for marginalized common people to delegitimize ruling ideology by mocking, parodying, and laughing at those values and hierarchies. The carnivalesque denaturalizes the prevailing order by offering other social arrangements and values. At the very minimum, excessiveness and hilarious caricature expose social hierarchies as mere social constructs.

If the carnivalesque denotes a way of being that celebrates human physicality and commonality, then "grotesque realism" refers to a complementary form of comic vernacular literature. Phrased another way, grotesque realism describes a "peculiar type of imagery" (18) amenable to the carnival, and this aesthetic operates in two ways.

First, grotesque realism presents "cosmic, social, and bodily elements" as an "indivisible whole. And this whole is gay and gracious" (19). In other words, the *way* an author presents the material body is "deeply positive" (19). Grotesque realism celebrates human existence by universalizing bodily functions and desires. It is less a matter of momentarily praising those who defecate, copulate, vomit, and ooze; instead, grotesque realism reminds us that *everyone*—man and woman, rich and poor, young and old, the high and the low—engages in these activities, and this imagery portrays these all too human bodies and behaviors in positive and appealing ways.

Second, if grotesque realism revels in bodily fluids and movement, it also levels the high, theoretical, and mighty: "The essential principle of grotesque realism is degradation, that is, the lowering of all that is high, spiritual, ideal, abstract; it is a transfer to the material level, to the sphere of earth and body in their indissoluble unity" (19–20). Note that Bakhtin does not use the term "degradation" pejoratively. Instead, he associates degradation with reproductive discourse: sowing, birthing, regenerating, reproducing, conceiving, and creating "the zone in which conception and a new birth take place" (21). By degrading the high-minded, spiritual, idealized, and abstract, grotesque realism unifies humans and promotes growth. Put yet another way, in its positive portrayals of the human body, grotesque realism degrades sex in the sense that copulation is not a clean, spiritual, and abstract activity. Instead, sex involves dirty, stinky, loud, and wet bodies, but the act brings people together and initiates new life. While grotesque realism degrades sex, it also celebrates this messy act by associating basic desires with fertility and new life. What could be more necessary and glorious than earthy, sweaty bodies coming together?

Carnivalesque and grotesque realism share a transgressive desire to transform the ordinary: "The grotesque image reflects a phenomenon in transformation, an as yet unfinished metamorphosis, of death and birth, growth and becoming" (24). This celebration of process contrasts with the "ready-made, completed being" (25). Yes, the carnivalesque crosses ideological, moral, and aesthetic boundaries, and the result may be that grotesque images are "ugly, monstrous, hideous from the point of view of 'classic' aesthetics" (25) because classic aesthetics values "the ready-made and the completed," (25) but Bakhtin, following Rabelais, celebrates the process of transformation and change.

For Bakhtin, the carnivalesque and the aesthetic of grotesque realism do not offer a utopian state, a mere alternative to the sterile and static unchanging social hierarchy. In fact, a ready-made vision of what society ought to be contradicts the very premise of the carnivalesque which thrives on transgression and fluidity. The carnivalesque and grotesque realism are always oppositional, for they are, by definition, "unofficial culture" (166). As Bakhtin explains, there is no place for the carnivalesque "in the culture of the ruling classes; here praise and abuse are clearly divided and static, for official culture is founded on the principle of an immovable and unchanging hierarchy in which the higher and the lower never merge" (166). Bakhtin suggests, then, that a society arranged by class and rules will, by its very structure, invite critique, and the carnivalesque is one form of opposition. By disrupting social norms, questioning hierarchies, and bringing "gloomy, disincarnated medieval truth … 'down to earth' through laughter" (176), the carnivalesque lays the groundwork for social change.

POTENTIAL PROJECTS

Remember that Bakhtin describes the carnivalesque as a way to respond to official culture, prevailing values, and hierarchies, and he explains how grotesque realism is one of the ways that we encounter the carnivalesque in language and imagery. We look for works that present a topsy-turvy world, and we are mindful of how an author, filmmaker, or artist presents that inverted world in form and content.

Subvert hierarchies and roles

Following Bakhtin, explore the subversive potential of texts or parts of texts that portray in content and/or form the carnivalesque impulse. In terms of content, texts may concern themselves "with the lower stratum of the body, the life of the belly and the reproductive organs; it therefore relates to acts of defecation and copulation, conception, pregnancy, and birth" (21). The work may portray scenes that describe moments of "temporary liberation from the prevailing truth and from the established order" (10). The text may present action that suspends "all hierarchical rank, privileges, norms, and prohibitions" (10). The language itself may be "grandiose, exaggerated, immeasurable" (19). The author's use of syntax, grammar, diction, form, and tone may transgress language codes and linguistic systems. Note how a work resists closure, scrambles chronology, and revels in multiple voices, registers, dialects, high and low discourse, folk and classic allusions. Pay attention to incongruous, expansive, excessive, and grotesque descriptions. In other words, how does the content and form of a work humorously "degrade" the social order and language itself in the sense that the author, artist, or filmmaker humanizes everyone, celebrates the collective human body, brings us down to earth, all in an effort to "bring forth something more and better" (21), especially through laughter?

Question boundaries

Some scholars have pointed out that carnival merely works as an escape hatch that siphons off revolutionary potential. Terry Eagleton, for example, points out that "Carnival, after all, is a *licensed* affair in every sense, a permissible rupture of hegemony, a contained popular blow-off as disturbing and relatively ineffectual as a revolutionary work of art" (148). While Bakhtinian scholars respond by saying that the carnivalesque offers a set of symbolic practices that revolutionaries and protesters employ during social conflicts, we should still examine ways that ruling groups use a temporary lapse in order to preserve their power. Therefore, explore how the work or practice portrays this particular power dynamic.

A variation on this project invites us to mark the limits of the carnivalesque in another way. Bakhtin insists that degradation destroys, but also regenerates: "Degradation digs a bodily grave for a new birth" (21). Portrayals of human corpulence and fleshy acts are not really about individuals *per se*, but humankind because the "material bodily principle is contained not in the biological individual, not in the bourgeois ego, but in the people, a people who are continually growing and renewed" (19). However, are there, perhaps, depictions of the body, "acts of defecation and copulation, conception, pregnancy, and birth" (21), that do not renew our sense of community and fail to suspend "all hierarchical rank, privileges, norms, and prohibitions" (10)? Does "degradation" take on different forms? Can we identify forms of degradation that renew and regenerate while others merely destroy and ruin? Can you theorize the difference between liberating and limiting forms of degradation?

WORKS CITED

Bakhtin, Mikhail. *Rabelais and His World*. 1965. Translated by Helene Iswolsky, Indiana UP, 1984.
Burning Man. burningman.org. Accessed 27 January 2018.
Eagleton, Terry. *Walter Benjamin or Towards a Revolutionary Criticism*. Verso, 1981.
Hawthorne, Nathaniel. "Young Goodman Brown." *Nathaniel Hawthorne's Tales*, edited by James McIntosh. Norton, 1987, pp. 65–74.

CHAPTER 5

Reading as writing

> Because the goal of literary work (of literature as work) is to make the reader no longer a consumer, but a producer of the text.
>
> (Roland Barthes *S/Z* 4)

PROBLEMS, PUZZLES, OR QUESTIONS

Sometimes we come across works that seem to demand something different of us. The form breaks from convention or uses technology in new ways. For example, Susan Howe's prose piece "Incloser" (1993) offers the reader a series of seemingly unrelated paragraphs: a definition of "to enclose," an Emily Dickinson poem, a description of how trappers used beaver dams as bridges, Howe's personal ruminations, a puritan catechism, a passage of literary theory, and a paragraph from Cotton Mather's *Magnalia Christi Americana*, among many other fragments. The types of citations range from historical documents, memoir, and poetry, to dictionary entries, academic scholarship, and religious works. This literary collage vexes readers because no transitions exist between passages. We can imagine Howe arranging random quotes that escaped from a library bookshelf.

In 1987, Michael Joyce published "afternoon, a story," a work of hypertext fiction. In 1990, Eastgate Systems published the story in diskette form. The story begins with a first-person narrator: "I try to recall winter." A short scene description follows. However, "afternoon, a story" differs from other narratives because the reader can choose from a collection of hyperlinks on each page, and these links lead to different narrative pathways. Given this freedom and sheer number of links, every reader will encounter a different experience and draw different conclusions.

Jonathan Safran Foer created *Tree of Codes* (2010) by excising words and passages from Bruno Schulz' 1934 short story collection *The Street of Crocodiles*. *Tree of Codes* is delicate and fragile because selected words and passages are literally cut out of the page, leaving holes that allow readers to see words and phrases that peek through from beneath. We are not sure if we should read one page at a time, two pages, or as many as possible.

These works make us pause because of their radical form, but they are not alone in their desire to celebrate multiplicity and intertextuality. Like many experimental poems, stories, plays, films, and art, they ask the reader to take an active role in constructing the text. They foreground the questions: What is the role of the writer and reader? What does the text ask us to do?

KEY PASSAGE

Roland Barthes' *S/Z* (1970) interprets in detail Honoré de Balzac's short story "Sarrasine." He describes five codes we can use to interpret the story, and while a discussion of these particular codes lies beyond our immediate interest, the core idea is that a text is a collection of woven codes: "*text, fabric, braid*: the same thing" (160). Barthes' textile metaphor suggests that writing is crisscrossed with overlapping discourses and conversations, asserting that we should "listen to the text as an iridescent exchange carried on by multiple voices, on different wavelengths" (41–42). This notion of layered voices speaking simultaneously helps us understand two kinds of texts—readerly and writerly—and these two categories help us understand a range of works that expect something different of a reader.

In the opening pages of *S/Z*, Barthes asserts that

> On the one hand, there is what it is possible to write, and on the other, what it is no longer possible to write: what is within the practice of the writer and what has left it: which texts would I consent to write (to re-write), to desire, to put forth as a force in this world of mine? What evaluation finds is precisely this value: what can be written (rewritten) today: the *writerly*. Why is the writerly our value? Because the goal of literary work (of literature as work) is to make the reader no longer a consumer, but a producer

> of the text. Our literature is characterized by the pitiless divorce which the literary institution maintains between the producer of the text and its user, between its owner and its customer, between its author and its reader. This reader is thereby plunged into a kind of idleness—he is intransitive; he is, in short, *serious*: instead of functioning himself, instead of gaining access to the magic of the signifier, to the pleasure of writing, he is left with no more than the poor freedom either to accept or reject the text: reading is nothing more than a *referendum*. Opposite the writerly text, then, is its countervalue, its negative, reactive value: what can be read, but not written: the *readerly*. We call any readerly text a classic text.
>
> (4)

Keep in mind this key shift: Barthes wants us to acknowledge the value of the "writerly text," and his theory of reading and writing will help us make sense of texts that ask us to actively "produce" rather than idly "consume."

DISCUSSION

Barthes invents the terms "readerly" and "writerly" (*lisible* and *scriptible* in French) to refer to different roles a text asks us to play.

Readerly texts

Barthes asserts that our literary institutions privilege conventional ways of thinking about and writing literature which separates writers from readers. Writers write; readers read. Writers produce; readers consume. When writers embrace this assumption, then "a reader is thereby plunged into a kind of idleness—he is intransitive" (4). A foray into grammar is useful here. An intransitive verb is a verb that does not take a direct object: I sneezed. He went to campus. They arrived late. She died. Notice that the subject of the sentence does not act on something else. The verbs do not transfer action to a person or to an object. On the other hand, a transitive verb—eat, wash, throw, write—suggests that the subject acts on something else: I'm eating a hot dog. They wash the car. We are throwing a ball. She writes a novel. Therefore, when Barthes says that readerly texts make readers intransitive, he is claiming that those works make readers inactive. As a result, a reader is "left with no more than the poor freedom either to accept or reject the text: reading is nothing more than a *referendum*" (4). In other words, a reader's task is to follow along, receive information, and arrive at a predetermined outcome. Note that when Barthes concludes that "any readerly text [is] a classic text" (4), he is not necessarily celebrating those works. Instead, he is asserting that they are merely conventional.

Writerly texts

If readerly texts encourage readers to be idle consumers, a writerly text transforms the reader into a "writer" because the goal is to make the reader "no longer a consumer, but a producer of the text" (4). Barthes maintains that a writerly text will allow a reader to actively create the text, someone who "constructs" the work. How so? The writerly text gives "access to the magic of the signifier, to the pleasure of writing" (4). As a result, a writerly text foregrounds these codes, thus drawing attention to the multiple, complex, and intertextual layers of meaning, and the act of connecting these codes provides pleasure, an issue we will return to shortly.

Two other works, one written before *S/Z*, the other written after, help us clarify Barthes' theory of the readerly and writerly.

Roland Barthes wrote the short essay "The Death of the Author" (1967), asserting that

> there is one place where this multiplicity is focused and that place is the reader, not, as was hitherto said, the author. The reader is the space on which all the quotations that make up a writing are inscribed without any of them being lost; a text's unity lies not in its origin but in its destination. ... The birth of the reader must be at the cost of the death of the Author.
>
> (148)

Barthes is interested in the source of coherence. Who gathers and unifies all the elements one finds in a text? The idea that the reader, the destination, provides unity may strike one as counterintuitive, for does not the author create the story? Instead, Barthes maintains that the reader is the producer or creator of meaning because the reader makes sense of the various elements in a text. However, it is not just a matter of connecting language, characters, settings, tone, etc. and drawing conclusions. Instead, Barthes points out that "a text is made of multiple writings, drawn from many cultures and entering into mutual relations of dialogue, parody, contestation" (148). In other words, the words and sentences we read endlessly refer to traces of other words, texts, references, influences, and representations that differ in resonance and significance. Imagine an endless web of connections and meaning. The reader "listens" to that dialogue and generates meaning and significance, thus becoming a "writer."

We note that Barthes associates writerly texts with pleasure, and in *The Pleasure of the Text* (1973), Barthes distinguishes between two kinds of pleasure: *plaisir* and *jouissance*, often translated as pleasure and bliss.

> Text of pleasure: the text that contents, fills, grants euphoria; the text that comes from culture and does not break with it, is linked to a *comfortable* practice of reading. Text of bliss: the text that imposes a state of loss, the text that discomforts (perhaps to the point of a certain boredom), unsettles the reader's historical, cultural, psychological assumptions, the consistency of his tastes, values, memories, brings to a crisis his relation with language.
>
> (14)

Readerly texts do provide pleasure. The works comfort us by staying within conventional boundaries and reinforcing common value systems and choices. We recognize characters, plots, and ways of speaking. However, writerly texts provide bliss, but notice that bliss is not just more pleasure. Bliss is uncomfortable. Bliss unsettles conventions and traditional ways of thinking, writing, and reading. Or as Jean-Michel Rabaté explains, "*Jouissance* calls up a violent, climactic bliss closer to loss, death, fragmentation, and the disruptive rapture experienced when transgressing limits, whereas *plaisir* simply hints at an easy going enjoyment, more stable in its reenactment of cultural codes" (48). While his terminology does not sound inviting or appealing—imposes a state of loss, discomforts, unsettles, brings to a crisis—Barthes celebrates these states because they transgress limits and boundaries in much the same way that positive events like spiritual rapture or sexual ecstasy exceed our conventional and ordinary experiences.

These concepts and ways of describing what texts expect of the reader and the kinds of enjoyment they offer help us make sense of a wide range of avant-garde and challenging works as well as understand familiar texts in a new way.

POTENTIAL PROJECT

Admittedly, all literature and cultural representations, no matter how simple, require readers to work and "construct" an interpretation. As

Italian scholar Umberto Eco reminds us, "Texts are lazy machineries that ask someone to do part of their job" (214). In other words, we are not talking about texts that are simply readerly or writerly. Instead, place texts on a continuum. Works are *more* or *less* readerly and writerly. Some texts depart from a *"comfortable* practice of reading" (*Pleasure* 14) and invite us to actively participate in the act of writing more than others. Thinking in terms of a spectrum gives us some freedom to focus on entire works or just key parts.

Categorize a text

Find a complicated, multilayered, even multimedia text, a text that *refuses* to leave the reader "with no more than the poor freedom either to accept or reject the text" (*S/Z* 4). The text may play with form and technology as my initial examples demonstrate, or they may experiment with narrative strategy as we see in James Joyce's *Ulysses* (1922) or *Finnegans Wake* (1939), William Faulkner's *Absalom, Absalom!* (1936), Virginia Woolf's *Orlando* (1928), T. S. Eliot's *The Waste Land* (1922), John Barth's *Lost in the Funhouse* (1968), Susan Griffin's *A Chorus of Stones: The Private Life of War* (1992), Leslie Marmon Silko's *Almanac of the Dead* (1991), Jennifer Egan's *A Visit from the Goon Squad* (2010), or Jeff VanderMeer's *City of Saints and Madmen* (2001). Films like *Citizen Kane* (1941), *Adaptation* (2002), *Memento* (2001), *Mr. Nobody* (2009), *Tristram Shandy: A Cock and Bull Story* (2005), and *Inherent Vice* (2014) invite viewers to actively provide coherence. These examples suggest that you are most likely to encounter these texts in high modern and postmodern circles, but that is not always the case.

The goal is not to use Barthes to interpret the text in a conventional sense. You are not deciphering what a text suggests, implies, or means. Instead, you are using Barthes to describe the *function* of the text, and that function is to transform readers into active "writers" of the text. If you follow Barthes' lead, your research questions will be along the lines of, Does the novel encourage the reader to be an idle consumer or an active producer of the text? Does the work satisfy a reader's expectations, follow convention, reinforce cultural codes, and provide a *"comfortable* practice of reading" (*Pleasure* 14), or does the text break conventions, unsettle "the reader's historical, cultural, psychological assumptions" (14), and question a reader's tastes, values, and memories? Does the story invite the reader to actively construct and complete the text? Does the text provide pleasure or bliss?

As always, and with a good sense of whether or not the text is writerly or readerly in mind, you should identify the strategies the author, filmmaker, or artist uses to create such a text. What is it about the text that makes the reader idle? What strategies does the author use that make the text a mere referendum? On the other hand, what is it about the work that invites the reader to actively construct new meanings? What methods does the filmmaker use to unsettle our assumptions? What strategies does the artist employ to multiply meaning and generate indeterminacy instead of limit meaning?

WORKS CITED

Barthes, Roland. *S/Z*. 1970. Translated by Richard Miller, Hill, 1974.

———. *The Pleasure of the Text*. 1973. Translated by Richard Miller, Hill, 1975.

———. "The Death of the Author." *Image/Music/Text*. 1967. Translated by Stephen Heath, Hill, 1977.

Eco, Umberto. *The Role of the Reader: Explorations in the Semiotics of Texts*. Indiana UP, 1979.

Joyce, Michael. "afternoon, a story." Hypertext. Eastgate. 1987/1990.

Rabaté, Jean-Michel. "Barthes, Roland." *The Johns Hopkins Guide to Literary Theory and Criticism*, edited by Michael Groden, Martin Kreiswirth, and Imre Szeman, Johns Hopkins UP, 2012, pp. 44–49.

CHAPTER 6

Simulating the real

> Simulation is no longer that of a territory, a referential being or a substance.
> (Jean Baudrillard 2)

PROBLEMS, PUZZLES, AND QUESTIONS

The Matrix (1999) portrays a world where humans, encased in womb-like pods, provide energy for machines, yet the wired humans experience a virtual reality they fail to recognize as unreal. Morpheus recruits Neo, reveals the truth of his condition, and with a small group of revolutionaries battle to rid themselves of the robots who enslave them. Paying homage to French sociologist Jean Baudrillard, Neo stashes his money and computer files in a hollowed out copy of *Simulacres et Simulation*. The shot is a heavy-handed and pretentious invitation to ponder the book's significance, but does Baudrillard's work really help explain the film? And why would Baudrillard himself declare, "The most embarrassing part of the film is that the new problem posed by simulation is confused with its classical, Platonic treatment. This is a serious flaw" (qtd. in Smith 180).

Fake news, in the sense of fabricated content presented as real, is not new, but the concept makes the headlines today. In response, educators, journalists, and others offer seemingly helpful advice. For example, the International Federation of Library Associations and Institutions provides a pedagogical infographic with a list of imperatives and questions: "Consider the source. Check the author. Check the date. Check your biases. Read beyond. Supporting sources? Is it a joke? Ask the experts." The problem and solution exemplify a rationalist approach to reality which assumes we live in a world of truth and error, and we can discern between the two if we use the right methods. However, in the age of TV, Internet, virtual reality, new media, populist leaders, and 10-minute news cycles, the boundary between real and fake seems porous. At what point does the imitation become the reality? When does the image precede the real? What happens when representations—substitutions for reality—become our reality? And how will we even know?

KEY PASSAGES

Often known as a key theorist of postmodernism, Jean Baudrillard addresses the problem of representation in *Simulacres et Simulation* (1981), a work that grows out of larger academic discussions about the relationship between symbols, media, power, ideology, and economic systems. Baudrillard also addresses what some call the "hermeneutics of suspicion," a phrase coined by Paul Ricoeur to refer to the writings of Marx, Freud, and Nietzsche who describe a world of hidden systems that lie beneath the surface. For these practitioners, the goal is to uncover and decode disguised meanings and hidden structures. Baudrillard questions this surface-depth model by exploring the relationship between the object and its representation, between the thing and the idea. His insights help us explain our contemporary condition that is saturated by mass media and new forms of communication.

> Simulation is no longer that of a territory, a referential being or a substance. It is the generation by models of a real without origin or reality: a hyperreal. The territory no longer precedes the map, nor survives it.
>
> (2)
>
> All of Western faith and good faith was engaged in this wager on representation: that a sign could refer to the depth of meaning, that a sign could *exchange* for meaning and that something could guarantee this exchange—God, of course.
>
> (10)
>
> So it is with simulation, insofar as it is opposed to representation. The latter starts from the principle that the sign and the real are equivalent (even if this equivalence is utopian, it is a fundamental axiom). Conversely, simulation

> starts from the *utopia* of this principle of equivalence, *from the radical negation of the sign as value*, from the sign as reversion and death sentence of every reference. Whereas representation tries to absorb simulation by interpreting it as false representation, simulation envelops the whole edifice of representation as itself a simulacrum.
>   This would be the successive phases of the image:
>
> —it is the reflection of a basic reality
> —it masks and perverts a basic reality
> —it masks the *absence* of a basic reality
> —it bears no relation to any reality whatever: it is its own pure simulacrum.
>
> (11)
>
> Disneyland is presented as imaginary in order to make us believe that the rest is real, when in fact all of Los Angeles and the America surrounding it are no longer real, but of the order of the hyperreal and of simulation. It is no longer a question of a false representation of reality (ideology), but of concealing the fact that the real is no longer real, and thus of saving the reality principle.
>
> (25)

Key words for Baudrillard are representation, simulation, simulacrum, reality, and hyperreality, and these concepts circle around questions like, Is there a difference between an object and its representation, an original and its copy? What role do representations play? How do simulations differ from representations? What is the difference between reality and hyperreality?

DISCUSSION

To answer those questions, a useful first step is to discuss the trajectory or "phases" Baudrillard describes that chart the relationship between reality or "the thing itself" and the image, sound, mark, etc. we use to represent the real.

First, when Baudrillard says that the image (a sign or representation) reflects a basic reality, he is referring to an idealized version of what images do. In this case, the representation is equivalent to the object we are trying to represent. The representation conveys truth.

For example, a drawing of a cow is the cow itself. While this idea seems far-fetched, we encounter versions of this one-to-one relationship between representations and reality in religion, and Baudrillard nudges us in this direction when he says this first phase is "of the order of sacrament" (12). A "sacrament" is an outward or visible sign of inward and spiritual grace. In other words, the sign and the moment of grace are equivalent. The sign *is* the moment of grace. Note, too, that the Christian communion wafer is both representation *and* body of Christ. Or, consider the first sentence of the Gospel of John in the New Testament: "In the beginning was the Word, and the Word was with God, and the Word was God." We often think that words represent or stand in for people, places, things, and actions, as well as thoughts, feelings, and experiences, but here Word and God become synonymous. Word and God are equivalent. In this utopian scenario, no gap exists between the representation and the thing itself, and that is why the image can reflect the basic reality.

Second, when Baudrillard writes that the image "masks and perverts a basic reality" (11), he suggests that we recognize that representations substitute themselves for reality. The word "cow," the sound "kou," or the drawing of a cow actually obscures the real cow. We recognize a gap between the object itself and the representation or sign we use to communicate what we see or hear. *The Diary of a Young Girl* (1947) "masks and perverts" Anne Frank's life; Claude Monet's *Poppy Field, Argenteuil* (1875) distorts a real poppy field in Argenteuil; Peter O'Toole only pretends to be T. E. Lawrence in *Lawrence of Arabia* (1962). We still think in terms of true and false, surface and depth. We recognize that we are looking at a copy, a mere imitation, but an original, reality itself, still exists. In short, representations mask reality because they are not equivalent to reality.

Third, declaring that the image "masks the *absence* of a basic reality" (11) describes a situation where the *idea* of the genuine article still exists, but access escapes us. Because of industrial methods of reproduction, copies proliferate, and we are awash in images, copies, and reproductions, and the result is that (1) the original, the thing itself, matters less to us, especially because the representation imitates the original so well, and (2) one copy is not more important than another copy. In fact, we cannot distinguish between the copies. The photo of the Eiffel Tower I purchase in Paris does not differ from the same photo you purchase. The version of *The Matrix* I watch at the theater does not differ from *The Matrix* you watch in your town. This development erodes the idea "that a sign could refer to the depth of meaning, that a sign could *exchange* for meaning" (10).

Before we discuss the final phase, notice the development Baudrillard maps for us so far. Initially, a representation is equivalent, equal, or true to reality, then copies come between us and reality, and then mass-produced copies of reality make the original increasingly irrelevant. That process still describes a "representation," and the *re-* of that word implies an original and a copy. A "presentation" arrives first, then a "re-presentation" appears later. We may lose sight of reality, but it lingers as a possibility. The last phase—simulation—erases that possibility.

In the final phrase, Baudrillard claims that we are living in a time of *simulation* and *simulacra* (words that suggest copy, but also counterfeit and fake), not representation, because the representation "bears no relation to any reality whatever: it is its own pure simulacrum" (11). In other words, we only have simulations because representations no longer exist because "presentations" no longer exist to "re-present." Instead, we encounter copies of copies without originals. To put it yet another way, Baudrillard not only reverses cause and effect by suggesting that "models of a real" (2) exist before reality (the representation arrives before the thing represented), but he is arguing that we never experience any reality…ever. Simulations, models of a real, generate a "hyperreal." An echo chamber illustrates the concept reasonably well in the sense that voices reverberate off the walls, and each reverberation copies another. What about the original voice? In Baudrillard's description of hyperreality, that original voice is long gone and inaccessible. Instead, we only have echoes of echoes, copies of copies, imitations of imitations. One might say, "But we can get to the bottom of this; we can ferret out the truth." However, we can never arrive at the truth because we have lost contact with any sense of the real that we can use to identify what is authentic and what is not.

Baudrillard also explains that simulations serve an important purpose: "Whereas representation tries to absorb simulation by interpreting it as false representation, simulation envelops the whole edifice of representation as itself a simulacrum" (11). As noted above, representations assume a difference between an original and its imitation, but simulations erase the boundary between original and imitation. Disneyland, for Baudrillard, epitomizes simulation and the hyperreal. This playground is a "perfect model of all the entangled orders of simulation" (23). The problem is not that Disneyland offers acreage of space dedicated to fantasy and illusion. Everyone knows that Disneyland is an imitation. We know that the site, characters, and narratives are fake. More to the point, by being a blatant imitation, Disneyland preserves the idea or concept of reality. Or, as Baudrillard phrases it,

> Disneyland is presented as imaginary in order to make us believe that the rest is real, when in fact all of Los Angeles and the America surrounding it are no longer real, but of the order of the hyperreal and of simulation.
>
> (25)

In other words, by contrasting so dramatically from the "outside," Disneyland hides the fact that the park is

> meant to be an infantile world, in order to make us believe that the adults are elsewhere, in the 'real' world, and to conceal the fact that real childishness is everywhere, particularly amongst those adults who go there to act the child in order to foster illusions as to their real childishness.
>
> (25)

To offer another analogy, I wear a costume on Halloween, but pretending to be a mummy "conceals the fact" that I pretend everyday. I am always in costume. I have no true identity.

But does this talk of concealment not remind us of the "hermeneutics of suspicion" with its desire to uncover hidden structures, systems, and desires? Not quite. For Baudrillard, simulations do not hide reality. Instead, simulations hide the fact that everything is a simulation. We live in a world where appearances do not differ from reality. We always and only encounter surfaces, for there is no depth to be found.

POTENTIAL PROJECTS

Unlike most projects in this textbook, Baudrillard is not giving us tools so that we can decipher, unmask, or uncover a hidden reality. He may help us rethink and reconceptualize the "real" as we saw in the Disneyland example, but he does not encourage us to think in terms of surface/depth models, and he does not ask us to search for reality lurking behind appearances. Instead, Baudrillard insists that we live in a world where those very boundaries blur and dissolve. He wants us to think more theoretically about the role representations play in our lives. He wants us to question what a representation even is and challenge the premise that representations convey reality. He also gives us a way of talking about texts that reflect on the same issues and concepts. As for representations, we ask, yet again, *not* what something *means*, but how it *functions*.

Question the relationship between nature and culture

Following Baudrillard, it would be easy enough to explore how all cultural representations (a literary work, film, art, media, advertising, news, TV, cultural practice, technologies, etc.) merely mask the fact we live in a hyperreal world, "the product of an irradiating synthesis of combinatory models" (3). That project is not very appealing because it just confirms Baudrillard's foundational claim. A more interesting path to take is to examine representations that explore, expose, and draw attention to the questionable boundaries between fact and fiction, virtual and real. Baudrillard himself draws attention to *The Truman Show* (1998), *Minority Report* (2002), and *Mulholland Drive* (2001). We could add *JFK* (1991), *Scott Pilgrim vs. the World* (2010), *Synecdoche, New York* (2008), or a film short by London designer Keiichi Matsuda aptly named *Hyper-Reality* (2016). We see similar meditations on how signs precede reality in John Barth's *Lost in the Funhouse* (1968), Art Spiegelman's *Maus I and II* (1986, 1991), David Foster Wallace's *The Pale King* (2011), Thomas Pynchon's *Mason and Dixon* (1997), Don DeLillo's *White Noise* (1985), and the works of William Gibson, among so many more. These works describe and comment on the fundamental relationship between reality and the signs we use to represent reality.

Your task, then, is to use Baudrillard's vocabulary and concepts to clarify and explain the ways these works address binaries like medium/message, surface/depth, truth/illusion, representation/reality, and representation/simulation. The key move is to focus on ways that texts explore the idea that reality has disappeared, and signs/images/representations create and only respond to each other. Or put another way, examine the ways that models, representations, and signs generate a simulation of reality that we then respond to as though it were reality. As you discuss the works, the goal is not to affirm Baudrillard's claims, but instead, use Baudrillard's concepts to frame your discussion, pointing out how the texts themselves may resist, clarify, modify, or extend his theory of representation and simulation.

Identify phases

While the first project focuses on the fourth phase, the image "bears no relation to any reality whatever: it is its own pure simulacrum" (11), Baudrillard's description of the "successive phases of the image" (11) offers a useful framework and vocabulary to discuss how a wide range of works approach the relationship between reality and the tools we use to represent the real. Does, say, Virginia Woolf's *To the Lighthouse* (1927) mask the *absence* of a basic reality? As a work of performative fiction, does Salman Rushdie's *The Satanic Verses* (1988) reflect a basic reality? In what sense might Barry Unsworth's historical fiction *Sacred Hunger* (1992) mask and pervert a basic reality? Your goal is not merely to confirm or deny that a work reflects, masks, or perverts a basic reality, but to use Baudrillard's outline to discuss *how* a literary work explores the problem of fiction and nonfiction, the imitation and the original, the present and the absent.

WORKS CITED

Baudrillard, Jean. *Simulations*. 1981. Translated by Paul Foss, Paul Patton, and Philip Beitchman, Semiotext(e), 1983.
"How To Spot Fake News." *International Federation of Library Associations and Institutions*, www.ifla.org/publications/node/11174. Accessed 16 January 2018.
Smith, Richard G. *Jean Baudrillard: From Hyperreality to Disappearance*. Edinburgh UP, 2015.

CHAPTER 7

Creating a space between

> These 'in-between' spaces provide the terrain for elaborating strategies of selfhood—singular or communal—that initiate new signs of identity.
>
> (Homi K. Bhabha 2)

PROBLEMS, PUZZLES, AND QUESTIONS

Consider three ways to think about identity:
    The metaphor that continues to guide the United States' view of national identity, the metaphor that exemplifies the national motto *e pluribus unum*, is, of course, the "melting pot," an image popularized by the English Jew Israel Zangwill, whose 1908 play about immigrants traveling to the United States became one of the most successful productions in the history of Broadway. Zangwill's *The Melting Pot* recasts the story of Romeo and Juliet. This time, instead of feuding families in a medieval Italian city, the lovers are from Russian Jewish and Russian Cossack families. The play emphatically presents the United States as a new country where the old hatreds have no place. God, our hero David suggests, is using the States as a "crucible" to melt Europeans into a metal from which He can cast Americans. The melting pot metaphor, more often than not, prompts people to conceptualize identity as a process of combining roles so that an "American" is a little bit of this and a little bit of that. That image is not quite correct. For Zangwill, the "great Alchemist" stirs the melting pot, whose "roaring fires of God are fusing our race with all the others" (95) and melting away "all race-differences and vendettas" (179). In short, the melting pot pours out a completely new identity, Americans, in the same way base metals produce gold. Nothing remains of old elements.

Tato Laviera's poem "AmeRícan" (1985) plays with accents: "with the big R and the / accent on the í!" (37–38). He sprinkles stanzas with Spanish: "la española," "jíbaro," "*que corta*," "*destino*." Linguistic mixing provides a home: "speaking new words in spanglish tenements" (41). And he focuses on movement: "across forth and across back / back across and forth back / forth across and back and forth / our trips are walking bridges!" (21–24). He uses a small "i" that dreams "to take the accent from / the altercation, and be proud to call / myself american, in the u.s. sense of the / word, AmeRícan, America!" (57–60). In short, the Puerto Rican gives "birth to a new generation" (5), a true hybrid identity.

Salman Rushdie's characters often find themselves in airplanes. Moraes Zogoiby, who boards a plane to Granada in *The Moor's Last Sigh* (1995), addresses us:

> You will see that I had entered an unfamiliar state of mind. The place, language, people and customs I knew had all been removed from me by the simple act of boarding this flying vehicle; and these, for most of us, are the four anchors of the soul.
>
> (383)

In *The Ground Beneath Her Feet* (1999), Ormus Cama, en route to London, feels euphoric: "As the plane lifts from his native soil, so his heart lifts also, he sheds his old skin without a second thought, crosses that frontier as if it didn't exist, like a shape-shifter, like a snake" (250). In *The Satanic Verses* (1988), a plane explodes en route to England, and Chamcha and Farishta transform as they fall to the ground. Along with all kinds of normal debris, a broken plane would spill as it falls from the sky, "there floated the debris of the soul, broken memories, sloughed-off selves, severed mother-tongues, violated privacies, untranslatable jokes, extinguished futures, lost loves, the forgotten meaning of hollow, booming words, *land, belonging, home*" (4–5). For Rushdie, being in-between presents new opportunities.

Melting and fusing European immigrants, accenting the í of Puerto Rican-Americans, and transforming Indians in mid-air all portray different ways to create identity, a new self. Rushdie's *The Satanic Verses* asks, perhaps, the most relevant questions of all. As Chamcha and Farishta fall toward the sea, the narrator ponders:

> How does newness come into the world? How is it born? Of what fusions, translations, conjoinings is it made? How does it survive, extreme and dangerous as it is? What compromises, what deals,

what betrayals of its secret nature must it make to stave off the wrecking crew, the exterminating angel, the guillotine? Is birth always a fall? Do angels have wings? Can men fly?

(8–9)

KEY PASSAGES

Homi Bhabha's *The Location of Culture* (1994) addresses these questions of identity in interesting ways. Writing amidst a surge of scholarship discussing postcolonial states, cosmopolitanism, and multiculturalism, Bhabha's work examines the formation of identity, particularly in the face of colonialism's legacy. For Bhabha, the source of our identity is not an essential, static, or primordial sense of self. Instead, identity is generated in liminal or "in-between spaces," the social zones where different identities encounter each other. As a result, the identities of the colonized and the colonizer are always interdependent, and Bhabha helps us understand that relationship as well as possible productive outcomes.

> The move away from the singularities of "class" or "gender" as primary conceptual and organizational categories has resulted in an awareness of the subject positions—of race, gender, generation, institutional location, geopolitical locale, sexual orientation—that inhabit any claim to identity in the modern world. What is theoretically innovative, and politically crucial, is the need to think beyond narratives of originary and initial subjectivities and to focus on those moments or processes that are produced in the articulation of cultural differences. These "in-between" spaces provide the terrain for elaborating strategies of selfhood—singular or communal—that initiate new signs of identity, and innovative sites of collaboration, and contestation, in the act of defining the idea of society itself.
>
> (2)
>
> It is in the emergence of the interstices—the overlap and displacement of domains of difference—that the intersubjective and collective experiences of *nationness*, community interest, or cultural value are negotiated.
>
> (2)

Political empowerment, and the enlargement of the multiculturalist cause, come from posing questions of solidarity and community from the interstitial perspective. Social differences are not simply given to experience through an already authenticated cultural tradition; they are the signs of the emergence of community envisaged as a project—at once a vision and a construction—that takes you "beyond" yourself in order to return, in a spirit of revision and reconstruction, to the political *conditions* of the present.

(4)

The "beyond" is neither a new horizon, nor a leaving behind of the past.... Beginnings and endings may be the sustaining myths of the middle years; but in the *fin de siècle*, we find ourselves in the moment of transit where space and time cross to produce complex figures of difference and identity, past and present, inside and outside, inclusion and exclusion. For there is a sense of disorientation, a disturbance of direction, in the "beyond": an exploratory, restless movement caught so well in the French rendition of the words *au-delà*—here and there, on all sides, *fort/da*, hither and thither, back and forth.

(1–2)

For the demography of the new internationalism is the history of postcolonial migration, the narratives of cultural and political diaspora, the major social displacements of peasant and aboriginal communities, the poetics of exile, the grim prose of political and economic refugees. It is in this sense that the boundary becomes the place from which *something begins its presencing* in a movement not dissimilar to the ambulant, ambivalent articulation of the beyond that I have drawn out: "Always and ever differently the bridge escorts the lingering and hastening ways of men to and fro, so that they may get to other banks.... The bridge *gathers* as a passage that crosses."

(6–7)

We could get far just by paying attention to Bhabha's geographic terminology: location, positions, terrain, in-between, spaces, sites, interstices, domain, beyond, disorientation, disturbance in direction, displacement, diaspora, boundaries, bridge, banks, and passage. He combines these spatial metaphors with the temporal: process, moments, transition, movement, ambulant, migration, and *presencing*. As we work through the passages, we will see how the temporal and the spatial come together, and this combination helps us understand the aesthetics and politics of hybridity.

DISCUSSION

We begin by noting that Bhabha, in just a few sentences, quickly summarizes debates about how we define identity. He reminds us that categories and concepts of identity have proliferated, and the sheer number of categories increases today. More importantly, Bhabha draws attention to the critique of essentialist notions of identity, what he calls "narratives of originary and initial subjectivities" (2). Instead of asserting that identity is fixed, natural, or inherent, something to salvage and preserve, Bhabha maintains that identity has always been based on an ongoing *process* that rejects the idea that our identities ever were or can be pure or complete. Our identity is the result of the encounter itself, or as Bhabha describes, "those moments or processes that are produced in the articulation of cultural differences" (2). As a result, instead of thinking of two independent and sovereign identities, with distinct histories and trajectories, we imagine groups—particularly postcolonial and migrant groups—inevitably and always contesting and collaborating with other communities as they vie for supremacy and recognition. These encounters, or what he calls "the emergence of the interstices—the overlap and displacement of domains of difference" (2), simultaneously form and reshape both identities and generate new hybrid versions of communities and social groups. Phrased yet another way, the meeting and mixing of groups can be productive, not always destructive, because the encounter and relationships initiate "new signs of identity" (2). In short, the history of a particular group, or even a particular individual, is actually the record of cultural negotiations.

When Bhabha talks about political empowerment and multiculturalism, he does not envision different cultural groups and social identities living in harmony in a kind of utopian multicultural society. The concept of "cultural diversity" often reinforces monolithic notions of identity, evident in phrases like "the black community," "Latino heritage," and "gay culture." Bhabha complicates our notion of community as an "already authenticated cultural tradition" (4) by insisting that we pose "questions of solidarity and community from the interstitial perspective" (4), a phrase that suggests that our groups are always and inevitably hybrid. Our identity forms when we interact with others. When we talk about building a community, we need to remember that the goal is "at once a vision and a construction" (4), a paradox that implies that a community is an ongoing, always incomplete goal that involves a constant process of collaboration, conflict, and movement.

Therefore, we think "beyond ourselves" in two senses. First, "beyond" implies a spatial relationship. If we normally think of identity as a container, then we need to imagine an identity that differs from where we are now, outside ourselves and beyond the border of our identity. Instead of thinking of ourselves inhabiting a fixed identity, we think of ways that we can change by crossing into a new space or subject position. Second, "beyond ourselves" also has a temporal sense. We live beyond the border of our time. We rethink our past and imagine a different future. But Bhabha also complicates our conventional ideas of time. "Beyond," for Bhabha, defines the border itself, for "the 'beyond' is neither a new horizon, nor a leaving behind of the past" (1). The "beyond" signals "the moment of transit where space and time cross to produce complex figures of difference and identity, past and present, inside and outside, inclusion and exclusion" (2). This indeterminate time, space, identity, and boundary cause "a sense of disorientation, a disturbance of direction" (2), but these are productive moments because they allow something new to emerge. The benefit, as Bhabha explains, is that when we live "beyond" our place and time, we live *today* "in a spirit of revision and reconstruction" (4).

This celebration of movement is why Bhabha foregrounds groups like postcolonial migrants, exiles, expatriates, refugees, and people living in a diaspora. These groups embody the emerging hybrid identities Bhabha admires. By inhabiting the terrain between identities, "the boundary becomes the place from which *something begins its presencing*" (7). Part of that citation comes from Martin Heidegger's essay "Building Dwelling Thinking" that asserts that

> A space is something that has been made room for, something that is cleared and free, namely within a boundary, Greek *peras*. A boundary is not that at which something stops but, as the Greek recognized, the boundary is that from which something *begins its presencing*.
>
> (152)

What Bhabha borrows from Heidegger is the idea that a boundary marks the place where identity emerges, as well as the idea that a boundary is a space "that is cleared and free" in the sense that the space is open to many possibilities, not barren or empty. Placed in the context of Bhabha's argument, new identities may emerge because a boundary marks a place that is free and clear. This in-between, interstitial perspective forms a bridge that allows one to generate a new identity. Note that what emerges from this border space is not always positive or progressive. Bhabha's point is that this "third space" (53) is a site of regeneration, but it is also ambivalent in the sense that the encounters can be contradictory, chaotic, and conflicted. Bhabha suggests the *possibility* of new and complex forms of identity that disrupt prevailing histories and conventional subject positions.

POTENTIAL PROJECTS

Bhabha's work speaks to any kind of identity formation, but his idea of an in-between space as the source of identity is especially relevant when we read postcolonial texts because of the inevitable encounters between competing cultures. The terms "beyond, interstitial, hybrid, in-between, crossing, in transit, process, bridge, boundary, third space" become almost synonymous because they all draw attention to a middle and contested ground. The projects below all ask you to question notions of pure identity.

Identify hybrid identities

With an eye on postcolonial, multicultural, and migrant works, build on Bhabha's observation that borders, interstices, and in-between spaces "initiate new signs of identity" (2). For example, Bhabha uses Renée Green's installation *Sites of Genealogy* to explain how art can display and displace "the binary logic through which identities of difference are often constructed—Black/White, Self/Other" (5). He explains how Green uses the liminal space of staircases to question fixed identities and create a hybrid identity in its place. Bhabha concludes that the "interstitial passage between fixed identifications" (5) that Green creates "opens up the possibility of a cultural hybridity" (5). To follow Bhabha's example, you need to explore how writers, filmmakers, and artists displace binary notions of identity and portray shared terrains as "innovative sites of collaboration, and contestation" (2). How does the work redefine or regenerate identity by drawing attention to the passages between fixed identities?

Recognize hybrid forms

Equally interesting would be an exploration of how a work moves beyond a coherent identity, escapes a boundary, works between identities, creates an interstitial perspective, engages us in a process, or offers us a third space. How does the work—in its very form— embody cultural hybridity? Consider ways the work rejects singularity in voice, content, language, and values and offers a truly multicultural hybrid text that crosses linguistic, cultural, social, geographic, and even textual borders. How does the work, in the particular way the creator designs it, "initiate new signs of identity, and innovative sites of collaboration, and contestation, in the act of defining the idea of society itself" (2)? For example, Gloria Anzaldúa is well known for her work on border identity, particularly the figure of the *mestiza*. "From this racial, ideological, cultural and biological cross-pollinization, an 'alien' consciousness is presently in the making—a new *mestiza* consciousness, *uno conciencia de mujer*. It is a consciousness of the Borderlands" (99). While Anzaldúa writes about *mestiza* culture, her book *Borderlands/La Frontera* (1987) embodies *mestiza* identity in its form. The work is at once cultural history, political and feminist theory, poetry, and narrative prose. The tone is both personal and academic as she discusses myth, history, and personal anecdote, and she conveys her argument–narrative in English, Tex-Mex, Mexican dialect, Castilian Spanish, and Nahuatl. *Borderlands/La Frontera* is a *mestiza*-hybrid text that creates a contested and collaborative identity.

Disrupt identity

Rather than focusing on the productive encounter of groups within borders, use Bhabha's concept of hybridity to question "narratives of originary and initial subjectivities" (2) or what he calls "primordial polarities" (5). In other words, explore works that undermine seemingly cohesive community identities or "an already authenticated cultural tradition" (4). Pay attention to the ways a work uses contested histories, multiple histories, contradictory and differentiated values, polylingualism, competing chronologies, varied voices, multiple genres, etc. to question a seemingly unified and coherent identity. For example, when we read Gerald Vizenor's *Heirs of Columbus* (1991), we notice a comic and subversive reversal: Native Americans are avant-garde scientists on the cutting edge of cybernetics whose research erases the difference between Native and non-Native, all in an effort to complicate our sense of what it means to be an "American."

To expand Bhabha's topographical vocabulary, your task is to explore how a work reveals that a group's identity, particularly groups that assume cultural purity, has always been run over, trespassed, invaded, encroached upon, marked, and stepped on by multiple cultural traditions, values, languages, customs, and identities. In short, explain how a work exposes a community's unfounded pretension to purity and coherence.

WORKS CITED

Anzaldúa, Gloria. *Borderlands/La Frontera: The New Mestiza*. 1987. Aunt Lute, 1999.
Bhabha, Homi K. *The Location of Culture*. 1994. Routledge, 2004.
Heidegger, Martin. *Poetry, Language, Thought*. 1971. Perennial, 2001.
Laviera, Tato. "AmeRícan." *Bendición: The Complete Poetry of Tato Laviera*, Arte Público, 2014, pp. 261–262.
Rushdie, Salman. *The Ground Beneath Her Feet*. Henry Holt, 1999.
———. *The Moor's Last Sigh*. 1995. Vintage, 1997.
———. *The Satanic Verses*. 1988. Viking, 1989.
Zangwill, Israel. *The Melting-Pot: Drama in Four Acts*. 1909. Macmillan, 1916.

CHAPTER 8

Performing gender

There is no gender identity behind the expressions of gender.

(Judith Butler 34)

PROBLEMS, PUZZLES, AND QUESTIONS

In Disney's *The Little Mermaid* (1989), Ariel trades her voice to become human so that she can encounter Eric, her love interest. We watch the purple and black octopus Ursula, with her short white hair, bright red lipstick, and bosomy strapless "dress" negotiating with Ariel in song: "The men up there don't like a lot of blabber. They think a girl who gossips is a bore. Yet on land it's much preferred for ladies not to say a word. And after all dear, what is idle babble for?" Ariel's romantic desires, her svelte figure, the loss of her signature voice, and her battle with Ursula certainly invite discussions of femininity, masculinity, sexuality, and identity. One question that immediately arises for contemporary viewers of *The Little Mermaid* is whether or not the film mirrors prevailing notions of gender or shapes them? We find it easy enough to critique the film because of its stereotypical representations, but even the word "stereotype" implies that there is an authentic yet hidden reality the film distorts. Does the film mask an authentic feminine identity that we need to uncover? Is the film problematic because the images of men and women do not reflect gender accurately?

Or, let us think about Lady Gaga's music video "Born This Way" (2011). With imagery reminiscent of *Metropolis* and other German expressionist films, the video begins with the "Manifesto of Mother Monster," a narration that offers an alternative origin story describing the birth of two competing human races, one that "bears no prejudice, no judgment but boundless freedom," the other evil. The images and lyrics are hip and progressive, but the title and repetition of "born this way," supported with lines such as, "I'm beautiful in my way 'cause god makes no mistakes. I'm on the right track baby. I was born this way," seem to invoke a notion of identity familiar with Enlightenment ideology: what is natural is good, and whatever is good is natural. What do we think of rooting identity in nature? Do we have an essential, fixed gender and sexual identity? Do we just need to stay true to our DNA? Is gender identity more nuanced and complicated than that?

While *The Little Mermaid* and "Born This Way" seem comfortable with binary notions of men and women, an actor, model, and drag queen like RuPaul disrupts that easy binary: "You can call me he. You can call me she. You can call me Regis and Kathie Lee; I don't care! Just as long as you call me." Drag differs from other representations of gender because the performance encourages us to ask some key questions: When a man appears in a skirt, blouse, high heels, and makeup, is the man merely wearing a costume, or do the clothes reveal a fundamental feminine identity? Does the parody of femininity reinforce authentic femininity or expose gender codes as malleable social codes?

KEY PASSAGES

Before Judith Butler published *Gender Trouble: Feminism and the Subversion of Identity* (1990), many in the feminist movement embraced the idea that women, as a group, share common characteristics and interests, and if the fundamental problem is that patriarchy has repressed that identity, then the political solution is representation of those suppressed authentic womanly concerns. However, in *Gender Trouble*, Butler asks, "Is the construction of the category of women as a coherent and stable subject an unwitting regulation and reification of gender relations?" (7). In other words, the categories "woman" and "man," however recoded or redefined, merely reinforce a binary view of gender identity and gender relations. She goes on to assert, following Michel Foucault, that "A genealogical critique refuses to search for the origins of gender, the inner truth of female desire, a genuine or authentic sexual identity that repression has kept from view" (xxxi). Instead of embracing the idea that women have an authentic, albeit obscured, identity, Butler maintains that identity categories are "the *effects* of institutions, practices, discourses with multiple and diffuse points of origin" (xxxi). In short, she reverses the way we think about cause, effect, and gender identity, proposing instead that gender is an effect not a cause. In an effort to help us rethink gender, Butler makes the following productive observation:

> Gender is always a doing, though not a doing by a subject who might be said to preexist the deed. ... There is no gender identity behind the expressions of gender; that identity is performatively constituted by the very "expressions" that are said to be its results.
>
> (34)

There is much to clarify in those two sentences, but a common thread is the notion of gender as a performative, a social construct, an effect.

DISCUSSION

To understand Butler's gender theory, we need to discuss identity, context, and performatives. When Butler insists that "there is no gender identity behind the expressions of gender," she resists the familiar idea that one's innate masculinity or femininity prompts one to play with guns or dolls. In other words, Butler questions the notion that chromosomes, gonads, internal reproductive organs, and external genitalia are the same as "gender," a term that refers to the qualities or attributes we assign to sex. In short, our body is not our identity.

If our body does not determine our gender, then what does? Let us take a linguistic turn. When I ask students to identify "beer" as a part of speech, without fail they answer "noun." However, when I write, following Homer Simpson's lead, "Beer me!" students recognize that "beer" is now a verb. And if I say, "You're so beer," then "beer" becomes an adjective. Notice that there are no inherent properties that make "beer" a noun, verb, or adjective. Instead, "beer's" location in the sentence, in the linguistic system, determines its identity. The value, meaning, and identity of a word, a sentence, a paragraph, a character, a setting, or an image—in fact, everything—depend on its relationship to other parts in a system.

And when we think about gender, our culture works in a similar way. Just as a sentence's syntax determines the identity of "beer," so, too, do network or system of codes, language, values, hierarchies, attitudes, and definitions embedded in institutions, practices, and discourses create our gender identities. To put it yet another way, masculinity and femininity do not exist before social definitions or categories; instead, masculinity and femininity are the *effect* of these social categories just as the word "beer" became a noun, verb, or adjective based on its location in the system. That is, we cannot determine beer's part of speech until we place it in a sentence. To extend this insight, our gender identity also depends on context, and our behavior lacks significance in the absence of definitions, categories, or relationships with other behaviors.

But what does Butler mean by the phrase, "performatively constituted by the very 'expressions' that are said to be its results"? The term "performative" grows out of work by J. L. Austin (1962) who worked in the field of speech act theory. As I explain in the chapter on Austin in this textbook, *constatives* are a kind of sentence that describes an action: It's six o'clock. I bought bread yesterday. She won the race. The Nile River flows north. *Performatives*, however, perform an action. Saying the words "I do… I name… I give and bequeath… I bet…" are the acts of agreeing to marry, christening a boat, giving one's possessions away, and making a wager. Words are practices. Or as Austin phrases it, "Here we should say that in saying these words we are *doing* something—namely, marrying, rather than *reporting* something, namely *that* we are marrying" (13). Expressed yet another way, these particular linguistic acts do not describe an event; they *are* the event. The marriage, christening, inheritance, and wager do not occur without saying those words in an appropriate context.

What do performatives have to do with Butler and gender? Butler argues that gender follows some of the same logic. We establish a stable gender identity by repeating the same acts that our society codes as masculine or feminine. So, when Butler says that "identity is performatively constituted by the very 'expressions' that are said to be its results," she is arguing against the idea that we first have an identity and subsequently perform or represent it. Instead, there is no gender identity until we act in ways that our culture has coded as masculine and feminine. Gender is based, not on what one *is*, but on what one *does*, and what one does is only meaningful in a particular context. Jeffrey Nealon and Susan Searls Giroux describe this process well:

> One is not born a man or woman or a homosexual; one becomes a man or woman or homosexual (becomes recognizable as such) only in the context of performing or not performing certain acts. Homosexual doesn't name a state of being; it names a being that performs certain acts, who's recognized and categorized by social categories rather than essential attributes.
>
> (188)

We can connect the dots by saying that institutions, practices, and discourses code behavior and construct gender categories, and we become masculine, feminine, or homosexual the moment we perform those acts, the moment we locate ourselves in the social system that we inherit.

But does this way of thinking mean that gender is a choice? Can I be a woman today, a man tomorrow, and a transgendered subject the next day? No. Butler explains that "Gender performativity is not a matter of choosing which gender one will be today. Performativity is a matter of reiterating or repeating the norms by which one is constituted: it is not a radical fabrication of a gendered self" ("Critically Queer" 22). To clarify, we inherit or are *subject to* preexisting laws, codes, categories, and definitions. Our agency is limited by the available ways of thinking, speaking, and writing. This network or discourse limits and constrains us.

On the other hand, the concept of performativity gives us room to question gender codes and expose them as mere codes. Butler points out that when we think of gender as a social construction, what she calls "a free-floating artifice" (*Gender Trouble* 9), then it is possible to slowly recode and redefine gender: "*man* and *masculine* might just as easily signify a female body as a male one, and *woman* and *feminine* a male body as easily as a female one" (9). Cultural representations are often engaged in this work, for gender is fluid, always in the process of being made and remade in specific social contexts.

POTENTIAL PROJECTS

Remember that representations like literature, film, and art are actively defining what it means to be a man and a woman, but also LGBTQ. Therefore, discuss gender and sexual identities in terms of "*effects* of institutions, practices, discourses" (*Gender* xxxi). These texts are not representing a preexisting reality. Instead, by assigning attributes, significance, and values to specific behaviors, representations make and remake perceptions we often embrace as real. Of course, there are competing codes or definitions, not one monolithic idea (although it may feel that way from time to time). Consider the following projects.

Identify consequences of gender coding

Explore how a text reaffirms normative gender and sexual identities. You could explain, for example, how a text naturalizes—portrays identities as natural, normal, and commonsensical—familiar forms of masculinity, femininity, or sexuality. Draw attention to the "gender codes" the text uses, how the text conveys those codes, and then discuss the function of those codes. For example, cross-dressing narratives are often comedies because we laugh at the ridiculous efforts men exert to imitate women, and this mismatch reinforces the idea that men and women need to remain true to their "given" genders.

Or, explain, for example, how a particular character encounters troubles or rewards because of the way the culture (within the narrative) treats that character. Characters "live" in contexts, and so your task is to explain the effects or consequences for a character who lives in a particular society with specific gender codes or gender norms. For example, *The Imitation Game* dramatizes the life of Alan Turing, a British code breaker during WWII. While the film's main plot focuses on Turing's ability to decipher the German enigma machine, the subplot addresses Turing's homosexuality, the question of normality, and the value of being different. In a series of on-screen texts, we learn that after Turing endures a year of estrogen treatments, he kills himself. Given this cause–effect relationship, we recognize that the film naturalizes homosexuality and celebrates difference: As friends Christopher and Joan, and Alan himself, proclaim, "sometimes it is the very people who no one imagines anything of, who do the things that no one can imagine."

Identify subversive strategies

Draw attention to methods and strategies the text uses to subvert conventional notions of gender and sexuality. Explain how the work redefines gender and sexuality in new and challenging ways. Or, you could discuss how certain texts subvert the binary nature of gender. As Butler notes, "Even if the sexes appear to be unproblematically binary in their morphology and constitution (which will become a question), there is no reason to assume that genders ought also to remain as two" (*Gender* 9). Therefore, find and discuss texts that question the binary notions of gender by multiplying or redefining genders. Works like Virginia Woolf's *Orlando* (1928), Ursula K. LeGuin's *Left Hand of Darkness* (1969), Melissa Scott's *Shadow Man* (1995), Joanna Russ' *The Female Man* (1975), and Ann Leckie's *Ancillary Justice* (2013) come to mind. A variation on this project asks you to explore how departures from gender norms have become institutionalized and become a new norm.

Draw attention to meta-strategies

In "Imitation and Gender Insubordination," Butler argues that "drag constitutes the mundane way in which genders are appropriated, theatricalized, worn, and done; it implies that all gendering is a kind of impersonation and approximation" (313). In other words, "drag" is potentially subversive because the practice "denaturalizes" social and gender codes we thought were natural, commonsensical, and predetermined. Drag makes us aware of gender codes as codes, exposing the network or discourse that limits and constrains us. Therefore, find a literary "drag-act," a text that draws attention to the very gender codes it is flaunting. Parodies and comedies are often a rich source for this kind of project. For example, the films *Mrs. Doubtfire* (1993) and *Kinky Boots* (2005) portray men in drag, while women perform masculinity in *Yentl* (1983), *Victor/Victoria* (1982), and *The Ballad of Little Jo* (1993). The films foreground the theatricality of gender and draw attention to gender as socially created codes, but be sensitive to the ways these portrayals of drag may also reinforce gender stereotypes.

WORKS CITED

Austin, John Langshaw. *How to Do Things with Words*. 1962. Oxford UP, 1965.
Butler, Judith. "Critically Queer." *GLQ*, vol. 1, 1993, pp. 17–32.
———. *Gender Trouble: Feminism and the Subversion of Identity*. 1990. Routledge, 2007.
———. "Imitation and Gender Insubordination." *The Lesbian and Gay Studies Reader*, edited by Henry Abelove, et al. Routleldge, 1993, pp. 307–320.
Lady Gaga, performer. "Born This Way." *Born This Way*. Streamline/Interscope, 2011.
The Little Mermaid. Directed by Ron Clements and John Musker, Buena Vista, 1989.
Nealon, Jeffrey and Susan Searls Giroux. *The Theory Toolbox: Critical Concepts for the Humanities, Arts, and Social Sciences*. Rowman, 2012.
RuPaul. *Lettin It All Hang Out: An Autobiography*. Hyperion, 1995.

CHAPTER 9

Locating trauma

> Trauma is not locatable in the simple violent or original event in an individual's past, but rather in the way that its very unassimilated nature ... returns to haunt the survivor later on.
>
> (Cathy Caruth 4)

PROBLEMS, PUZZLES, AND QUESTIONS

At once biography, autobiography, history, novel, and comic strip, Art Spiegelman's two-volume *Maus* (1986/1991) records the life of Art Spiegelman's father Vladek, from prewar Poland to Auschwitz to Rego Park, New York. Importantly, this story is told within a self-reflexive and guilt-ridden frame tale, blurring the boundary between Art Spiegelman the artist and "Art Spiegelman" the character. In addition to portraying Jews as mice and German Nazis as cats, the volumes contain several features that differ from the black and white drawings: the insertion of a short narrative published in *Short Order Comix* in 1973 entitled "Prisoner from the Hell Planet: A Case History," photographs of Spiegelman's brother Richieu, and a "souvenir" photograph of Vladek after surviving Auschwitz. These elements serve the larger narrative, but they also jar the reader. They either interrupt the flow of the narrative or break the conceptual metaphor of Jews as mice and Nazis as cats. How do we make sense of these elements that do not seamlessly integrate into the rest of the narrative? What can they suggest about the nature of trauma, memory, and representation?

Set in the 19th century, Toni Morrison's novel *Beloved* (1987) describes the experiences of Sethe, a mother who kills her two-year-old daughter to prevent her from being returned to the Kentucky plantation she fled. Years later, a mysterious woman appears on Sethe's property. Believed to be the ghost of the daughter Sethe killed, Beloved haunts the household, driving out Sethe's sons, wreaking havoc, and consuming Sethe's life. At one point, Sethe seems to converse with Beloved: "You rememory me? Yes. I remember you" (215). Beloved eventually disappears, and the family finds its balance. The novel challenges readers on many levels, and Morrison draws attention to the process of memory, re-memory, and disrememberment. In what sense does trauma haunt us? How do we make sense of Sethe's "rememory" and Beloved's departure? What is the relationship between memory and healing? What allows us to exorcise our past?

The 9/11 Memorial & Museum opened in 2014, a mere thirteen years after the terrorist attacks. The museum accompanies Michael Arad's memorial Reflecting Absence, two giant pools with cascading water that occupy the Twin Towers' footprints and bear the names of the dead. The exhibitions detail the events and aftermath of September 11th, commemorate individual victims, honor first responders, and invite personal reflection. The 9/11 Museum immerses its visitors in suffering and loss. But what is so striking about the museum is that it commemorates a traumatic event that occurred in the lifetimes of most visitors. Whether they lived in New York City and experienced the attack firsthand or watched the news in horror from thousands of miles away, people vividly remember 9/11 and continue to live with its effects. What is the purpose of visiting a museum that depicts, sometimes in excruciating detail, an event one lived through? What compels people to visit and relive that trauma, moving through the day minute by minute?

Spiegelman's memoir, Morrison's novel, and the 9/11 Museum & Memorial prompt us to ask even more questions: What makes an event "traumatic"? Why represent trauma? Does representing trauma cause more pain or provide closure and healing? What is the role of literature and representations of trauma?

KEY PASSAGES

Trauma comes to us via the Greek word for "wound," and the image suggests both an open sore and a scar. The enduring effect of the past implies a failure to heal and understand, but what is it about the nature of trauma that resists healing? Cathy Caruth's *Unclaimed Experience: Trauma, Narrative, and History* (1996) addresses the relationship between past and present, experience and representation, wounds and healing, and she reminds us that the idea of trauma as a deferred experience—not grasped as it occurs, returning later to haunt the survivor repeatedly—has struck a chord, likewise, in artists, survivors, activists, and others who work in the public sphere, and who have responded creatively to the powerful call of this enigmatic notion.

(117)

But what is it about traumatic experiences that escape our understanding? With countless narratives, performances, and representations exploring the effect of the traumatic past on the present, Caruth's explanation of how trauma works helps us make sense of these deferred experiences.

> In its later usage, particularly in the medical and psychiatric literature, and most centrally in Freud's text, the term *trauma* is understood as a wound inflicted not upon the body but upon the mind. But what seems to be suggested by Freud in *Beyond the Pleasure Principle* is that the wound of the mind—the breach in the mind's experience of time, self, and the world—is not, like the wound of the body, a simple and healable event, but rather an event that, like Tancred's first infliction of a mortal wound on the disguised Clorinda in the duel, is experienced too soon, too unexpectedly, to be fully known and is therefore not available to consciousness until it imposes itself again, repeatedly, in the nightmares and repetitive actions of the survivor.
>
> (3–4)
>
> Trauma is not locatable in the simple violent or original event in an individual's past, but rather in the way that its very unassimilated nature—the way it was precisely *not known* in the first instance—returns to haunt the survivor later on.
>
> (4)
>
> The accident, that is, as it emerges in Freud and is passed on through other trauma narratives, does not simply represent the violence of a collision but also conveys the impact of its very incomprehensibility. What returns to haunt the victim, these stories tell us, is not only the reality of the violent event but also the reality of the way that its violence has not yet been fully known.
>
> (6)

> Is the trauma the encounter with death or the ongoing experience of having survived it? At the core of these stories, I would suggest, is thus a kind of double telling, the oscillation between a *crisis of death* and the correlative *crisis of life*: between the story of the unbearable nature of an event and the story of the unbearable nature of its survival.
>
> (7–8)
>
> In its most general definition, trauma describes an overwhelming experience of sudden or catastrophic events in which the response to the event occurs in the often delayed, uncontrolled repetitive appearance of hallucinations and other intrusive phenomena.
>
> (11–12)
>
> Traumatic experience, beyond the psychological dimension of suffering it involves, suggests a certain paradox: that the most direct seeing of a violent event may occur as an absolute inability to know it; that immediacy, paradoxically, may take the form of belatedness.
>
> (94)

Caruth personifies trauma: it haunts, intrudes, inflicts, cries out, and addresses us. We cannot escape its effect. We cannot locate trauma because it arrives too soon, yet the story of trauma delays its return. It breaches the mind, yet we cannot comprehend its meaning or significance. How do we interpret Caruth's temporal and spatial language when we discuss traumatic experiences? In what sense does trauma arrive too early and return too late? What is the relationship between past and present, or, as Caruth asks, "Is the trauma the encounter with death, or the ongoing experience of having survived it?"

DISCUSSION

Although the original definition of trauma focused on physical wounds, the late 19th century turned inward. What is traumatic is psychological, not physical: "the term *trauma* is understood as a wound inflicted not upon the body but upon the mind" (3). These particular events inflict our consciousness in the sense that they disrupt and disorient our "experience of time, self, and the world" (3). Traumatic events confuse our sense of time and place, unsettle our moral codes, and undermine a sense of who we are and how we relate to others. We may lose our very notion of what constitutes normal and appropriate behavior.

But traumatic events differ from other painful experiences in another way because they refer to an "overwhelming experience of sudden or catastrophic events in which the response to the event occurs in the often delayed, uncontrolled repetitive appearance of hallucinations and other intrusive phenomena" (11–12). The seemingly unstoppable reappearance of the original event disrupting the victim is familiar territory. We experience an event that stresses, disturbs, and shatters us, and while we survive the incident, the real effects arrive later, forcing us to relive the horrifying event. We cannot escape these recollections. Imagine the psychological version of frost-bitten fingers. We do not notice the pain when we are outside as much as we do when our fingers thaw in front of the fire. We fully experience the impact of the original event in another place and time.

But why does the mind not heal just as a gash in the arm improves over time? Why do memories continue to distress us? And why do certain events disrupt us, often in the form of "nightmares and repetitive actions," while other memories, even painful or terrifying ones, do not? The difference has to do with our inability to assimilate and integrate those memories. Caruth frames the answer in terms of timing. We experience the event "too soon, too unexpectedly" (4), and as a result, we do not have time to process the experience, to make sense of it. The event lies beyond our conceptual framework. The episode does not fit our modes of understanding, and that is why the experience is "unclaimed." In a sense, an event's "meaninglessness" is what traumatizes us, for

> trauma is not locatable in the simple violent or original event in an individual's past, but rather in the way that its very unassimilated nature—the way it was precisely *not known* in the first instance—returns to haunt the survivor later on.
>
> (4)

Phrased yet another way, what defines trauma is surviving what we have not fully understood, but at the same time we reexperience the draining emotional effects.

Therefore, when Caruth asks, "Is the trauma the encounter with death, or the ongoing experience of having survived it?" (7), we should answer, "both." Trauma narratives dwell on the aftermath of the original violence, its effects and impact, and Caruth describes this process as a "kind of double telling": "the story of the unbearable nature of an event and the story of the unbearable nature of its survival" (7–8). Paradoxically, Caruth suggests that the representation of the event, the belated retelling of the original trauma, offers us the best opportunity to understand the truth: the "most direct seeing of a violent event may occur as an absolute inability to know it; that immediacy, paradoxically, may take the form of belatedness" (94). However, this paradox does not simplistically imply that trauma narratives tell us the truth while firsthand experiences do not. Rather, literary texts embody trauma in a "language that defies, even as it claims, our understanding" (5). In other words, literary language is itself paradoxical: narratives and representations offer the possibility of understanding even as they make certainty impossible. Therefore, trauma narratives simultaneously refer to the original event even as they remind us that they are mere substitutions. And yet, while literary narratives do not promise "ultimate" knowing, they do offer ways of understanding a traumatic experience.

POTENTIAL PROJECTS

The projects described below depend on a few key foundational claims. First, trauma haunts survivors who reexperience events they did not fully process when they occurred the first time. Second, the original event does not traumatize as much as the inability to assimilate, integrate, or understand the event. Third, due to their indirect and allusive approach, narratives and representations have the potential to convey trauma's immediacy. In short, trauma narratives and representations reflect on and explore the (im)possibility of meaning and understanding.

Tell it twice

Trauma narratives tell two stories. Therefore, consider texts that engage in this kind of "double telling." First, explain how the narrative describes "the unbearable nature of an event" (7). We learn, for example, about the horrors of Auschwitz, child abuse, firefights, marriages gone awry, epic neglect, accidents, etc. Second, and more importantly, examine how the narrative describes "the unbearable nature of its survival" (8). How does the narrative try to make sense of the original event? Does the narrator or character succeed in integrating or assimilating the experience? If so, how so? If not, then what continues to defy comprehension? What prevents the narrator or character from understanding the original wound? As with trauma theory itself, trauma narratives do not "simply make a new claim to knowledge," but instead, they articulate a "kind of not-knowing at the heart of catastrophic experience, a resistance to conceptual assimilation, an intimate bond between knowing and not-knowing" (117). In short, your task is to identify the ways the narrative engages in a form of "double telling" and offers either a successful integration or "a kind of not-knowing" that continues to haunt the narrator or character.

Explore the paradox

Build on Caruth's claim that traumatic experience suggests "a certain paradox: that the most direct seeing of a violent event may occur as an absolute inability to know it; that immediacy, paradoxically, may take the form of belatedness" (94). Therefore, explain how the retelling of a horrific event in words, on canvas, on film, or on the stage allows us to experience the event in a more immediate and intimate way. In other words, how does the representation of an event allow us to know and understand the experience in a way that firsthand experience cannot provide? For example, Caruth discusses the film *Hiroshima, mon amour* (1959), and she explains that filmmaker Alain Resnais initially gathered archival footage to make a documentary about the bombing. He abandoned the project and instead created a fictional narrative about a French actress and a Japanese architect. Caruth argues that "In his refusal to make a documentary on Hiroshima, Resnais paradoxically implies that it is direct archival footage that cannot maintain the very specificity of the event" (28). She adds that "the interest of *Hiroshima mon amour* lies in how it explores the possibility of a faithful history in the very indirectness of this telling" (28). Follow Caruth's lead by exploring the ways a representation or an indirect treatment of a traumatic event may help us understand the event itself. Explain how being faithful to the past may require a kind of literary betrayal.

WORKS CITED

Caruth, Cathy. *Unclaimed Experience: Trauma, Narrative, and History*. 1996. Johns Hopkins UP, 2016.
Morrison, Toni. *Beloved*. Plume, 1987.

CHAPTER 10

Intersecting identities

Single-axis framework erases Black women in the conceptualization, identification and remediation of race and sex discrimination.
(Kimberle Crenshaw 140)

PROBLEMS, PUZZLES, AND QUESTIONS

In "Who Said It Was Simple" (1973), Audre Lorde begins by reminding us that "There are so many roots to the tree of anger / that sometimes the branches shatter / before they bear" (1–3). She describes an image of, we infer, white women preparing to march in behalf of some cause. More observer than participant, the narrator notices an "almost white counterman" (8) who passes a "brother" to serve these women. The narrator shifts to herself: "But I who am bound by my mirror / as well as my bed / see causes in colour / as well as sex" (12–15). The lines direct our attention to the narrator's identity that depends on skin color and gender roles. The notion of multiple identities becomes more apparent in the next lines: "and sit here wondering / which me will survive / all these liberations" (16–18). How do we make sense of Lorde's exploration of multiple identities? Are there, in fact, multiple identities, or does the image of the tree suggest consolidation? Does the narrator separate woman from Black, or encourage us to see them as one coherent identity?

In 2015, Patricia Arquette won an Oscar for Best Supporting Actress, and she used her acceptance speech to insist on gender and pay equity. "To every woman who gave birth, to every taxpayer and citizen of this nation," she declares, "we have fought for everybody else's equal rights. It's our time to have wage equality once and for all, and equal rights for women in the United States of America." Backstage, she elaborated,

> The truth is, right under the surface, there are huge issues that are at play that do affect women, and it's time for all the women in America and all the men that love women and all the gay people and all the people of color that we all fought for to fight for us now.
>
> (qtd. in McDonald)

Some critiqued Arquette's assumption that LGBTQ communities and people of color have achieved equality when that is clearly not the case. Andrea Grimes in the online site *Rewire* entitles her critique, "Patricia Arquette's Spectacular Intersectionality Fail." Megan Kearns at *Bitch-Media* insists that "We white women need to do a much better job to make feminism an intersectional, inclusive movement." Both Grimes and Kearns defend their views, but what does "intersectionality/ intersectional" even mean? What did Arquette fail to do, notice, or say?

Leslie Marmon Silko draws on her experience living on the Laguna Pueblo Reservation in her short story "Lullaby" (1981) that describes the strong-willed Ayah who laments the loss of her son Jimmie in Vietnam. Ayah takes care of her husband Chato whom she eventually finds walking home from a bar. The story ends with a maternal image of Ayah singing an ancient song as she comforts him during a snow storm, no doubt dying. As Ayah reminisces, she recalls when white doctors coerced her into signing documents she could not read, allowing them to take away her children Danny and Ella and place them in white schools and homes. Like all Natives in the story, Ayah suffers at the hands of whites, but her poverty limits her as well. After Chato loses his ranch job, they are destitute. Men at the bar fear Ayah, and Silko presents her as a key link between past and present, nature and culture, life and death. To grasp the story well, do we focus on Ayah's Navajo tribal affiliation, her poverty and limited resources, or her gender? Can we separate those identities? A "destitute Navajo woman." Is that three identities or one? And why does that question matter?

These examples address the difficulties of identity and discrimination. Does one identity describe us? Do we have multiple identities? Do our identities "add up" or do they merge? Does a Black woman encounter a different form of discrimination than, say, a white woman or a Black male? Does a gay woman experience bigotry in ways that a gay man or straight woman does not? In short, do (or how do) multidimensional forms of identity compound prejudice?

KEY PASSAGES

Professor of Law, Kimberlé Crenshaw published "Demarginalizing the Intersection of Race and Sex: A Black Feminist Critique of Antidiscrimination Doctrine, Feminist Theory and Antiracist Politics" (1989) as part of a volume on "Feminism in the Law: Theory, Practice and Criticism" in *The University of Chicago Legal Forum*. Working within a legal context, Crenshaw describes situations when courts ruled against Black women because their legal cases insisted that being both Black and female, not just one or the other, was central to their argument. By critiquing these cases, Crenshaw wants to develop "language which is critical of the dominant view and which provides some basis for unifying activity. The goal of this activity should be to facilitate the inclusion of marginalized groups" (167). In other words, Crenshaw offers us a way to rethink privilege, visibility, inclusion, and institutional power in ways that acknowledge the complexity and interactivity of identity and discrimination.

> I will center Black women in this analysis in order to contrast the multidimensionality of Black women's experience with the single-axis analysis that distorts these experiences. Not only will this juxtaposition reveal how Black women are theoretically erased, it will also illustrate how this framework imports its own theoretical limitations that undermine efforts to broaden feminist and antiracist analyses. With Black women as the starting point, it becomes more apparent how dominant conceptions of discrimination condition us to think about subordination as disadvantage occurring along a single categorical axis. I want to suggest further that this single-axis framework erases Black women in the conceptualization, identification, and remediation of race and sex discrimination by limiting inquiry to the experiences of otherwise-privileged members of the group.
> (139–140)
>
> Because the intersectional experience is greater than the sum of racism and sexism, any analysis that does not take intersectionality into account cannot sufficiently address the particular manner in which Black women are subordinated.
> (140)

> Black women can experience discrimination in ways that are both similar to and different from those experienced by white women and Black men. Black women sometimes experience discrimination in ways similar to white women's experiences; sometimes they share very similar experiences with Black men. Yet often they experience double-discrimination—the combined effects of practices which discriminate on the basis of race, and on the basis of sex. And sometimes, they experience discrimination as Black women—not the sum of race and sex discrimination, but as Black women.
>
> (149)
>
> The paradigm of sex discrimination tends to be based on the experiences of white women; the model of race discrimination tends to be based on the experiences of the most privileged Blacks. Notions of what constitutes race and sex discrimination are, as a result, narrowly tailored to embrace only a small set of circumstances, none of which include discrimination against Black women.
>
> (151)
>
> I have stated earlier that the failure to embrace the complexities of compoundedness is not simply a matter of political will, but is also due to the influence of a way of thinking about discrimination which structures politics so that struggles are categorized as singular issues.
>
> (166–167)

These key passages signal the core contrasts: single axis vs. multidimensionality, singular discrimination vs. double discrimination, simple vs. compoundedness, theory vs. experience, and center vs. margin. In sum, Crenshaw wants us to recognize that identity and discrimination are not singular issues, and she returns time and again to the ways a Black woman's identity shapes the discrimination she faces. Finally, she reminds us that our solutions must consider the ways Black women experience the compounding effect of multiple forms of discrimination.

DISCUSSION

The terms "intersectionality" and "intersectional experience" are rooted to everyday life: traffic. Crenshaw describes how discrimination may flow in different directions. Sexism enters from one direction, racism from another. "If an accident happens in an intersection," Crenshaw reminds us,

> it can be caused by cars traveling from any number of directions and, sometimes, from all of them. Similarly, if a Black woman is harmed because she is in the intersection, her injury could result from sex discrimination or race discrimination.
>
> (149)

However, she explains that the legal system is not equipped to rule on issues that involve complex notions of identity. "Sometimes the skid marks and the injuries simply indicate that they occurred simultaneously, frustrating efforts to determine which driver caused the harm" (149). The intersection is where these multiple drivers collide simultaneously.

Crenshaw uses this traffic analogy to illustrate the ways the legal system erases Black women. In what sense are they erased or rendered invisible? Crenshaw describes three exemplary legal cases. A group of Black women sued General Motors on the grounds that the company discriminated against Black women. The court stated, "plaintiffs have failed to cite any decisions which have stated that Black women are a special class to be protected from discrimination" (141). The company proved that they had hired white women, so they were not guilty of sex discrimination. The plaintiffs could only proceed on racial grounds. In another case, Black women sued in behalf of women and all Blacks, but the court "refused to certify Black females as class representatives in race *and* sex discrimination actions" (143). The Black female plaintiffs could only represent Black employees, not white women. In a third case, Black female plaintiffs sued on behalf of all Black employees. However, the court narrowed the class to Black women only. Despite the fact that the women won their case, Crenshaw reminds us that the case demonstrates that these Black women "cannot represent an entire class of Blacks" (148). These cases illustrate the contradictions and limitations in the legal system. In terms of erasure, what is rendered invisible is part of a Black woman's identity. She is either Black or female, never both, and that is why "Black women are protected only to the extent that their experiences coincide with those of either of the two groups" (143). In other words, Black women can pursue sex discrimination cases so long as their experience is analogous to what white women experience, and Black women can sue for racial discrimination if their experience echoes what Black men experience. However, the courts refused to acknowledge that "Black woman" is an identity or believe Black women experience discrimination differently than white women and Black men.

The fact that "Black women can experience discrimination in ways that are both similar to and different from those experienced by white women and Black men" (149) does not mean Black women need to choose which form of discrimination they should combat. Plus, Crenshaw reminds us that what Black women face is not just sexism and racism arriving in two different directions. There is a multiplying and compounding effect. "Sometimes, they experience discrimination as Black women—not the sum of race and sex discrimination, but as Black women" (149). In other words, it is not a matter of simple arithmetic: racism plus sexism. Instead, being a Black woman is a third category that encounters a specific form of discrimination because racism and sexism interact. As a result, any solution requires us to reject a form of politics that categorizes racism and sexism (and any other form of discrimination) as singular issues. As Crenshaw explains, if we think of our struggles as singular issues, then our politics will be equally singular, and the result is that we will never completely combat the struggles of groups who are "multiply-disadvantaged."

Crenshaw's argument suggests that identity itself is more complex than we often conceive. Instead of thinking in strict gender or racial terms—one is a woman or one is Black—Crenshaw's argument recognizes a hybrid identity that is more complex than the sum of the parts. This more nuanced view of identity is why she returns time and again to the "multidimensionality of Black women's experience" (139). Intersectionality undermines essentialist and reductive notions of identity because we need to recognize a plurality of identities that depends on context and subject position. Crenshaw encourages us to pay attention to the ways that differences exist among classes of people. While we are not saying that white middle-class straight women enjoy pay equity with white men, they do experience greater privilege than white gay women, Black women, or poor white women.

POTENTIAL PROJECTS

Although Crenshaw's essay focuses on Black women in legal contexts, the concept of intersectionality offers many opportunities to rethink identity, discrimination, and visibility. We can move beyond legal cases to examine intersectional experiences in cultural representations and daily life. Activists have seized on this idea of intersectionality to build social movements like #WhyWeCantWait and "Say Her Name" and other social justice campaigns. The projects below invite you to consider ways that current events and texts of all kinds continue to operate on single-axis assumptions of identity, or examine how social movements and representations complicate identity and explore the various ways that classes of people experience multiple and compounding forms of discrimination. While acknowledging that intersectionality permeates every academic field and social practices, we limit ourselves to the way writers, filmmakers, and artists portray intersectional experiences.

Identify intersectional experience

Extend Crenshaw's insights to literary texts by exploring how writers represent the experience of Black women as a social category. Do writers perpetuate the idea that Black women are either Black or female, or does the work complicate our perceptions of single-axis identities? How do these authors limit or expand our understanding of Black women as "multiply-burdened"? Note that it is not enough to just add different forms of discrimination. For example, Edwidge Dandicat often writes about Haitian women who make their way to the United States, and these women encounter any number of problems. Instead of merely suggesting that her young protagonists encounter racism plus sexism plus xenophobia, implying that these forms of oppression work independently of each other, we need to ask how Dandicat portrays what these Haitian female immigrants experience. How does Dandicat help us understand (or not) how racism, sexism, xenophobia, particularly of Haitians, always and inevitably interact with each other and compound the discrimination Haitian women face when they try to find a new life in the United States? This nuanced analysis will also encourage us to identify differences *among* women, for certain combinations can construct privilege as well.

No matter the project you choose, adopt key phrases like "intersectional experiences," "multiply-burdened," "multiply-disadvantaged class," "double-discrimination," "crosscurrents of racism and sexism," "crosscutting forces," "multidimensionality of Black women's experience," and "complexities of compoundedness." This specialized vocabulary shapes the way you write about how texts construct identity, define discrimination, address visibility, and empower or disenfranchise Black women.

Extend the project

Crenshaw writes, "With Black women as the starting point, it becomes more apparent how dominant conceptions of discrimination condition us to think about subordination as disadvantage occurring along a single categorical axis" (140). The phrase "With Black women as the starting point" suggests that Crenshaw is well aware of how other groups experience multiple forms of discrimination. In an interview with the *Washington Post*, she adds that

> Intersectional erasures are not exclusive to black women. People of color within LGBTQ movements; girls of color in the fight against the school-to-prison pipeline; women within immigration movements; trans women within feminist movements; and people with disabilities fighting police abuse—all face vulnerabilities that reflect the intersections of racism, sexism, class oppression, transphobia, able-ism and more. Intersectionality has given many advocates a way to frame their circumstances and to fight for their visibility and inclusion.

Building on Crenshaw's insights into the intersectional experiences of Black women, explore other forms of multidimensional identity and the compounding effect of discrimination that other identities encounter. As a literary or cultural critic, your task is to explain how novels, films, poems, plays, and art portray (or fail to portray) the complexities of identity and explore how different forms of discrimination intersect and interact in ways that erase some groups but endow others with privilege.

WORKS CITED

Crenshaw, Kimberlé. "Demarginalizing the Intersection of Race and Sex: A Black Feminist Critique of Antidiscrimination Doctrine, Feminist Theory and Antiracist Politics." "Feminism in the Law: Theory, Practice and Criticism" in *The University of Chicago Legal Forum*, vol. 1989, no. 1, Article 8, 1989, pp. 139–167.
———. "Why Intersectionality Can't Wait." *The Washington Post*, www.washingtonpost.com/news/in-theory/wp/2015/09/24/why-intersectionality-cant-wait/?utm_term=.2c095018c844. Accessed 16 January 2018.
Grimes, Andrea. "Patricia Arquette's Spectacular Intersectionality Fail." *Rewire*, www.rewire.news/article/2015/02/23/patricia-arquettes-spectacular-intersectionality-fail. Accessed 16 January 2018.

Kearns, Megan. "Patricia Arquette Undermined Her Own 'Most Feminist Moment' of the Oscars." *Bitchmedia*, www.bitchmedia.org/post/patricia-arquette-undermined-the-most-feminist-moment-of-the-oscars. Accessed 16 January 2018.

Lorde, Audre. "Who Said It Was Simple." *From a Land Where Other People Live*. Broadside, 1973, p. 39.

McDonald, Soraya Nadia. "Ripping Patricia Arquette to Shreds." www.washingtonpost.com/news/morning-mix/wp/2015/02/24/why-some-activists-were-offended-by-patricia-arquette/?utm_term=.b8aa05c0c1d6. Accessed 16 January 2018.

CHAPTER 11

Locating alterity

> Deconstruction opens a reading by locating a moment of alterity within a text.
> (Simon Critchley 28)

PROBLEMS, PUZZLES, AND QUESTIONS

As a film like *Return of the Living Dead* (1985) reminds us, zombies threaten us by attacking and eating our brains. However, the real threat is that zombies disrupt our conceptual order. They present themselves as our radical Other. We are used to the logic of *either/or*. Thinking in terms of binaries governs our identities, categories, relationships, and value systems. Zombies, however, escape our ways of thinking about being dead and alive. We cannot assimilate zombies into our intellectual frameworks. As the "undead," zombies are both dead and alive, or they are not really dead, but they are not really alive either. They are *undecidable*. They embrace the logic of *both/and* and *neither/nor*. Fortunately, zombies do not chase us, but we do encounter language and texts. But how are texts like zombies?

In 1942, American General John L. DeWitt issued an order to relocate a group of Japanese Americans (citizens or not) to an internment camp in Manzanar, California. Prominently displayed on the order are the words "INSTRUCTIONS TO ALL PERSONS OF JAPANESE ANCESTRY," and the document describes how and when Japanese people should leave Los Angeles and other California coastal cities. In 1993, Lawson Fusao Inada published a poem entitled "Instructions to All Persons" that appropriates the vocabulary of DeWitt's relocation order and transforms and recodes the original document into an invitation that strengthens the community, perhaps even drawing our attention to an absent Japanese identity erased by nationalist and racist categories. While it is easy enough to discuss Inada's poem in terms of subversive mimicry and appropriation, we can also question whether his use of the document's vocabulary makes the poem complicit with the very assumptions Inada hopes to reject. Does Inada's poem embrace the logic of *either/or* or *both/and*?

Hannah Webster Foster published *The Coquette; or, The History of Eliza Wharton* (1797) in the shadow of the American Revolution. A "founded on fact" episodic narrative, the collection of letters recounts the dating dilemmas faced by a beautiful young woman. Eliza must choose between the fun and adventurous rake Peter Sanford and a safe and conventional marriage to Reverend Boyer. Of course, she chooses poorly, and she finds herself abandoned and destitute with a child, and both die. Unabashedly didactic, a letter penned by Eliza's friend Lucy declares, "I wish it engraved upon every heart, that virtue alone, independent of the trappings of wealth, the parade of equipage, and the adulation of gallantry, can secure lasting felicity" (167–168). Despite her choices, we sympathize with Eliza, especially when she laments her options: "What a pity, my dear Lucy, that the graces and virtues are not oftener united!" (22). The novel exudes confidence in its morality, but Eliza's observation suggests blind spots. Foster attempts to speak with one voice to demonstrate that a conventional marriage trumps personal freedom and pleasure, but the literal competing voices seem to trouble that easy conclusion. How, then, might the novel critique the very system Foster seems to privilege? How might the novel simultaneously critique patriarchal culture and its celebration of the domestic sphere while at the same time challenge it?

Zombies, Inada, and Foster invite us to explore the relationship between undecidability and alterity. How does undecidability leave space for the Other? Is a text undecidable, or do readers render texts undecidable? Can we answer "yes" to both questions?

KEY PASSAGES

The examples above encourage us to ask other related questions: What is our responsibility as readers? Is there such a thing as "reading responsibly?" Should we be loyal to the author, text, or the unspoken elements within a text? Do we direct our attention to what is visible or absent? Simon Critchley published *The Ethics of Deconstruction: Derrida and Levinas* (1992) to respond to those who assert that the exposure of Martin Heidegger and Paul de Man's Nazi affiliations compromise

Jacques Derrida's signature work: deconstruction. As Critchley explains in a 2014 interview with Jeremy Butman of the *Los Angeles Review of Books*, "Well, the charge is usually a charge about nihilism. Deconstruction is kind of value nihilism—it has no politics, it has no sense of responsibility, it takes us nowhere." Critchley explains in his introduction to *The Ethics of Deconstruction* that "I will attempt to respond to this question by arguing that an ethical moment is essential to deconstructive reading and that ethics is the goal, or horizon, towards which Derrida's work tends" (2). Although the word *deconstruction* appears throughout this chapter, our focus is not on deconstruction *per se*. Instead, we will focus on Critchley's contribution, his insights and observations, his particular way of describing what he calls "*clôtural* reading," which is based on his study of Derrida. What Critchley provides is a way of thinking about alterity or the condition of absolute otherness in a text, and that attention to what is absent in a text opens up ways of understanding cultural representations and addressing our responsibility as a reader.

> The very activity of thinking, which lies at the basis of epistemological, ontological, and veridical comprehension, is the reduction of plurality to unity and alterity to sameness. The activity of philosophy, the very task of thinking, is the reduction of otherness. In seeking to think the other, its otherness is reduced or appropriated to our understanding. To think philosophically is to comprehend—*comprendre, comprehendere, begreifen*, to include, to seize, to grasp—and master the other, thereby reducing its alterity. As Rodolphe Gasché points out, "Western philosophy is in essence the attempt to domesticate Otherness, since what we understand by thought is nothing but such a project."
>
> (29)
>
> Deconstruction opens a reading by locating a moment of alterity within a text.
>
> (28)
>
> If the first moment of reading is the rigorous, scholarly reconstruction of the dominant interpretation of a text, its intended meaning (*vouloir-dire*) in the guise of a commentary, then the second moment of reading, in virtue of which deconstruction obeys a double necessity,

> is *the destabilization of the stability of the dominant interpretation*. It is the movement of traversing the text, which enables the reading to obtain a position of alterity or exteriority, from which the text can be deconstructed. The second moment brings the text into contradiction with itself, opening its intended meaning, its *vouloir-dire*, onto an alterity which goes against what the text wants to say or mean (*ce que le texte veut dire*).
>
> (26–27)
>
> As the attempt to attain a point of exteriority to logocentrism, deconstruction may therefore be "understood" as the desire to keep open a dimension of alterity which can neither be reduced, comprehended, nor, strictly speaking, even *thought* by philosophy.
>
> (29)
>
> *Clôtural* reading articulates the ethical interruption of ontological closure, thereby disrupting the text's claims to comprehensive unity and self-understanding.
>
> (30)
>
> A *clôtural* reading of a text would consist, first, of a patient and scholarly commentary following the main lines of the text's dominant interpretation, and second, in locating an interruption or alterity within that dominant interpretation where reading discovers insights within a text to which that text is blind.
>
> (30)

Difficult prose. The terminology and concepts imply a familiarity with long and complex philosophical debates, but the stated and implied pairings that frame the discussion—Self and Other, comprehend and exclude, interior and exterior, sight and blindness, intended and unintended, single reading and double reading, closed and open—provide us with a reasonable way to understand Critchley's argument.

DISCUSSION

Critchley asserts that "the very activity of thinking" (29), the act of conceiving, imagining, or bringing a person, place, object, event, or idea into our consciousness inevitably reduces what is complex and plural to something simpler. He points out that our spatial metaphors for understanding—"*comprendre, comprehendere, begreifen*, to include, to seize, to grasp" (29)—give us the image of drawing a circle around what we read, watch, and experience. And what encircles what we encounter? It is our way of thinking: our intellectual frameworks, categories, principles, codes, images, and language. This textbook, this chapter that you are reading right now, exemplifies this move. The entire goal and greatest limitation of this textbook is its desire to simplify and rephrase difficult theoretical concepts in more familiar language. Any analogy or example I use to clarify an idea or experience replaces the new and unfamiliar with the old and recognizable. Consider as well the way the Judeo-Christian tradition comprehends, domesticates, or reduces "God." God, for many theologians, exceeds a human's ability to understand or grasp. God is completely Other. However, sacred texts like the Bible reduce God to our own forms of understanding, for God is father, potter, shepherd, bread of life, light, rock, fortress, deliverer, prince, redeemer, king, ruler, physician, fire, property owner, and vine, among so many other metaphors. These figures domesticate and simplify the divine, but they are inevitable substitutions if we want to comprehend or grasp God.

To be more tangible, imagine the moment when an explorer encounters new lands, people, and customs. The explorer meets his Other, an experience that exceeds his understanding. How does he make sense or give meaning to what appears so alien? Unavoidably, the explorer uses his language, categories, cultural codes, and imagery to comprehend, frame, and describe what he experiences. As a result, the explorer now understands what is radically Other in his own terms. He comprehends and grasps the Other. Embracing a similar process, a novel, poem, film, work of art, speech, or essay presents itself as a unified representation that encloses a topic or draws discussion to a close. Inevitably, through the use of language and literary devices like narrative, figures, characterization, setting, tone, etc., the work simplifies and reduces otherness. The text appropriates the subject "to our understanding." The work cannot do otherwise, but something is lost and made invisible in the process.

If thinking is the act of reducing, simplifying, and enclosing, then to read ethically is to allow the Other to assert itself, a process Critchley calls "*clôtural* reading." First, by *clôture*, Critchley asserts that "understood temporally or spatially, it is necessary to understand *clôture* as a limit, a moment in time or points in space which delimit a given area and seek to circumscribe it" (63). *Clôture* conveys a movement toward closure, "the bringing of a process to its conclusion" (62) or enclosing and surrounding a space. Second, he asserts that *"clôtural* reading articulates the ethical interruption of ontological closure, thereby disrupting the text's claims to comprehensive unity and self-understanding" (30). In other words, *clôtural* reading resists the idea that all parts of a text work together to form a unified meaning. We read by paying "attention to the opening, or breakthrough, that occurs within the closure, violating its vows and breaching its barriers, thereby offering the *promise* of a new beginning" (63). In place of reduction, we seek enlargement. In lieu of unity and sameness, we promote plurality and alterity. We do not domesticate; we embrace wildness. Instead of comprehending, we liberate. We do not enclose; we open. In keeping with his spatial metaphor, Critchley encourages us to "attain a point of exteriority to logocentrism" (29). If logocentrism refers to the belief in a center of knowledge and meaning, a belief in an authoritative source of significance and sense, then our goal is to escape that framework, foundation, and orbit.

Phrased yet another way, we seek to "keep open a dimension of alterity which can neither be reduced, comprehended, nor, strictly speaking, even *thought* by philosophy" (29). What does it mean to "keep open a dimension of alterity," or allow space for an Other that philosophy cannot even conceive? The process sounds rather mystical and impossible. Without delving into the idea of infinite regress and transcendence, suffice it to say that what matters is an ardent and earnest attempt to constantly draw attention to the unacknowledged Other in the text, and that Other can take the form of identities, principles, philosophies, assumptions, ideologies, values, and hierarchies. In short, we are identifying elements in the text that exceed the text's grasp.

In short, there are two moments of reading. The first refers to a "rigorous, scholarly reconstruction of the dominant interpretation of a text, its intended meaning *(vouloir-dire)*" (26). The second destabilizes the text, "brings the text into contradiction with itself, opening its intended meaning" (27). Reading ethically requires us to point to what escapes the grasp of the text and identify what the text excludes or ignores.

POTENTIAL PROJECT

Clôtural reading differs from other methodologies because we are not trying to interpret the text in a traditional sense. We are not reading closely so that we can say, "The story is not saying this; the story really means that." Instead, the purpose of *clôtural* reading is the act of drawing attention to the complexities and indeterminate elements in a text. We succeed when we allude to the possibility of a radical Other. To "speak Critchley," we talk about how texts or even how interpretations of texts "reduce otherness," "domesticate otherness," "simplify and domesticate," explain how "otherness is reduced or appropriated to our understanding," reduce "plurality to unity and alterity to sameness," and "master the other, thereby reducing its alterity." On the other hand, we seek to "disrupt and interrupt unity," disrupt "the text's claims to comprehensive unity and self-understanding," "keep open a dimension of alterity," and locate "a moment of alterity."

PRODUCE A DOUBLE-READING

As noted above, Critchley presents a two-part reading protocol:

> A *clôtural* reading of a text would consist, first, of a patient and scholarly commentary following the main lines of the text's dominant interpretation, and second, in locating an interruption or alterity within that dominant interpretation where reading discovers insights within a text to which that text is blind.
>
> (30)

What does "a patient and scholarly commentary following the main lines of the text's dominant interpretation" involve? Some call this move "reading with the grain" because we work hard to understand a text's "intended meaning" or what it wants to say. The word "intended" misguides to a degree. It is less a matter of asking the author what she meant than paying attention to the work's literary devices, rhetorical strategies, cause-effect relationships, historical context, juxtapositions, and any other tool may we use to make sense of the text. We read closely, gather evidence, and draw conclusions based on how the parts work together to convey meaning. In short, we act like a traditional critic who interprets the text.

The next step invites us to read with an eye on alterity. But what does "in locating an interruption or alterity within that dominant interpretation where reading discovers insights within a text to which that text is blind" (30) ask us to do? Some call this strategy "reading against the grain" because we notice elements that contradict the dominant reading. We pay attention to unreconcilable parts, unassimilable values, unstated assumptions, inconsistencies, confusions, and latent connections. If trying to connect all the parts into a unified whole characterizes reading *with* the grain, then reading *against* the grain "brings the text into contradiction with itself, opening its intended meaning, its *vouloir-dire*, onto an alterity which goes against what the text wants to say or mean" (27). The plurality and competing elements undermine its singular vision. We work hard to preserve a text's complexity and complications, resisting summaries. We may note that the text affirms the very value systems, hierarchies, and structures it seeks to reject, subvert, oppose, or transgress. We note its unspoken complicity with particular philosophical assumptions. And for Critchley, this act of locating alterity, the unassimilated Other in the text, is an *ethical* act. That is, we are responsible readers when we draw attention to what the text excludes and marginalizes. We open rather than close. We "arrive" when we identify the blind spots in a text, when we reveal the logic of *both/and* and *neither/nor* in the work.

Risking over simplification, consider, for example, the ways texts written by explorers establish their rights to colonize while at the same time reveal that their very identity and value are based on those they conquer. Note how critiques of gender binaries may simultaneously reinstate those same binary structures. Pay attention to the ways that a text may affirm the value of transgressing boundaries even as it applauds new boundaries. Explore the ways that critiques of feminism also undermine the very notion of patriarchy. Examine the ways that interrogations of racial superiority belie their own racial essentialism. How do attempts to glorify God end up humanizing the divine and deifying the human? Or, how do images intended to differentiate human and animal ultimately blur those boundaries? These brief hypothetical questions exemplify the need to write in terms of *both/and*, not *either/or*. As noted above, your task is not to point out what the text is "really" saying or doing. Rather, invite the Other—the unreconcilable parts, unassimilable values, unstated assumptions, inconsistencies, confusions, and latent connections—in the text to interrupt, disrupt, contradict, and speak.

WORKS CITED

Butman, Jeremy. "No Exist for Derrida." *Los Angeles Review of Books*, https://lareviewofbooks.org/article/exit-derrida#! Accessed 20 January 2018.

Critchley, Simon. *The Ethics of Deconstruction: Derrida and Levinas*. Purdue UP, 1992.

Foster, Hannah Webster. *The Coquette; or, The History of Eliza Wharton*. 1797. Oxford UP, 1986.

CHAPTER 12

Poaching texts

> Everyday life invents itself by *poaching* in countless ways on the property of others.
>
> (Michel de Certeau xii)

PROBLEMS, PUZZLES, AND QUESTIONS

For years, *Star Trek* fans (followed by fans of *Star Wars*, *Buffy*, *Xena*, and so on) have, with no compensation expected, reworked episodes, created games, generated a wide range of art, coded computer programs, produced personal films, designed countless websites, composed songs, developed languages, designed costumes, and engaged in far-ranging role-playing games, just to name a few activities. A lot of critics mock this kind of behavior, concluding that participants are prolonging adolescence, submitting to consumerism, or escaping from real-world concerns. How do we explain this behavior? Are these consumers falling prey to consumer capitalism, or are they engaged in socially relevant acts of appropriation, or are they doing something else?

Barbie dolls are an easy target when it comes to consumer items that encourage unhealthy body images, consumerism, heterosexual norms, and vapid ideas about beauty, among other potential problems. However, how do we make sense of consumers who do not always use the toys as designed and promoted? For example, some Barbie owners disfigure her body, redesign her clothes, create subversive narratives, marry her to other Barbies, hook her up with several Ken dolls, or even use her as a sex toy. Is Barbie, then, oppressive or empowering? Are Barbie owners (young and old) consumers who mindlessly accept normative social values, or can consumers resist corporate intentions and designs? And are there limits to how one can recode Barbie and other consumer products?

FanFiction, Quotev, Kindle World, Archive of Our Own (AO3), and Asianfanfic, along with other websites and venues, offer readers countless fanfiction texts. For example, over two million readers use FanFiction, and the site offers over 650,000 stories inspired by the Harry Potter series alone. While some authors describe short scenes that describe, say, Hogwarts teachers' after-class encounters with students, others narrate, at length, "missing" romantic moments between Harry and Hermione, fill in narrative gaps, or elaborate on subplots. How do we account for the popularity of these sites? What prompts authors to rewrite scenes, invent new scenarios, and tie up loose threads?

All these questions draw our attention to popular culture, those works that do not often appear on university syllabi. The questions also shift our attention away from the original product to the particular ways consumers—in the broadest sense of the term—actually use what they buy, read, and watch. And we can pose more challenging and expansive questions: Where should we direct our critical attention, to the products and texts or the ways consumers use them? Are consumers pawns or players? To what degree do they have power to resist what society makes available to them?

KEY PASSAGES

Michel de Certeau's *The Practice of Everyday Life* (1980) questions the common idea that consumers are passive dupes who yield to the values, attitudes, and hierarchies consumer society imposes on them. In other words, de Certeau focuses on how people resist social forces that seem to erase an individual's ability to subvert and assert a degree of control. He investigates "the ways in which users—commonly assumed to be passive and guided by established rules—operate" (xi). In particular, de Certeau is not interested in cultural products *per se* than he is in how consumers use the products within limited contexts. He champions, in a sense, those whom "elite culture" ignores, for he wants "to bring to light the clandestine forms taken by the dispersed, tactical, and makeshift creativity of groups or individuals already caught in the nets of 'discipline'" (xiv–xv). He recognizes that consumers engage in legitimate production, and as a result, he advises us that "it is always good to remind ourselves that we mustn't take people for fools" (176). His insights redirect our critical attention in useful ways.

Everyday life invents itself by *poaching* in countless ways on the property of others.

(xii)

Far from being writers—founders of their own place, heirs of the peasants of earlier ages now working on the soil of language, diggers of wells and builders of houses—readers are travellers; they move across lands belonging to someone else, like nomads poaching their way across fields they did not write, despoiling the wealth of Egypt to enjoy it themselves.

(174)

The efficiency of production implies the inertia of consumption. It produces the ideology of consumption-as-a-receptacle. The result of class ideology and technical blindness, this legend is necessary for the system that distinguishes and privileges authors, educators, revolutionaries, in a word, "producers," in contrast with those who do not produce. By challenging "consumption" as it is conceived and (of course) confirmed by these "authorial" enterprises, we may be able to discover creative activity where it has been denied that any exists, and to relativize the exorbitant claim that *a certain kind* of production (real enough, but not the only kind) can set out to produce history by "informing" the whole of a country.

(167)

The reader takes neither the position of the author nor an author's position. He invents in texts something different from what they "intended." He detaches them from their (lost or accessory) origin. He combines their fragments and creates something un-known in the space organized by their capacity for allowing an indefinite plurality of meanings. Is this "reading" activity reserved for the literary critic (always privileged in studies of reading), that is, once again, for a category of professional intellectuals (*clercs*), or can it be extended to all cultural consumers?

(169)

Note that de Certeau redefines readers as travelers, poachers, and nomads who invent, detach, combine, and create. But we need to better understand these new roles, especially in the context of critical theorists who lean toward presenting consumers as mindless pawns or hapless victims in a system they cannot control.

DISCUSSION

Much is embedded in that first sentence: "Everyday life invents itself by *poaching* in countless ways on the property of others" (xii). By "everyday life," de Certeau refers to seemingly routine activities completed by what he calls the "dominated element in a society" (xi–xii), the users, not the makers. "Poaching" conveys not only a kind of theft, but also a trespass. This spatial metaphor is important, for talking about illegally crossing boundaries reminds us that poachers are encroaching on property they do not own or control, but they momentarily make it their own. Inhabiting that space "transforms another person's property into a space borrowed for a moment by a transient" (xxi). We are not talking about gaining territory. Instead, a poacher briefly takes advantage of the land, and the strategy allows the weak to make use of the strong.

To make the poaching metaphor more tangible, note that de Certeau is referring, first, in the broad sense, to language: "speaking operates within the field of a linguistic system; it effects an appropriation, or reappropriation, of language by its speakers" (xiii). That is, we inherit a linguistic system with vocabulary and syntax that defines acceptable sentences. Although users cannot change the fundamental grammar, for working outside the linguistic system would produce incomprehensible and unrecognizable speech, they do demonstrate creativity by using the vocabulary and sentence structure that is available. In this sense, language users travel onto and poach from a linguistic field in order to say what they want to say. They work within the system to serve their own interests.

Second, de Certeau also describes social systems and ideologies as a kind of territory or social space. Institutions of various sorts exercise power, normalizing and legitimizing particular values, hierarchies, and practices. As with language, a social system determines acceptable behavior, privileging certain ideologies while critiquing others. These value systems or social frameworks define social boundaries. People "travel" upon this social field and poach what they can by appropriating, redefining, remaking, and recombining the values, practices, and meanings these social systems offer. For example, de Certeau draws attention to colonized groups that use the rituals and practices imposed upon them in ways that the colonizers never intended.

Finally, the notion of owners and poachers echoes de Certeau's division between writers and readers. When de Certeau suggests that writers are "founders of their own place, heirs of the peasants of earlier ages now working on the soil of language, diggers of wells and builders of houses" (174), he is really comparing writers to property owners. A novel is a kind of territory, an organized space, a "system of verbal or iconic signs" (169) that one can travel to and inhabit. Portraying writing as a kind of property and the reader as a traveler or nomad who poaches, despoils, and enjoys what she finds reverses the common misconception that readers and consumers are passive "receptacles" who simply receive and accept what they read and watch. Instead, de Certeau portrays writing as static and inert, and the reader is actively making meaning. In other words, by privileging the professional class of writers and intellectuals, we miss the ways that consumers actually produce and demonstrate their creativity. By redefining what it means to consume, we discover "creative activity where it has been denied that any exists" (167), and we can question the top-down social arrangement that assumes that only those in power contribute to society.

In short, de Certeau blurs the boundaries between writers and readers, producers and users. Just as a poacher travels on land she does not own, uses what she finds to serve her own interests, and works hard to avoid the property owner, a reader ignores an author's intention, makes new connections, and generates new meanings. The common reader assumes the role of literary critic, teacher, or professional intellectual, decontextualizes elements of the text, and "combines their fragments and creates something un-known in the space organized by their capacity for allowing an indefinite plurality of meanings" (169). By "indefinite plurality of meanings," de Certeau asserts that the complex and rich nature of texts makes them endlessly open to interpretation, and the poaching reader ignores the "authorized" interpretations and finds what is relevant to her instead.

POTENTIAL PROJECT

Remember that de Certeau does not suggest that consumers are romantic individualists, free of any constraint. More to the point, consumers work within linguistic, social, and textual systems and frameworks they did not make. De Certeau is interested in consuming and reading as a creative process. As a result, no matter which project you choose, you need to be one part ethnographer and one part interpreter, and that means you need to focus less on the texts readers read and watch and more on what they produce in response.

Identify acts of resistance

To follow de Certeau's lead, you need to choose a text and make two interpretive moves. First, use any number of strategies in this textbook to understand what values, attitudes, and behaviors a particular text celebrates or critiques. For example, in what ways does the text legitimize particular social hierarchies or ideologies? How does the text shape, articulate, and reproduce cultural boundaries through a process of praising and blaming?

Second, shift your focus away from the text to how the readers, viewers, fans, and consumers modify, use, and make sense of the text. Because consumers of culture are travelers who "move across lands belonging to someone else, like nomads poaching their way across fields they did not write" (174), explain how readers, fans, and viewers have "poached" the text in ways that serve their interests. And by "poach," remember that we are referring to the process of inventing "something different from what they 'intended'" (169), detaching or decontextualizing elements from their original source, combining parts in new ways to create something new, all in order to make the text relevant to the consumer, reader, or viewer. Therefore, use interviews, blog postings, podcasts, remixes, websites, and other forms of social media to understand how consumers and users appropriate the text in ways that serve their needs and circumstances. These acts of appropriation may take the form of noting how readers have reinterpreted a story or image. What do they find useful or relevant? What do their choices reveal about what users value, praise, critique, and disparage? Or, concentrate on remakes and remixes, fan fiction, and other kinds of extensions. What elements of the original does the poacher delete, modify, or add? To what end or purpose?

We are, as de Certeau explains, looking at two forms of production, the first by the makers and the second by the users. And by comparing the values embodied in the original with the poacher's creation or interpretation, what do we learn about competing value systems and goals? Put another way, de Certeau insists that "the tactics of consumption, the ingenious ways in which the weak make use of the strong, thus lend a political dimension to everyday practices" (xvii). And if politics have to do with power, then how do poachers resist the values, attitudes, and social order of the text, the property owner?

Consider the seminal work of John Fiske who explores how Madonna fans make sense of her music videos and images. He acknowledges that Madonna's persona, images, music, performances, films, etc. exploit her sexuality and embody masculine fantasies that make her rich, but that is only part of the analysis. More importantly, he interviews fans and examines how they read Madonna's image and music in ways that challenge typical notions of masculinity and femininity. For these fans, Madonna models ways to construct and control female sexuality and identity and reverses the relationship between object and voyeur. The anecdotes in the Problems, Puzzles, and Questions section also invite you to explore how fans and readers have poached a dizzying array of films and stories. How, for example, does fan fiction that portrays Spock and Captain Kirk as lovers help us understand a desire to question heterosexual norms? How might alternative endings to Jane Austin novels critique Austin's values and social order and provide an opportunity to explore and articulate countervalues and hierarchies? How could a fictional elaboration on a minor character in *The Hunger Games* trilogy (2008–2010) offer an empowering fantasy or another way to construct identity? Every "What if...?" narrative invites us to ask, "How does the poaching reader question the status quo and offer an alternative identity and social environment?" In short, this project encourages you to understand ways that readers and viewers rewrite specific value systems and social realities.

WORK CITED

De Certeau, Michel. *The Practice of Everyday Life.* 1980. Translated by Steven Rendall. U of California P, 1984.

CHAPTER 13

Cultivating rhizomes

Any point of a rhizome can be connected to anything other, and must be. This is very different from the tree or root, which plots a point, fixes an order.
(Gilles Deleuze and Félix Guattari 7)

PROBLEMS, PUZZLES, AND QUESTIONS

The word "encyclopedia" derives from two Greek words that, when combined, suggest "complete instruction" or "complete knowledge." Communities have compiled what they have learned for at least two thousand years, but our modern notion of the encyclopedia arrives in the 18th century. For writers of the 1755 *Encyclopédie*, structure and order improve the random selection of memorable citations in commonplace books, evident when Denis Diderot and Jean le Rond d'Alembert cite the ancient poet Horace on the title page of their massive work: "What grace may be added to commonplace matters by the power of order and connection" (qtd. in Furbank 83).

Contrast this compendium of knowledge with the Internet. Designed in the shadow of the Cold War for military purposes, the Internet lacks a central command, thus allowing for multiple points of communication, especially useful when a nuclear strike threatens to destroy the headquarters. Consisting of interconnected computer networks that convey information globally, the Internet connects a wide variety of networks to other networks, and as a result, metaphors like the "web," the "net," "cyberspace," or "cloud" underestimate its complexity. Does the Internet merely expand the encyclopedia's purpose and organizational logic? Do these sources of knowledge just differ in size and scope, breadth and depth? Does the absence of a core or center within the

Internet mean that the Internet is more democratic or even anarchic, or does the Internet's decentralized and global coverage merely allow those in power to extend their reach? In its desire for "order and connection," does the encyclopedia offer the same potential? How so, or why not?

As mentioned in different places in this textbook, Susan Griffin's *A Chorus of Stones: The Private Life of War* (1992) and Susan Howe's prose poem "Incloser" (1993) surprise us with their unusual form. In lieu of connected and coherent paragraphs, Howe and Griffin offer us verbal collages composed of seemingly random fragments that cross genres, discourses, tones, and styles. We strain to locate a central thesis, a common denominator, or a conceptual center. Julia Kristeva's essay "Stabat Mater" (1977) examines the cult of the Virgin Mary as well as observations about her own experience as a mother. What is striking about Kristeva's essay is its form. The main body of the text, written in academic prose, is periodically interrupted by a parallel column that presents personal and sensory-rich observations about maternity and motherhood. In 1974, philosopher Jacques Derrida published *Glas* (1974), a dual-column work that discusses Georg Hegel and Jean Genet, but the format and style cross genres. Is it a collage, philosophical treatise, literary critique, commentary, or art object? Roland Barthes produces his own set of instructions to create *A Lover's Discourse: Fragments* (1977). A series of highly organized fragments that meditate on specific images common in a love affair, *A Lover's Discourse* blurs the boundaries between fact and fiction, academic argument and personal memoir, public and private discourse. How do we make sense of these radical experiments in form? Can we identify a core or center? Does the text's design merely reinforce and embody the content? Or, does the form invite a kind of linguistic play, replacing thesis-driven arguments and its desire to explain and interpret with an indeterminate text?

These examples and questions circle around the larger issues of identity and desire, boundaries and liminal spaces, being and becoming. Framed yet another way, how do bodies and fragments connect? How do parts relate? What allows them to relate? Who controls these connections? Are some systems more appealing than others?

KEY PASSAGES

Questions about systems and parts, control and freedom, center and periphery, and order and connection are often at the heart of our discussions about social organizations, personal and social psychology, and literature and culture. With a desire to understand how parts relate to wholes, Gilles Deleuze and Félix Guattari collaborated to produce *A Thousand Plateaus: Capitalism and Schizophrenia* (1980), an avant-garde work whose form challenges readers as much as the concepts. While the work elaborates on terms we encounter in previous Deleuze and Guattari publications, like "body without organs," "deterritorialization/reterritorialization," "assemblages," "nomadism," "schizoanalysis," and "desiring machines," we will focus on an especially rich concept: rhizomes. Rhizomes have everything to do with how one thing relates to another, and as a result, this flexible plant metaphor allows us to discuss a range of systems, from aesthetics, memory, and identity to the way we discuss psychology, politics, and philosophy.

> Any point of a rhizome can be connected to anything other, and must be. This is very different from the tree or root, which plots a point, fixes an order.
> (7)
>
> Arborescent systems are hierarchical systems with centers of significance and subjectification, central automata like organized memories. In the corresponding models, an element only receives information from a higher unit, and only receives a subjective affection along preestablished paths.
> (16)
>
> To these centered systems, the authors contrast acentered systems, finite networks of automata in which communication runs from any neighbor to any other, the stems or channels do not preexist, and all individuals are interchangeable, defined only by their *state* at a given moment—such that the local operations are coordinated and the final, global result synchronized without a central agency.
> (17)
>
> Unlike a structure, which is defined by a set of points and positions, with binary relations between the points and biunivocal relationships between the positions, the rhizome is made only of lines: lines of segmentarity and stratification as its dimensions, and the line of flight or deterritorialization as the maximum dimension after which the multiplicity undergoes metamorphosis changes in nature. These lines, or lineaments, should not be confused with lineages of the arborescent type, which are merely

> localizable linkages between points and positions. Unlike the tree, the rhizome is not the object of reproduction: neither external reproduction as image-tree nor internal reproduction as tree-structure. The rhizome is an antigenealogy. It is a short-term memory, or antimemory. The rhizome operates by variation, expansion, conquest, capture, and offshoots. Unlike the graphic arts, drawing, or photography, unlike tracings, the rhizome pertains to a map that must be produced, constructed, a map that is always detachable, connectable, reversible, modifiable, and has multiple entryways and exits and its own lines of flight. It is tracings that must be put on the map, not the opposite. In contrast to centered (even polycentric) systems with hierarchical modes of communication and preestablished paths, the rhizome is an acentered, nonhierarchical, nonsignifying system without a General and without an organizing memory or central automaton, defined solely by a circulation of states.
> (21)
>
> A rhizome has no beginning or end; it is always in the middle, between things, interbeing, *intermezzo*. The tree is filiation, but the rhizome is alliance, uniquely alliance. The tree imposes the verb "to be," but the fabric of the rhizome is the conjunction, "and...and...and..." This conjunction carries enough force to shake and uproot the verb "to be."
> (25)

The terminology is a bit unconventional. When we read theory, we are not used to talking about tubers and trees, rhizomes and arborescent systems, and antigeneology and lineages. We have to admit, however, that it is refreshing to read sentences like this in a work of cultural theory: "We're tired of trees. We should stop believing in trees, roots, and radicles. They've made us suffer too much" (Deleuze and Guattari 15). But understanding why trees are a problem invites our next step and provides a key to understanding the rhizome's appeal.

DISCUSSION

For Deleuze and Guattari, a tree exemplifies a particular kind of hierarchical system with limited pathways and a central command. When they write that "arborescent" or tree-like systems have "centers of significance and subjectification, central automata like organized memories" (16), they are asserting that these structures follow a binary logic characterized by up and down lines of communication, and as a result, "an element only receives information from a higher unit, and only receives a subjective affection along preestablished paths" (16). A military "chain of command" illustrates this system well, but about any kind of bureaucratic structure—academic, corporate, political—exemplifies organizational trees. Note as well that one gains value and significance, and one becomes a "subject" and acquires an identity, only by being part of these preestablished paths. Phrased yet another way, to be recognized, individuals must integrate themselves into the preexisting system that moves back and forth from the root to the uppermost branches. If we are not part of the chain of command, we do not exist, and we do not have value.

One might ask, "But what about the expansive growth both above and below the ground? Does not that complexity generate individuality and freedom?" For Deleuze and Guattari, this branching out, no matter how extensive, is merely a form of lineage or genealogy, or as they explain, "a set of points and positions, with binary relations between the points and biunivocal relationships between the positions" (21). In other words, one can still trace rather direct pathways along those roots and branches, for one "line" leads directly to another; one line is always more secondary to its source branch. Using the word "lineage" and "genealogy" also brings to mind a pedigree chart with its vast, predictable, and hierarchical system that limits and regulates connections. In short, tree systems think in linear terms as they search for roots and sources as well as conclusions and outcomes.

In contrast to trees, Deleuze and Guattari celebrate rhizomes, subterranean stems of plants that grow horizontally and send out roots and shoots, not by design, but by chance and opportunity. And if trees are centered, hierarchical systems preoccupied with cause and effect, then rhizomes are "acentered systems, finite networks of automata in which communication runs from any neighbor to any other, the stems or channels do not preexist, and all individuals are interchangeable, defined only by their *state* at a given moment" (17). In contrast to a tree's rigid binary structure, a rhizome offers a nonhierarchical, opportunistic system that operates at the local level. Desire expresses itself in unsanctioned and unregulated ways. As the word "network" implies, rhizomes are groups of random and unpredictable nodes that interconnect. And just as we see in a huge net, there is no central point, no governing body, no "General" that guides, directs, and designs.

Deleuze and Guattari also explain that a "rhizome is made only of lines: lines of segmentarity and stratification as its dimensions, and the line of flight or deterritorialization as the maximum dimension after which the multiplicity undergoes metamorphosis, changes in nature" (21). The first part of that vexing sentence refers to the impossibility of identifying lines in clear, linear, and hierarchical ways. A rhizome is "antigenealogy" and "antimemory" because "a rhizome has no beginning or end; it is always in the middle, between things, interbeing, *intermezzo*" (25). In other words, just as we cannot pick a blade of grass and follow its roots to the first original blade, and just as the Internet does not have an original or central server that governs all other servers, a rhizomatic network has no genealogy or long-term memory in the sense of a traceable, chronological path. We only have decentralized and interconnected segments and groups, and that is why "the fabric of the rhizome is the conjunction, 'and…and… and…'" instead of "to be" which suggests a single, identifiable identity. As implied by the repetition of "and," rhizomes are nomadic and constantly on the move. They are always in the process of "becoming."

The second half of that sentence is even more difficult. First, "line of flight or deterritorialization" (21) refers to a moment of transformation and escape. As translator Brian Massumi explains in "Notes on the Translation and Acknowledgments," the words "flight" and "escape"

> translate *fuite*, which has a different range of meanings than either of the English terms. *Fuite* covers not only the act of fleeing or eluding but also flowing, leaking, and disappearing into the distance (the vanishing point in a painting is *a point de fuite*). It has no relation to flying.
>
> (Massumi xvi)

A "line of flight" and "deterritorialization," then, refer to the possibility of leaving of a territory and initiating a new segment that may connect to other segments in unpredictable ways. Second, a "multiplicity" is another way to describe a rhizome which is a gathering of connections that have no center or hierarchy. In sum, a rhizome forms relationships in such a way that this collection of segments has no center, no sense of beginning and ending, and there are moments when elements break away or escape to form yet another node, and this transformation changes the identity of the entire assemblage or structure.

POTENTIAL PROJECTS

And what does all this talk about rhizomes and trees have to do with literary and cultural criticism? We can think of short stories, plays, poems, films, art, and public events as systems that belong to larger systems.

And as noted earlier, Deleuze and Guattari's highly abstract language offers a way to discuss relationships and systems, from organizations as broad as science, bureaucracies, terrorist cells, and guerrilla warfare to something as narrow as the way an author designs a novel or portrays a character. The common focus, however, is a desire to understand how a system or structure channels or liberates, represses or emancipates. We explore our place (or a character's place) within (or outside) of that system. Note, too, that the form of the text is equally important to its content. *How* a novel portrays events demands as much attention as *what* a novel portrays. A narrative may portray and comment on rhizomatic relationships, or it may embody or be organized like a rhizome.

Categorize: tree or rhizome?

Use Deleuze and Guattari's discussion of arborescent and rhizomatic structures to make sense of narratives, organizations, or performances that depart from preestablished aesthetic forms, politics, and ways of thinking. Rhizomatic texts often confuse us because they appear incoherent, aimless, unpredictable, and disorganized. They do not always seem complete. Some narratives lack a central character or coherent plot. Some resist traditional reading strategies and categories. Some works of art ask us to participate in ways the artist cannot predict or control. Contrasting these rhizomatic works with arborescent systems help us understand their design and purpose.

Therefore, discuss your text or organization in terms of trees vs. rhizomes, preestablished paths vs. open channels, centered vs. acentered systems, organized memory guided by a General vs. local operations coordinated and synchronized without a central agency, binary relations between points vs. lines of flight and deterritorialization, genealogy vs. antimemory, points vs. middles, filiations vs. alliances, and "to be" vs. conjunctive connections. Discuss how "arborescent structures" embody hierarchical systems governed by a coherent, centralized, stable, and reproducible identity, while rhizomatic assemblages operate by variation, expansion, conquest, capture, and offshoots that generate detachable, connectable, reversible, modifiable, and multiple entryways and exits. Finally, remember that it is not enough to say, for example, that this novel is a tree while that poem is a rhizome. Instead, explain the effect and purpose of these competing ways of organizing social organizations and texts. Simply put, works that operate like trees control and direct desire *for* something, while rhizomatic texts liberate desires, allowing them to move as opportunities arise. Their effect or purpose is unpredictable and indeterminate.

Identify strategies of resistance

Rhizomes subvert trees. Rhizomes are nomadic. They send out shoots when the opportunity arises. In fact, rhizomes act a bit like water in that they want to flow unobstructed, and even when someone reroutes the water into pipes, the water finds weak spots, fissures, and cracks. Deleuze and Guattari seize on this comparison:

> Lines of flight, for their part, never consist in running away from the world but rather in causing runoffs, as when you drill a hole in a pipe; there is no social system that does not leak from all directions, even if it makes its segments increasingly rigid in order to seal the lines of flight.
>
> (204)

The fact that a system always leaks provides hope for change, for this inability to create a water-tight system means that subversion is always possible.

With this subversive potential in mind, explore texts that "leak" from a system that seeks to create established pathways. The goal is to discuss how these works offer identities that do not have a "center," that are constantly on the move and always in the process of creation. These texts portray how desire is expressed in multiple, unsanctioned, and unregulated ways. These works roam in-between established hierarchical pathways and escape attempts to "seal the lines of flight" (204). They constantly seek connections from any direction, and as a result, identity is a never-ending process of becoming. For example, scholars have used Deleuze and Guattari to understand the gender/transgender continuum in new ways. Following their lead, you could discuss how rhizomatic texts subvert binary notions of gender, multiply the connections among other identity groups, and generate new identity pathways that resist any kind of unifying concepts by multiplying and transforming identities. Others have explored how postcolonial narratives deterritorialize colonized identity and replace a colonial impulse to establish a stable genealogy with a postcolonial antimemory. They have examined how these subversive texts, in form and content, undermine hierarchical, arborescent forms of control. Still others have explained how postcolonial narratives reject "preestablished paths" and embrace the "middle, between things, interbeing, *intermezzo*" (25). With an eye on race, scholars rethink representations of race and ethnicity, foregrounding the subversive potential of the conjunction, "and…and…and…." In short, discuss the various strategies these texts use to resist the language and concepts of roots, hierarchies, stability, and centered systems that seek to control and channel desire and identity.

WORKS CITED

Deleuze, Gilles and Félix Guattari. *A Thousand Plateaus: Capitalism and Schizophrenia*. Translated by Brian Massumi, U of Minnesota P, 1987.
Furbank, Philip Nicholas. *Diderot: A Critical Biography*. Secker, 1992.
Massumi, Brian. "Translator's Foreword." *A Thousand Plateaus: Capitalism and Schizophrenia*, by Gilles Deleuze and Félix Guatarri, U of Minnesota P, 1987.

CHAPTER 14

Reconciling double consciousness

> It is a peculiar sensation, this double-consciousness, this sense of always looking at one's self through the eyes of others.
>
> (W.E.B Du Bois 5)

PROBLEMS, PUZZLES, AND QUESTIONS

Captured in West Africa in the mid-1700s when she was probably seven years old, Phillis Wheatley was raised by a Boston couple who taught her to read and write, and this foundation gave her to access to an education few slaves enjoyed. In her most famous poem "On being brought from *Africa* to *America*" (1773), Wheatley describes her capture in surprisingly positive terms: "TWAS mercy brought me from my *Pagan* land" (1), but she encounters racism: "Some view our sable race with scornful eye, / 'Their colour is a diabolic die'" (5–6). She concludes by chiding her readers: "Remember, *Christians*, *Negroes* black as *Cain* / May be refin'd, and join th'angelic train" (7–8). Notice her awareness of multiple identities: she moves from a biographical "I" to "some view our sable race," to "*Negroes*, black as *Cain*." What do we make of these multiple identities? How can we account for the shift in perspective?

Gwendolyn Bennett graduated from Columbia University and the Pratt Institute in 1924, and she soon landed a teaching position at Howard University where she taught art. After a brief stay in Paris, she returned to New York where she worked for *Opportunity Magazine*. In "Heritage" (1923), she describes "lithe Negro girls" among palm trees, a sunset, silent sands, a lotus flower, and the Nile. Her persona wants "to hear the chinting / Around a heathen fire / Of a strange black race" (10–12). She concludes with an unfulfilled desire: "I want to feel the surging / Of my sad people's soul / Hidden by a minstrel smile"

(16–18). The last four words remind us of the gap between Africa and America, between authenticity and artifice. Why does her yearning remain unfulfilled? Why does authentic identity remain hidden?

A Jamaican immigrant, Claude McKay flourished during the Harlem Renaissance. In "America" (1921), we recognize a familiar tension: "Although she feeds me bread of bitterness, / And sinks into my throat her tiger's tooth, / Stealing my breath of life, I will confess / I love this cultured hell that tests my youth!" (1–4). America offers "vigor," "strength," and "bigness," but at the same time "hate," "terror," and "malice." Above all, the "wonders" America offers are "Like priceless treasures sinking in the sand" (14), visible, but not quite accessible.

Whether it is Wheatley who endures a "scornful eye," Bennett who draws attention to a "minstrel smile," or McKay who loves "this cultured hell," we recognize not only expressions of alienation and marginalization, but a kind of split identity. How do we make sense of texts like these that address identity, belonging, alienation, and marginalization? How do these figures arrive at an understanding of self, or what prevents them from doing so? Can they inhabit plural identities, and does a hybridized self offer any advantages, or do multiple identities merely suggest an incoherent or fragmented self? Importantly, is there a connection between these experiences and being African American?

KEY PASSAGES

W. E. B. Du Bois published *The Souls of Black Folk* in 1903, a sprawling work that combines anthropology, autobiography, poetry, philosophy, and history. However, the theme that binds the work together is Du Bois' observation that "the problem of the Twentieth Century is the problem of the color-line" (1). Du Bois goes on to describe conflicts, obstacles, and possible solutions. The first chapter, "Of Our Spiritual Strivings," focuses on the effect of racial discrimination that is both material and psychological. To be Black in America is to be divided, split, and at odds with one's "self":

> After the Egyptian and Indian, the Greek and Roman, the Teuton and Mongolian, the Negro is a sort of seventh son, born with a veil, and gifted with second-sight in this American world,—a world which yields him no true self-consciousness, but only lets him see himself through the revelation of the other world. It is a peculiar sensation, this

> double-consciousness, this sense of always looking at one's self through the eyes of others, of measuring one's soul by the tape of a world that looks on in amused contempt and pity. One ever feels his two-ness,—an American, a Negro; two souls, two thoughts, two unreconciled strivings; two warring ideals in one dark body, whose dogged strength alone keeps it from being torn asunder.
>
> (5)
>
> The history of the American Negro is the history of this strife—this longing to attain self-conscious manhood, to merge his double self into a better and truer self. In this merging he wishes neither of the older selves to be lost. He would not Africanize America, for America has too much to teach the world and Africa. He would not bleach his Negro soul in a flood of white Americanism, for he knows that Negro blood has a message for the world.
>
> (5)

These passages address the problem of identity, alienation, and marginalization, and Du Bois' attention to "self-consciousness," "double-consciousness," and hybridized identity offers a useful way to make sense of texts that explore the struggles and aspirations of those who seek a "better and truer self."

DISCUSSION

Keep in mind that Du Bois is writing in the shadow of Booker T. Washington, a leading African American at the turn of the century who advocated a gradual approach to ending racism and discrimination. In his "Address at the Atlanta Exposition" (1895), or what is known as "The Atlanta Compromise," Washington roots his solution in the separation of economic, social, and cultural spheres, and he asserts that African Americans will "prosper in proportion as we learn to dignify and glorify common labour, and put brains and skill into the common occupations of life" (138). He maintains that "In all things that are purely social we can be as separate as the fingers, yet one as the hand in all things essential to mutual progress" (139). Steering away from politics, he concludes that "the agitation of questions of social equality is the extremist folly" (140).

Du Bois rejects this "separate but equal" approach and demands equal rights in every sphere. *The Souls of Black Folk* critiques racist policies and advances a solution, but his foregrounding of the psychological and social effect of racism is especially useful when we examine questions of identity, community, and alienation. Let us examine a few of his concepts in detail.

True self-consciousness

The phrase "true self-consciousness" seems steeped in the 19th-century Romanticism which posits and privileges an authentic "self" that is independent of culture. This "self" is natural and suggests that one can understand who one is, often by intense introspection. The "self" is the best form of knowledge. Du Bois points out that this process is subverted by a racist culture which "only lets him see himself through the revelation of the other world" (5). In other words, the African American looks at him or herself through a cultural filter that acts as a "veil." The African American sees through a veil, and white Americans also see African Americans through a veil. One can only experience a "false" self-consciousness, and it is "false" because this awareness comes from outside one's self.

Double Consciousness

Du Bois also complicates the 19th-century notion of self by suggesting that one can simultaneously experience two perceptions, two forms of awareness. On the one hand, by "double consciousness," Du Bois may be referring to the fact that an awareness of self is one step removed from reality. "I perceive myself only as you perceive me." Or, as Du Bois phrases it, "this sense of always looking at one's self through the eyes of others, of measuring one's soul by the tape of a world that looks on in amused contempt and pity" (5). When we look at a mirror, our image is doubled. We see ourselves looking at ourselves. We view only a reflection of our self, not our true self. We experience alienation and fragmentation.

And what is the effect of this fragmentation and contradiction? Du Bois reminds his readers that

> This waste of double aims, this seeking to satisfy two unreconciled ideals, has wrought sad havoc with the courage and faith and deeds of ten thousand thousand people,—has sent them often wooing false gods and invoking false means of salvation, and at times has even seemed about to make them ashamed of themselves.
>
> (6)

Du Bois emphasizes that "inevitable self-questioning, self-disparagement, and lowering of ideals" (9) result from double consciousness. Note that the shame and lack of self-esteem come from within; it is part of what it means to be African American at the turn of the century in America. Du Bois points out the difficulty of responding to external contempt and shaming, but he identifies the sinister effects of the situation when African Americans themselves—as a result of experiencing double consciousness—are the source of shame, doubt, and critique.

Hybridity

On the other hand, this doubling of consciousness refers to the fact that one has to negotiate two identities: African and American. Note that Du Bois does not merely assert that African Americans must rid themselves of any "American" or "white" influence. He does not speak of "de-colonizing" identity, nor does he suggest African Americans can return to a pre-colonized state. Instead, he wants to merge his identities, reconcile the "two warring ideals in one dark body" (5).

Admittedly, Du Bois does not offer a clear method for merging "his double self into a better and truer self" (5) beyond gaining equal rights, thus legitimizing Black identity. However, we need to recognize Du Bois is not celebrating a hyphenated identity. He would, no doubt, flinch at my use of "African-American." He does not seem interested in a "self" that alternates between two or more identities. Instead, Du Bois suggests that the identity that remains should be unified, coherent, and whole. The "self" should be a seamless synthesis of both African and American, thus creating a completely new identity.

POTENTIAL PROJECTS

Du Bois is most useful when we discuss African American literature, art, and politics, particularly during the first half of the 20th century, for that is the context that engaged Du Bois in the first place. However, the power of his description of identity, alienation, discrimination, and double consciousness reaches well beyond his own historical moment. Consider the following projects.

Explore the Harlem Renaissance

We can use Du Bois to make sense of the literature and art of the Harlem Renaissance. How did the writers of the Harlem Renaissance address double consciousness? How did these writers respond to Du

Bois' theory of identity, manhood, and equality? How did any of these writers and artists find a way to "merge his double self into a better and truer self" (5)? One path is to discuss a character's psychological experience of discrimination. We can use Du Bois' notion of double consciousness to explain the alienation and divided identity that a marginalized character experiences. We can examine as well if characters woo "false gods" and invoke "false means of salvation" (6) that make them feel ashamed of their own identity. On the other hand, we can identify ways that characters reconcile their "two souls, two thoughts, two unreconciled strivings; two warring ideals in one dark body" (5). Or, more broadly, how did any of these writers and artists find a way to remove the "veil," eliminate his or her "twoness," and "merge his double self into a better and truer self" (5)?

Extend insight to other groups

Search databases for books and articles that apply Du Bois' notion of double consciousness to other groups who also experience "this sense of always looking at one's self through the eyes of others, of measuring one's soul by the tape of a world that looks on in amused contempt and pity" (5). Discuss how other groups face "two souls, two thoughts, two unreconciled strivings; two warring ideals" (5). For example, relying on the concept of double consciousness, scholars have written about representations of the disabled, Jewish American fiction, Native American literature, George Eliot, representations of immigrants, Latino literature, and Hong Kong cinema, among so many more. Read a range of articles and notice how they build upon Du Bois and apply his insights to other identity groups and contexts, then follow their lead.

WORKS CITED

Bennett, Gwendolyn. "Heritage." *Opportunity*, vol. 1, no. 12, 1923, p. 371.

Du Bois, William Edward Burghardt. *The Souls of Black Folk*. 1903. Yale UP, 2015.

McKay, Claude. "America." *The Heath Anthology of American Literature*. Volume D, 7th ed., edited by Paul Lauter, Wadsworth, 2014, p. 2163.

Washington, Booker T. "Address at the Atlanta Exposition." *American Speeches: Political Oratory from Abraham Lincoln to Bill Clinton*, edited by Ted Widmer, Library of America, 2006, pp. 137–141.

Wheatley, Phillis. *Poems on Various Subjects, Religious and Moral*. U of Virginia P, Generic NL, 1996.

CHAPTER 15

Shocking readers

> Shock, then, names a reaction to what is startling, painful, even horrifying.
> (Rita Felski 105)

PROBLEMS, PUZZLES, AND QUESTIONS

The opening scene of *Un Chien Andalou* (1929) portrays a man swiping a straight-edge razor across a leather strop. He walks to his balcony where we see a woman sitting on a chair. He uses his fingers to keep her eye open, and we see the razor near her eye. Thankfully, the film cuts to a thin cloud moving horizontally across a round moon, sparing us from the violent scene, but then the film returns to the woman, and we watch close-up the razor slicing the eye. Vitreous spills from the eyeball. When my students watch this scene, they inevitably and involuntarily express their dismay. I have seen the film over 50 times, and I always flinch. Despite this warning, the image will make you wince, too.

A cursory review of late 20th-century art offers its own set of shocking artworks: Chris Burden has himself crucified atop a WV Beatle. French artist Orlan uses plastic surgery to match her chin with Botticelli's "Venus," her nose with Gérôme's "Psyche," her lips with Boucher's "Europa," her eyes with a 17th-century painting of Diana, and her forehead with da Vinci's "Mona Lisa." Milo Moire creates art by squirting paint-filled eggs out of her vagina. More recently, Russian artist Petr Pavlensky, during three separate performances, sewed his mouth shut, wrapped himself in barbed wire, and nailed his scrotum to Moscow's Red Square.

We err if we think that these kinds of representations are new. Jonathan Swift's "A Modest Proposal" satirically offers advice to the "thrifty" who, after having eaten a *"good fat Child,"* may "flay the Carcase; the Skin of which, artificially dressed, will make admirable *Gloves for Ladies,* and *Summer Boots for fine Gentlemen*" (234). *King Lear* offers this shocking image as Gloucester speaks with Regan: "Because I would not see thy cruèl nails / Pluck out his poor old eyes, nor thy fierce sister / In his anointed flesh [rash] boarish fangs" (3.7.56–3.7.58). Instead of Regan gouging his eyes, servants bind Gloucester, and Cornwall blinds him by stomping on his eyes: "Lest it see more, prevent it. Out, vild jelly! / Where is thy lustre now?" (3.7.83–3.7.84). No matter how many times we read the passage or watch it performed, "Out, vild jelly!" still shocks.

What do we think of these images, scenes, and works of art? Why do these representations and performances shock us? While we might be able to explain the shock of the new, what about the shock of the old? And how do we account for the way Swift and Shakespeare continue to shock us? How do we account for our response? And is there a Goldilocks Zone of shock, not too shocking, not too tame? Why do we read *for* shock?

KEY PASSAGES

Rita Felski explores why shocking images, narratives, and language appeal to us in *Uses of Literature* (2008) which responds to two critical approaches. What Felski calls a "theological" approach is "any strong claim for literature's other-worldly aspects" (4), while "ideological critics insist that works of literature, as things of this world, are always caught up in social hierarchies and struggles over power" (7). Simply put, one approach celebrates literature's transcendent qualities, while the other firmly roots literature to social and material conditions. Felski wants to expand our options by proposing that "the meaning of literature lies in its use" (8) because looking at how readers use literature exposes "a vast terrain of practices, expectations, emotions, hopes, dreams, and interpretations" (8). More specifically, Felski wants to examine literature's effect on readers. Instead of high theory with its esoteric concepts, she encourages us to reflect on common "modes of textual engagement" (14) when we read and watch something. We recognize ourselves in characters. Texts enchant us. We learn something from them, and strangely enough, we seek out works that shock us. Interrogating this last form of engagement, what Felski says, "names a reaction to what is startling, painful, even horrifying" (105), is particularly interesting and timely.

> Shock builds on a sense of fear, serving as a synonym for terror or intense fright, while also shading towards rather different associations of disgust and repulsion. If we find ourselves shocked by graphic portrayals of organs or orifices, secretions or excretions, our reaction does not

spring from any real or imagined threat to our safety; the affront is to our moral or aesthetic sensibilities rather than our physical well-being. Alternatively, shock may trigger a notable absence of emotion, conjuring up a state of numbness or blankness much canvassed by trauma theorists. Shock, then, tells us less about the specific content of an affective state than about the qualitative impact of a text or object on the psyche. It denotes a sudden collision, an abrupt, even violent, encounter; the essence of shock is to be jarring.

(112–113)

Shock thus marks the antithesis of the blissful enfolding and voluptuous pleasure that we associate with enchantment. Instead of being rocked and cradled, we find ourselves ambushed and under assault; shock invades consciousness and broaches the reader's or viewer's defenses. Smashing into the psyche like a blunt instrument, it can wreak havoc on our usual ways of ordering and understanding the world.

(113)

Shock is both an adaptive defense to the swirling chaotic sensations of city life and a purposeful act of aggression on the part of the writer striking out at his public, fashioning a phenomenology of literary assault. The modern experience of discontinuity and suddenness, abruptness and surprise, is echoed in poetic forms that undercut the reader's certainties, court perversity, engage in discordant juxtapositions and poetic dissonance, plant punches and counter-punches.

(122)

If shock aims too low, its efforts to provoke are likely to go entirely unremarked or to risk being mocked as lame, tame, or risible. At any given moment, audiences are likely to have become immune or indifferent to the impact of certain subjects or styles of representation, to remain irritatingly unperturbed by what aims to disturb. Conversely, if shock-effects are ratcheted up too high, they are likely to trigger intense waves of revulsion or indignation that drive audiences out of theaters or cause them to slam shut their books, cutting off all further engagement with the work of art.

(130)

We often talk about "shock value," but we often use the phrase to signal some attempt to grab our attention. Felski, however, encourages us to think of the various effects and even uses of shock, and that is where we now turn our attention.

DISCUSSION

Writers, filmmakers, and artists often act aggressively toward us. Felski uses fighting metaphors to signal the hostility. "Striking out at his public" (122), a writer may engage in "literary assault" (122) and "plant punches and counter-punches" (122). We feel "ambushed and under assault" (113). Shock "invades consciousness and broaches the reader's or viewer's defenses" (113), smashing "into the psyche like a blunt instrument" (113). For Felski, shocking literary works are thugs, and readers are victims who endure what is "startling, painful, even horrifying" (105).

But why do we react this way? What, exactly, shocks us?

First, a text may shock by creating discord when we want harmony. The work engages in "discordant juxtapositions and poetic dissonance" (122). In other words, the form itself, the very way that a writer, filmmaker, or artist convey meaning, may shock us. Felski, for example, refers us to a shocking juxtaposition in a Baudelaire poem: An "animal carcass, its legs thrown up in the air, its belly exposed, roasting in the sun, brings to the speaker's mind the picture of a woman burning in the throes of desire" (122). Equating a lustful woman with a sensory-rich image of a putrefying corpse is a "brutal attack on visual, olfactory, and auditory modes of perception, a vile synesthesia of the repellent and obscene" (123). Or, if we want something more contemporary, it is easy enough to point to films that shock, not because of the content *per se*, but because of a particular use of editing, cinematography, *mise-en-scene*, or sound. "Rather than serving up suffering at a distance," Felski insists, these images "allow us to witness it close up, magnified to the nth degree, sometimes in lurid and blood-spattered detail. What they lack in factual truth they more than make up for in emotional force" (114).

Second, a text may go beyond our moral codes or "court perversity" (122). This form of shock varies from audience to audience, from cartoons that portray Muhammad in demeaning ways and voices that take the name of the Judeo-Christian God in vain to "graphic portrayals of organs or orifices, secretions or excretions" (112–113). Even if we limit ourselves to literary history, we have seen how influential readers find some novels morally perverse, particularly because of sexual imagery or graphic language: Marquis de Sade's *Justine* (1797), D.H. Lawrence's *Women in Love* (1920), *Lady Chatterley's Lover* (1928), Allen

Ginsberg's "Howl" (1955), Philip Roth's *Portnoy's Complaint* (1969), and Judy Blume's *Forever* (1975), and that is just scratching the surface of canonical works.

Third, shocking texts may question a sense of reality by undercutting "the reader's certainties" (122). That is, some texts may show us that our world view fails to adequately interpret our experience, our information is flawed, or what we thought was true is not true after all. A text shocks by sowing doubt, not in beliefs we hold at a distance, but beliefs we hold close and dear. As a result, the world grows more chaotic and incomprehensible. More painful still, letting go of uncertainties means we let go of part of ourselves, our identity. This kind of shock reaches who we think we are. When a text affects our psyche, the change suggests something deeper and unknown, and the event will likely have long-term ripple effects.

Shock runs along a continuum. "If shock aims too low," Felski explains, "its efforts to provoke are likely to go entirely unremarked or to risk being mocked as lame, tame, or risible" (130). On the other hand,

> If shock-effects are ratcheted up too high, they are likely to trigger intense waves of revulsion or indignation that drive audiences out of theaters or cause them to slam shut their books, cutting off all further engagement with the work of art.
>
> (130)

Phrased differently, to be effective, shock needs to be truly discordant and dissonant in form, trespass important moral codes, and undermine foundational assumptions, all without going to the extremes. What makes our task difficult, however, is that what shocks one audience does not shock another. Some readers find Salman Rushdie's *The Satanic Verses* to be yet another work of magical realism, while religious leaders in Iran issued a *fatwā*. A vivid description of one's wedding night may amuse friends, but the same content and delivery over the pulpit shocks. Context and audience matter.

POTENTIAL PROJECTS

Shock is a mode of engagement, a way to connect with a text. Instead of ignoring our "reaction to what is startling, painful, even horrifying" (105), we interrogate it. When we ask why we find the text disturbing, appalling, and provocative, we can better understand the work and ourselves. Felski reminds us as well to resist the argument that we have grown numb or indifferent to shocking content and form. Yes, we may roll our eyes at the fact that women may have shocked Puritan men by the mere act of writing poetry, but pedophilia sparks more moral outrage today than it did, say, in 5th-century Athens. Finally, we are not looking for some kind of transcendent principle of shock. Rather, we explore how particular contexts shape our responses.

Understand shock

First, choose a shocking text, and remember that it may shock us in different ways: Does its form "engage in discordant juxtapositions and poetic dissonance" (122)? Does its content affront our "moral or aesthetic sensibilities" (113)?

Second, ask some version of "to what end or purpose?" What is the effect or use of this shocking form or content? For example, does what we read or watch undermine our "usual ways of ordering and understanding the world" (113)? Does it "undercut the reader's certainties" (122)? For example, when Felski analyzes Euripides' *The Bacchae*, she draws attention to its gruesome images, but more importantly, she discusses how the play dissolves boundaries between "male/female, human/animal, reason/madness" (111). Plus, the play "offers no standpoint from which such horror can be condemned as aberrant or exceptional...no clear ethical foothold, no means to pass judgment" (112). That inability to redeem the text is what shocks us. When discussing Heinrich von Kleist's *Penthesilea* (1808), Felski sympathetically refers to how Michel Chaouli claims that the play "violates the prohibition against representations of the disgusting" and "forces itself upon us as a visceral response beyond our control" (117). She concludes by suggesting that the play "blurs the line between taste as reflective aesthetic judgment and taste as animalistic appetite and cannibalistic craving" (117). That is why the work shocks us. When she addresses modernism, Felski argues that "the sharp stab of pain, the electrifying jolt of disgust" that some modernist works generate "offers a welcome release from the numbness of not being able to feel" (121). While unpleasant, shock wakes one up. What these sample interpretations show is the need to think more deeply about why a work really shocks us, moving beyond surface reactions to more disturbing, life-altering reasons.

Find Goldilocks

To be effective, to actually engage us, a shocking text cannot aim too low or too high. The work needs to provoke us, but not appall us. Or as Felski explains, "Shock thus teeters precariously between the threat of two forms of failure, caught between the potential humiliation of audience indifference and the permanent risk of outright and outraged refusal" (131). Can you find such a text? Discuss a range of texts and explore the extremes as well as texts that hit the mark. Generate a theory of "appropriately shocking." To complicate matters, historicize your theory of shock. Pay attention to how audiences have reacted to particular works in reviews, newspapers, blogs, and fan sites, then compare reactions to similar works in different contexts. Resist "repression to enlightenment" narratives as you link shock or the failure to be shocked with particular historical moments. Remember as well that even though "readers of different periods may be shocked by the same works [it] does not mean that they are shocked in the same way" (120). In short, this project requires an attention to the specificities of reader response and historical context.

Explore the old and the new

Respond to Felski's own questions. Consider the following:

> How, then, do we explain that works from the distant past can be more disquieting and disturbing than those of the present? Why do texts that are venerated, widely analyzed, and indisputably canonized pack a more powerful emotional punch than their successors? How do we account for the shock of the old?
>
> (114)

This project invites a comparative analysis. Felski reminds us that novelty does not necessarily shock us. Shock's power lies elsewhere, and your task is to locate it.

WORKS CITED

Felski, Rita. *Uses of Literature*. Blackwell, 2008.
Shakespeare, William. *King Lear*. *The Riverside Shakespeare*, 2nd ed., edited by Dean Johnson et al., Houghton, 1997.
Swift, Jonathan. "A Modest Proposal." *A Modest Proposal and Other Writings*, edited by Carole Fabricant, Penguin, 2009, pp. 231–239.

CHAPTER 16

Joining power and knowledge

He is seen, but he does not see; he is the object of information, never a subject in communication.

(Michel Foucault 200)

PROBLEMS, PUZZLES, AND QUESTIONS

Consider several narratives that describe people whom others watch. With a nod toward *Sesame Street*, we can ask, "Which one of these narratives is not like the others?"

Narrative of the Life of Frederick Douglass, an American Slave (1845) recounts Frederick Douglass' experience as a slave in Maryland. He describes a particularly terrible master, Edward Covey, who "acquired a very high reputation for breaking young slaves" (180). Douglass describes one strategy Covey used to control his slaves:

> His work went on in his absence almost as well as in his presence; and he had the faculty of making us feel that he was ever present with us. This he did by surprising us. He seldom approached the spot where we were at work openly, if he could do it secretly. He always aimed at taking us by surprise. ... This being his mode of attack, it was never safe to stop a single minute. His comings were like a thief in the night. He appeared to us as being ever at hand. He was under every tree, behind every stump, in every bush, and at every window, on the plantation.
>
> (47)

In 1949, George Orwell published *1984*, a dystopian novel that follows Winston Smith, his affair with Julia, their attempts to escape state control, and their eventual "re-education." The novel ruminates on the workings of an authoritarian state and its ability to maintain order. The narrator describes the living conditions:

> There was of course no way of knowing whether you were being watched at any given moment. How often, or on what system, the Thought Police plugged in on any individual wire was guesswork. It was even conceivable that they watched everybody all the time. But at any rate they could plug in your wire whenever they wanted to. You had to live—did live, from habit that became instinct—in the assumption that every sound you made was overheard, and, except in darkness, every movement scrutinized.
>
> (Orwell 90–91)

The Truman Show (1998) portrays Truman Burbank who was adopted by a corporation and becomes an unwitting star of "The Truman Show," a 24/7 TV reality show. His entire life is artificial: every location a set, every person an actor, every conversation a script. Millions watch the show every day until Truman finally realizes another life exists outside his tiny town, and he eludes the director's efforts to maintain his entirely constructed reality.

So, which narrative does not fit in the set? All three address the perils of constant surveillance, and they remind us that power and knowledge are connected, but *The Truman Show* differs because Truman is unaware that TV viewers are watching him. What difference does that awareness make? What is the relationship between power and knowledge? What effect does visible but unverifiable surveillance have on us? Is there a way to resist?

KEY PASSAGES

In *Discipline and Punish: The Birth of the Prison* (1975), Michel Foucault provides us with not only a history of prisons but also a theory of power: its sources, users, subjects, mechanisms, and effects. A key chapter focuses on Jeremy Bentham's *Panopticon*, an innovative circular prison designed in the late 18th century that allows a single guard to potentially survey all the prisoners, but the prisoners are never really certain if anyone is watching them, and they cannot communicate with other prisoners. This connection between knowledge and power offers a flexible way to rethink our identity and relationships with others.

Our society is one not of spectacle, but of surveillance.

(217)

He is seen, but he does not see; he is the object of information, never a subject in communication. The arrangement of his room, opposite the central tower, imposes on him an axial visibility; but the divisions of the ring, those separated cells, imply a lateral invisibility. And this invisibility is a guarantee of order.

(200)

Hence the major effect of the Panopticon: to induce in the inmate a state of conscious and permanent visibility that assures the automatic functioning of power. So to arrange things that the surveillance is permanent in its effects, even if it is discontinuous in its action; that the perfection of power should tend to render its actual exercise unnecessary; that this architectural apparatus should be a machine for creating and sustaining a power relation independent of the person who exercises it; in short, that the inmates should be caught up in a power situation of which they are themselves the bearers. To achieve this, it is at once too much and too little that the prisoner should be constantly observed by an inspector: too little, for what matters is that he knows himself to be observed; too much, because he has no need in fact of being so. In view of this, Bentham laid down the principle that power should be visible and unverifiable. Visible: the inmate will constantly have before his eyes the tall outline of the central tower from which he is spied upon. Unverifiable: the inmate must never know whether he is being looked at at any one moment; but he must be sure that he may always be so.

(201)

It is an important mechanism, for it automatizes and disindividualizes power. Power has its principle not so much in a person as in a certain concerted distribution of bodies, surfaces, lights, gazes; in an arrangement whose internal mechanisms produce the relation in which individuals are caught up.

(202)

Foucault treats Bentham's *Panopticon* as a historical artifact and part of a larger history of incarceration but also as a metaphor to explain how power and information function in our society. He is also interested in how particular social arrangements provide order and discipline, effects we need to understand by reading those passages more closely.

DISCUSSION

What does Foucault mean when he says that "Our society is one not of spectacle, but of surveillance" (217)? By "spectacle," Foucault refers to older civilizations' desire to "render accessible to a multitude of men the inspection of a small number of objects" (216). Spectacle depends on a public display, and the architecture and activities of the day (temples, theaters, circuses, as well as festivals, parades, pageants, sporting events, and public performances) were designed to focus the attention of the masses on a few people or objects. Display, openness, and visual exhibition are characteristic of spectacles, and Foucault argues that these public events "formed for a moment a single great body" (216). He argues that communities develop when large groups of people come together and participate in public events. In short, the many watch the few.

He then argues that "The modern age poses the opposite problem: 'To procure for a small number, or even for a single individual, the instantaneous view of a great multitude'" (216). This reversal is due to a shift from community and public life to private individuals and the bureaucratic state. For Foucault, communities—those in power and those subject to that power—began to organize their relationship differently, and this rearrangement includes maintaining order by surveilling citizens. We encounter surveillance not only in prisons, of course, but also at school, work, hospitals, airports, city streets, etc. More recently, we notice the efforts of government institutions and private entities that surveil citizens by using CCTVs, the Internet, phone records, financial transactions, social media, etc. In contrast to the spectacle, the few watch the many.

Bentham designed the *Panopticon* in such a way that the prisoner is "seen, but he does not see; he is the object of information, never a subject in communication" (200). The consequences of this unequal relationship are profound. First, given the fact that one has knowledge and the other does not, the potential of surveillance never disappears. That's why "surveillance is permanent in its effects, even if it is discontinuous in its action" (201). The possibility of being watched always exists, and as a result, inmates always feel authority's presence, and this perceived presence is why panopticism differs from mere voyeurism. Second, this lack of communication helps maintain order: "The crowd, a compact mass, a locus of multiple exchanges, individualities merging together, a collective effect, is abolished and replaced by a collection of separated individualities" (201). In other words, isolating individuals prevents partnerships, collaboration, and collusion. Third, inmates monitor themselves, for they are "caught up in a power situation of which they are themselves the bearers" (201). Placed in a situation where those in power have the ability to constantly watch, separated from others who could provide information and connections, subject to discipline or punishment caused by disobedience, the inmates comply. They assume the responsibility for monitoring their own behavior. They police themselves.

Foucault reminds us that "The Panopticon, on the other hand, must be understood as a generalizable model of functioning; a way of defining power relations in terms of the everyday life of men" (205). In other words, he is not talking just about architecture. Instead, he is talking about particular social and political arrangements. He calls it a "political technology" we can use "whenever one is dealing with a multiplicity of individuals on whom a task or a particular form of behaviour must be imposed" (205). This flexibility means that panoptic relationships can surface in a variety of institutions and social arrangements.

And what does he mean when he asserts that this panoptic arrangement "automatizes and disindividualizes power" (202)? "Automizes" refers to making something automatic and habitual. No one has to enforce power; the unequal arrangement makes it happen: "a state of conscious and permanent visibility … assures the automatic functioning of power" (201). The term "disindividualize" suggests that power depends on the arrangement itself, not certain kinds of people or particular motivations. For example, if an inmate stands in Bentham's watch tower while a guard sits in his cell, the power relationship still exerts the same force because power derives from the technology, social system, and spatial arrangement, not particular people who may be benevolent or full of malice. Or, as Foucault explains, "any individual, taken almost at random, can operate the machine: in the absence of the director, his family, his friends, his visitors, even his servants" (202). Powerful people do not sit in the watchtower. Instead, the watchtower makes people powerful. The position we inhabit, the relationship we maintain with others, determines whether or not we control others.

To put it yet another way, Foucault wants us to think in terms of systems, networks, and relationships, not in terms of individuals, choices, or motives. Our position within the system, role in the institution, or place in a hierarchy empowers us. Panopticism's lesson is that power derives from the ability to look, but avoid being seen, to know, but not be known.

POTENTIAL PROJECTS

Discipline and Punish is less literary theory than cultural history combined with a history of ideas, intellectual history, and social history. Plus, we have only focused on his discussion of panopticism. Nevertheless, we can use Foucault's observations in a variety of ways to make sense of narratives that address spectacles, surveillance, visibility, the gaze, knowledge, systems, institutions, networks, norming, and the process of disindividualizing power. We can apply his insights not only to narratives, but also to institutions, practices, and social arrangements.

Analyze power relationships

Foucault's reading of the Panopticon focuses on how systems and social arrangements create and sustain power or control, and he is particularly interested in how knowledge empowers while ignorance disables. Therefore, choose a text, institution, event, or physical space and ask, How do social structures in a narrative, specific institutional practices in our society, a particular form of technology, a social event, or the design of a physical space separate individuals from the group and transform them into an "object of information, never a subject in communication" (200)? In other words, explore how systems create and sustain a "power relation independent of the person who exercises it" (201), especially in terms of who controls information and knowledge. Consider, for example, the difference between voyeuristic control in Alfred Hitchcock's *Rear Window* (1954), the more panoptic "Eyes" in *The Handmaid's Tale* (1985), and the use of both spectacle and panopticism in *The Hunger Games* trilogy (2008–2010). While those narratives describe rather literal forms of surveillance, you can also explore more subtle panoptic and norming effects communities may have on individual characters.

Explore the function of (in)visibility

Given what Foucault says about the Panopticon's function—"to induce in the inmate a state of conscious and permanent visibility that assures the automatic functioning of power" (201)—explore fictional characters or real groups who empower themselves by remaining invisible or "unknowable." In other words, characters and people may disrupt "the automatic functioning of power" (201) by eluding the literal vision or awareness of others, and they may also empower themselves by escaping another's categories, classifications, or definitions. By remaining outside of any intellectual framework, they maintain their complexity, contradictions, idiosyncrasies, and subversive potential. For example, does Toni Morrison's "Recitatif" (1983) resist our desire to categorize or "know" what it means to be black or white? Does Gloria Anzaldua's *mestiza* figure question our ideas about stable and consistent identity? Gerald Vizenor's trickster characters avoid easy classification, but does that unknowability grant them a degree of power? Postcolonial theorists like Edward Said assert that an Orientalist "makes the Orient speak, describes the Orient, renders its mysteries plain for and to the West" (20–21). Therefore, explore texts that resist this colonial gaze by resisting the very idea of knowability.

WORKS CITED

Douglass, Frederick. *Narrative of the Life of Frederick Douglass, an American Slave. The Frederick Douglass Papers. Series Two: Autobiographical Writings. Volume 1: Narrative,* edited by John W. Blassingame et al., Yale UP, 1999.

Foucault, Michel. *Discipline and Punish: The Birth of the Prison.* 1975. Translated by Alan Sheridan, Pantheon, 1977.

Orwell, George. *Animal Farm/1984.* Harcourt, 1983.

Said, Edward. *Orientalism.* 1978. Vintage, 1979.

CHAPTER 17

Revealing the uncanny

The uncanny is that species of the frightening that goes back to what was once well known and had long been familiar.

(Sigmund Freud 124)

PROBLEMS, PUZZLES, AND QUESTIONS

In his photographic installation *Writing on the Wall* (1991–1992), Shimon Attie projects pre-World War II photographs of Jewish families and shop owners onto the original or nearby locations in Berlin, and the result displays old and new overlapping. "By using slide projection on location," Attie explains, "fragments of the past were thus introduced into the visual field of the present. Thus parts of long destroyed Jewish community life were visually simulated, momentarily recreated." What viewers of the installation saw at the time, and what we see as we peruse the book which records the project, is both familiar and unfamiliar. On the one hand, we have seen the images before: Jewish book handlers, peddlers selling their wares, a woman gazing out of her window, children sitting in the street. On the other hand, decaying buildings distort the images. The black and white photographs appear like ghosts amid the more colorful buildings and lights. Contemporary graffiti contrasts with Hebrew letters. What happens when the repressed appears anew? What do the images suggest about Berlin's identity? What kind of effect does Attie create?

As with all the chapters in Susan Griffin's *Chorus of Stones: The Private Life of War* (1993), "Our Secret" has an unusual form. Instead of a thesis-driven essay with coherent arguments, we encounter a collage of textual fragments: private memories, excerpts from Heinrich

Himmler's journal, details of V-1 and V2 rockets, descriptions of a cell's nucleus, meta-commentary on the act of writing, historical accounts, and comments about Käthe Kollwitz's art, among other passages. The fragments Griffin describes play with the image of inside and outside, known and unknown, secrets and revelations, and the juxtaposition of fragments blurs boundaries between personal and public history, prompting Griffin and us to ask, "even if a feeling has been made secret, even if it has vanished from memory, can it have disappeared altogether?" (150).

In Joseph Conrad's *Heart of Darkness* (1899), Charles Marlow narrates his voyage up the Congo River. He sees firsthand the evils of colonialization, from dying laborers and decimated jungle to madmen and severed heads. The novel seems to juxtapose the "civilized" with the "savage," but by moving through physical and psychological space, what does Marlow realize? Returning from Africa, Marlow aligns Kurtz's fiancée with an African woman who also mourns for Kurtz:

> She put out her arms as if after a retreating figure, stretching them black and with clasped pale hands across the fading and narrow sheen of the window. Never see him! I saw him clearly enough then. I shall see this eloquent phantom as long as I live, and I shall see her, too, a tragic and familiar Shade, resembling in this gesture another one, tragic also, and bedecked with powerless charms, stretching bare brown arms over the glitter of the infernal stream, the stream of darkness.
>
> (108)

Marlow speaks with the fiancée in the present, but his memory of the African woman, a "tragic and familiar Shade," haunts the scene. What comes to light in this passage? What is the relationship between the familiar and the strange? What does the past have to do with the present, the self with the other? What really frightens Marlow?

KEY PASSAGES

Uncomfortable intrusions of the past into the present prompt Sigmund Freud to write *The Uncanny* (1919). Normally concerned with psychological disorders, Freud notices a gap in scholarship discussing unpleasant aesthetics: "we find virtually nothing in the detailed accounts of aesthetics, which on the whole prefer to concern themselves with our feelings for the beautiful, the grandiose and the attractive" (123). Instead, Freud explores negative feelings, "feelings of repulsion and distress" (123). He is interested, in particular, in the "uncanny," or "the realm of the frightening, of what evokes fear and dread" (123). Like the questions posed above, Freud wants to understand the source of the uncanny, and his explanations offer us a useful tool when we read and watch narratives that portray characters who experience a particular kind of "repulsion and distress."

> The uncanny is that species of the frightening that goes back to what was once well known and had long been familiar.
>
> (124)
>
> In the first place, if psychoanalytic theory is right in asserting that every affect arising from an emotional impulse—of whatever kind—is converted into fear by being repressed, it follows that among those things that are felt to be frightening there must be one group in which it can be shown that the frightening element is something that has been repressed and now returns.
>
> (147)
>
> For this uncanny element is actually nothing new or strange, but something that was long familiar to the psyche and was estranged from it only through being repressed. The link with repression now illuminates Schelling's definition of the uncanny as "something that should have remained hidden and has come into the open."
>
> (148)
>
> This is the fact that an uncanny effect often arises when the boundary between fantasy and reality is blurred, when we are faced with the reality of something that we have until now considered imaginary, when a symbol takes on the full function and significance of what it symbolizes.
>
> (150)

As the key passages indicate, Freud is not interested in just any form of fear or dread. He acknowledges that "it seems obvious that something should be frightening precisely because it is unknown and unfamiliar" (124–125), and he is aware that "the converse is not true: not everything new and unfamiliar is frightening" (125). He suggests that "something must be added" (125) to make the unfamiliar dreadful, and that extra element is what we now discuss.

DISCUSSION

To understand the first key passage—"The uncanny is that species of the frightening that goes back to what was once well known and had long been familiar" (124)—we need to follow Freud and study the word's complicated usage. *Uncanny* in German is *unheimlich*. The root word is *heim*, which means home but also suggests familiar and comfortable, a feeling Freud calls "homely." The *-lich* turns the noun into an adjective, but the word *heimlich* actually means secret, clandestine, covert, and hidden. We might think that adding *-un* would signify "open, revealed, disclosed," but *unheimlich* actually means eerie, weird, spooky, creepy, and "unhomely." German usage complicates and even conflates the meaning, for Freud concludes that "the one relating to what is familiar and comfortable, the other to what is concealed and kept hidden" (132). In other words, the uncanny, a particular kind of fear, dread, or repulsion, has to do with the familiar and common. But why? What does the familiar and comfortable have to do with the concealed and hidden? How can the familiar and homely frighten us?

As the second and third passages indicate, the answer has to do with repression. What startles and frightens us is the unexpected reappearance of what we have tried to forget or deny. For one reason or another, we suppress an experience, thought, memory, feeling, person, place, thing, etc. This very act of repression converts that "emotional impulse" (147) into fear. We tuck it away in the "psyche," and in the process, we place it beyond our consciousness. However, this estranged element, this hidden fear, unexpectedly comes back into view, and as the phrase "should have remained hidden" (148) suggests, its reappearance surprises us, arrives against our will. This intrusion into our otherwise comfortable life frightens us and fills us with dread.

Freud identifies a number of occasions that may invite uncanny sensations, but one that is particularly important for readers has to do with fictional narratives. Freud asserts that we experience an uncanny effect "when the boundary between fantasy and reality is blurred, when we are faced with the reality of something that we have until now considered imaginary, when a symbol takes on the full function and significance of what it symbolizes" (150). Boundary is the key word here. Just as a repressed fear frightens us when it unexpectedly crosses a boundary—from hidden to revealed, unconscious to conscious, safe to threatening—a story disturbs us when what we thought was real turns out to the false, and what we thought was imaginary turns out to be real. What we repress is the possibility that we cannot distinguish between fantasy and reality, and when a story crosses that border, we lose, perhaps, confidence in our ability to understand what is real and what is not. We no longer feel at home, secure, and comfortable, for our world and its normal boundaries—real and fantasy, living and dead, copy and original, past and present—are now indeterminate and undecidable.

POTENTIAL PROJECTS

As you consider texts that invite discussions of the uncanny, keep in mind the key concept and vocabulary. Think first of the sentence by Schelling that Freud cites: "something that should have remained hidden and has come into the open" (148). Narratives often describe moments when familiar and well-known experiences, thoughts, memories, feelings, people, places, things, etc. are repressed, ignored, denied, or set aside in some way, but they unexpectedly return, and recognizing the reappearance frightens characters. Therefore, think in terms of what characters repress, and note the form the repressed takes when it returns. Pay attention to hidden yet familiar elements that intrude upon and disturb secure, safe, and comfortable settings. Explore as well the crossing of boundaries: real and fantasy, living and dead, copy and original, past and present. Finally, pay attention to what happens when the repressed returns. What does its reappearance and unveiling suggest or imply?

Trace uncanny effects

As noted above, choose texts that explore the uncanny effect of recognizing the reoccurrence of what has been repressed. Some genres invite such analysis. For example, the gothic produces many uncanny effects, for we encounter eerie settings that are both familiar and unfamiliar, a past that intrudes upon the present, taboo desires and behavior, and the presence of ghosts. Stories like Edgar Allan Poe's "Ligeia" (1838) and "The Fall of the House of Usher" (1839), Mary Shelley's *Frankenstein* (1818), or Charles Brockden Brown's *Wieland* (1798) all portray and explore the uncanny reoccurrence of hidden thoughts and desires. But the uncanny goes beyond Romantic fiction. Among many involuntary memories, Toni Morrison's *Beloved* (1987) explores the moment when

Sethe combs Denver's hair, throwing a bit into the fire. The smell of burning hair recalls a disturbing memory of her mother: "She [Sethe] had to do something with her hands because she was remembering something she had forgotten she knew" (61). What did she remember? What did she try to forget? What does this passage suggest about memory and history? In short, the uncanny surfaces throughout literature and film, particularly when characters recognize that the repressed is intruding into the present. Your task is to recognize those moments and explain their significance. What do we learn about desire, memory, trauma, reality, and truth when characters encounter what they thought they successfully repressed, denied, and forgot?

Identify what really frightens us

When Freud writes that "an uncanny effect often arises when the boundary between fantasy and reality is blurred, when we are faced with the reality of something that we have until now considered imaginary, when a symbol takes on the full function and significance of what it symbolizes" (150), he invites us to focus on the effect a story may have on us, as readers. In other words, we experience the uncanny when a story portrays an event in such a way that we can no longer differentiate between reality and fiction, between a symbolic creation and literal truth. Margaret Atwood's *The Handmaid's Tale* (1985) comes to mind. On the one hand, the events in the novel seem prophetic, for we see, as she says, the novel as a "blueprint of the kind of thing that human beings do when they're put under a certain sort of pressure" (Riley). One might find evidence of Atwood's cautionary tale in contemporary politics. On the other hand, Atwood reveals that "As I say, there's nothing in the book that hasn't already happened" (67). We experience the uncanny when we read *The Handmaid's Tale* because the events blur the boundary between fantasy and reality. Are the events fictional? Yes, but no. They have, in fact, already happened in various ways. It is not the possibility of *The Handmaid's Tale* coming to life that frightens us; it is the fact that Atwood unveils what has already happened and reminds us of what we may have repressed in our history.

Watch the repressed return

Many scholars have used Freud's concept to discuss postcolonial theory and literature. In this context, "the repressed" becomes more literal, for colonizing powers try to erase traces of colonized groups' histories and identities. As a result, the West experiences the uncanny when the colonized unexpectedly make their presence known. Plus, understanding the process of colonization brings into the light familiar, yet repressed ideologies, assumptions, and practices. In this sense, colonialism returns to disturb the colonizer's tranquility. The past returns to the present and casts the West's identity in doubt. How so? One answer has to do with the idea of the "double" or *Doppelgänger*, "the appearance of persons who have to be regarded as identical because they look alike" (141). One becomes a "co-owner of the other's knowledge" (141), and "a person may identify himself with another and so become unsure of his true self; or he may substitute the other's self or his own" (142). While admittedly abstract, this notion of the double who unsettles one's identity and the involuntary encounter with familiar yet repressed ideologies offer us useful ways to think about the colonized's relationship with the colonizer.

WORKS CITED

Attie, Shimon. "The Writing on the Wall." *Shimon Attie*, http://shimonattie.net/portfolio/the-writing-on-the-wall. Accessed 21 January 2018.

Atwood, Margaret. "There Is Nothing in the Book That Hasn't Already Happened." *Quill and Quire*, vol. 51, no. 9, 1985, pp. 66–67.

Conrad, Joseph. *Heart of Darkness*. 1899. Everyman's Library, 1993.

Freud, Sigmund. *The Uncanny*. 1919. Translated by David McLintock, Penguin, 2003.

Griffin, Susan. *A Chorus of Stones: The Private Life of War*. Anchor, 1993.

Morrison, Toni. *Beloved*. Plume, 1987.

Riley, Theresa. "Margaret Atwood Reflects on 'The Handmaid's Tale'." *Moyers and Company*, http://billmoyers.com/story/margaret-atwood-on-the-handmaids-tale. Accessed 21 January 2018.

CHAPTER 18

Questioning human/nonhuman boundaries

Sameness, not difference, provokes our greatest anxiety.

(Diana Fuss 3)

PROBLEMS, PUZZLES, AND QUESTIONS

One would think that we could recognize a monster if we saw one. Mary Shelley's monster, for example, is hideous: "When those muscles and joints were rendered capable of motion, it became a thing such as even Dante could not have conceived" (61). Of course, the monster goes on to commit heinous crimes, but when the monster confronts Dr. Frankenstein, he speaks eloquently:

> 'Hateful day when I received life!' I exclaimed in agony.
> 'Accursed creator! Why did you form a monster so hideous that even *you* turned from me in disgust? God, in pity, made man beautiful and alluring, after his own image; but my form is a filthy type of yours, more horrid even from the very resemblance. Satan had his companions, fellow-devils, to admire and encourage him; but I am solitary and abhorred.'
>
> (117)

A fiendish creation confronts Dr. Frankenstein, but the monster offers an emotional and human argument, wrapped in biblical allusion, elevated vocabulary, rhetorical questions, and a moving comparison. The introspection, the intelligence, the intense emotion startle us, but what makes the monster so hideous and stirring? Is it his repulsive form and his terrible acts, or does our reaction have more to do with the monster's observation that "my form is a filthy type of yours, more horrid even from the very resemblance" (117)? Does the monster frighten us because he differs so radically from us or because he resembles us?

Narrative of the Life of Frederick Douglass (1845) reminds us that most slave owners did not want to teach their slaves to read and write. Mr. Auld prohibits his wife from teaching Douglass because literacy would "spoil" him, for teaching him to read "would forever unfit him to be a slave" (31). Douglass recognizes that "the white man's power to enslave the black man" (32) has everything to do with repressing the slave's voice, for the ability to read and write "gave tongue to interesting thoughts of my own soul" (35). But does an ability to read and write threaten simply because, in the words of Mr. Auld, slaves will become "discontented and unhappy" or "unmanageable"? Does literacy, perhaps, destabilize slavery's foundation, and if so, why?

Ridley Scott's *Blade Runner* (1982) questions the human/nonhuman binary in an early scene when businessman and inventor Eldon Tyrell asks "blade runner" Deckard, who is assigned to kill runaway replicants, to test Rachel, Tyrell's latest creation. After an extensive interrogation that involves a machine that tests emotional responses to provocative questions, Tyrell excuses Rachel and reveals that she is, in fact, a replicant, a genetically engineered human, but she is unaware of her identity. Deckard asks, "How can it not know what it is?" Do these replicants threaten the city because they are physically dangerous or because they are, in Tyrell's words, "more human than human"?

We are more than familiar with stories, films, and art that define and challenge what it means to be human, but a key question is, "Why does questioning the human/nonhuman boundary threaten us?"

KEY PASSAGES

In *Human, All Too Human* (1996), Diana Fuss offers us a useful context by citing Jean-François Lyotard who asks, "What shall we call human in humans?" Fuss reminds us of the importance of the question:

> The political stakes of this preeminently philosophical question today pose themselves with special urgency, as debates over the significance of genetic surgery, virtual reality, reproductive technology, artificial intelligence, and other forms of 'posthuman' reconstruction dramatically disorganize traditional Enlightenment conceptions of the human. The question of what it means to be human has never before been

> more difficult—and more contested. In the wake of humanism's recession, what has become of the human? Our task here is to rethink the category of the human, opening a door to an encounter with what one of our most fearless poets of humanity calls the 'human after human.'
>
> (1)

Indeed, the stakes are high. What once seemed so simple (but it never was) is now complex, and the implications are vast.

In her effort to examine the "cultural, historical, social, and political borders" (4), Fuss makes an insightful observation that helps us rethink the effect of the nonhuman:

> The vigilance with which the demarcations between humans and animals, humans and things, and humans and children are watched over and safeguarded tells us much about the assailability of what they seek to preserve: an abstract notion of the human as a unified, autonomous, and unmodified subject. It is as if the alienness of these borderlanders lies not in their distance from the human, but in their proximity. Sameness, not difference, provokes our greatest anxiety (and our greatest fascination) with the "almost human." Indeed, whenever we are called to become "more human" we are reminded that the human is never adequate to itself, and may be defined more by its likeness to these alien others than by its unlikeness.
>
> (3)

Fuss draws attention to the paradoxical nature of the human and the nonhuman, but we need to sort out the implications of this relationship.

DISCUSSION

Geographic terms like "boundaries," "frontiers," and "borders" abound in Fuss' anthology, so let us return to that first sentence. She reminds us that we are keen on maintaining our identity categories: "humans and animals, humans and things, and humans and children" (3) differ from one another, but an increased attention to policing boundaries suggests that our traditional notions of the "human" require protection. Despite all our effort, our experiences encourage us to question whether or not our identity as human is as "unified, autonomous, and unmodified" (3) as we thought. Consider the recent deluge of research discussing the degree to which our bodies play host to invisible critters, bacteria, viruses, etc. In light of this biological research, David Barash asks, "Who R we? Well, that depends on what the meaning of 'who' is. Who's left after the parasites and pathogens and other fellow travelers are removed? And after 'you' are separated from your genes?" If being "human" were unquestionable, then we would not have to pay attention to our definitions. But the definition of "human" is far from settled, and many are vigilant when it comes to maintaining boundaries.

Fuss' next two sentences embrace the paradox and even irony of identity: "It is as if the alienness of these borderlanders lies not in their distance from the human, but in their proximity. Sameness, not difference, provokes our greatest anxiety (and our greatest fascination) with the 'almost human'" (3). While the insight may feel contradictory, dramatic difference actually comforts us, for there is no mistaking who "they" are, and as a result, we can take measures to protect ourselves. While admittedly frightening, the more alien and hideous, the safer we are because we can identify the threat. In other words, distance does not mark our objection to the unfamiliar, disturbing, distasteful, or foreign. Instead, we worry most when the "nonhuman" blurs those boundaries, especially when we find it difficult to distinguish between "us" and "them." This insight echoes roboticist Masohiro Mori's "uncanny valley" theory which asserts that as robots begin to look and act more like humans, we find them appealing...up to a point. Then we find them creepy. We want our robots to look like us, but not too much like us.

This reversal in how we think about the nonhuman is what makes Fuss' idea so useful and interesting, for this counterintuitive observation helps us explain not only why certain robots, stuffed animals, and monsters do not bother us as much as zombies, corpses, prosthetic limbs, and vampires do. More importantly, the idea that "sameness, not difference, provokes our greatest anxiety (and our greatest fascination)" (3) also helps explain our relationships with other people.

While Fuss initially focuses on new technologies and innovations, the question of "what makes one a human?" takes us back in time as well, particularly to travel narratives, colonialism, cultural encounters, slavery, etc. The question preoccupied those who theorize Humanism and Enlightenment principles. Andrew Bennett and Nicholas Royle remind us that

> it is not by chance that the invention of the human takes place at a time when European imperial expansion

> makes it necessary to distinguish fundamentally between European colonizers and colonized natives (who can then be appropriated, enslaved, exploited, slaughtered). Indeed, inventions of the human, definitions of 'man' or 'mankind', always seem to be bound up with the exploitation of their others (whether these others are defined in animal, gender, ethnic or racial, class or religious terms). Humanism, the logic of humanity, in other words, is also a dehumanizing discourse.
>
> (255)

In this colonial and postcolonial context, we can see why the theorist Homi Bhabha asserts that "The success of colonial appropriation depends on a proliferation of inappropriate objects that ensure its strategic failure, so that mimicry is at once resemblance and menace" (123). As colonized subjects begin to approximate those who colonize them, their success questions the very assumptions and system used to justify the social hierarchies that spawned colonization in the first place. Thus, "sameness" threatens more than difference. Mimicry can subvert colonial and postcolonial powers because similarity delegitimizes those in power. If the colonized and the colonizer are similar, then why should one rule the other?

POTENTIAL PROJECTS

The observation that "Sameness, not difference, provokes our greatest anxiety (and our greatest fascination)" (3) is rich and flexible enough to allow us to cross disciplines and explore a wide array of representations and cultural events, as well as examine theories of identity. Interrogating the "human" and "nonhuman" generates a large number of projects, but they all examine cultural, historical, social, and political borders, and these borders have everything to do with identity, power, and hierarchies. Consider the following projects:

Explore human/nonhuman boundaries

Some writers have focused on films and TV shows like the *Star Trek* series, *Star Wars* saga, *Close Encounters of the Third Kind* (1977), *Alien* (1979), *Blade Runner* (1982), *Blade Runner 2049* (2017), *Terminator* (1984), *Robocop* (1987), *The Matrix* (1999), *Ex Machina* (2014), *Chappie* (2015), *Black Mirror* series, *I, Robot* (2004), and *A.I.* (2001). Others have focused on literary works that describe human and pet relationships, as well as paranormal figures like vampires, zombies, and werewolves. In each case, the narratives describe encounters with an "Other" that defies categorization or questions the boundaries of the human. To be more specific, ask questions along the lines of, How does the text define what it means to be human? How does the text define the nonhuman? How does the text challenge or reinforce the boundary of the human and nonhuman? How does the text represent the consequences of maintaining or blurring identity boundaries?

Focus on colonial relationships

As Andrew Bennett and Nicholas Royle note, "inventions of the human, definitions of 'man' or 'mankind', always seem to be bound up with the exploitation of their others" (255). For example, Rudyard Kipling's "The White Man's Burden: The United States and the Philippine Islands" (1899) justifies imperialism in the name of civilizing the Other: "Your new-caught, sullen peoples, / Half devil and half child" (7–8) and "reap his old reward: / The blame of those ye better / The hate of those ye guard" (18–20). Or, consider a few of the more than fifty poetic responses to Kipling's poem. Henry Labouchère's "The Brown Man's Burden" (1899) mocks British platitudes: "Pile on the brown man's burden / And, if ye rouse his hate / Meet his old-fashioned reasons / With Maxims up to date" (9–12). H. T. Johnson's "The Black Man's Burden: A Response to Kipling" (1899) redirects the critique toward American racism: "Pile on the Black Man's Burden / His wail with laughter drown / You've sealed the Red Man's problem / And will take up the Brown" (9–11). Finally, J. Dallas Bowser's "Take up the Black Man's Burden" (1899) addresses a different audience: "Take up the Black Man's burden / Black men of every clime / What though your cross be heavy / Your sun but darkly shine" (33–36). Consider the following questions: How does the text justify colonization and exploitation along human/nonhuman lines? How do texts resist colonization and exploitation? How do characters challenge hierarchies and power structures by imitating and approximating their "masters"? How does the text use mimicry to resemble and menace colonial or postcolonial powers?

Examine child/human/adult relationships

As Fuss points out, children inhabit a kind of borderless realm: "Variously idealized, demonized, eroticized, patronized, and publicized, the child emerges as a highly mystified figure whose claim to the category 'human' is, from the very start, governed and circumscribed by political ideology, cultural mythology, legal doctrine, and social policy" (5). While it might feel strange to consider a child as less than human, reflect on how texts portray the "child" as a kind of human/nonhuman figure. Charles Kingsley's *Water-Babies* (1863), for example, tells the story of a misbehaving chimney sweep who confronts his nonhuman self. In Christina Rossetti's *Speaking Likenesses* (1874), a naughty girl is transported into another realm where she encounters a boy who "bristled with prickly quills like a porcupine" and "one girl exuded a sticky fluid and came off on the fingers" and "another, rather smaller, was slimy and slipped through the hands" (qtd. in Sigler 59). Violet Beauregard in *Charlie and the Chocolate Factory* (1964) behaves badly and swells into a giant blueberry, and squirrels toss Veruca Salt down the garbage chute because she is a "bad nut." Other novels explore how technology compromises young people. For example, the young adult novel *Feed* (2002) portrays a dystopian world where computer networks connect directly to most of the population via an implant, and *iBoy* (2010) describes a young man who becomes a walking app after gun shrapnel embeds phone fragments in his head. Others blur the boundary between adult and child in different ways. Henry James in "The Turn of the Screw" (1898) and William Golding in *Lord of the Flies* (1954) portray children as anything but innocent and vulnerable. William Faulkner's Caddy in *The Sound and the Fury* (1929) and Frankie Addams in Carson McCullers' *The Member of the Wedding* (1946) explore adult forms of sexuality. These are just a few examples, but in every case, ask questions along the lines of, How does the work distinguish the child from the adult or human world? Is this separation empowering or limiting? What allows the child to enter, periodically or completely, the adult or human world? What are the consequences if a child becomes or fails to become an adult or human?

Analyze animal/human boundaries

Fuss asserts that

> In a post-Darwinian culture that ceaselessly recalls us to our own status as animals, demarcating just where the human begins and the animal leaves off may be a difficult enterprise. The borders between human and animal are as much social as they are natural, a point that poses rather interesting problems for the classical representation of the human as *animal rationale*.

(4)

Consider Elizabeth Bishop's "The Man-Moth" (1979), the young black men in Ralph Ellison's "Battle Royale" chapter in *Invisible Man* (1952), and Sylvia Plath's honey-drudgers and queen bee in "Stings" (1965), all of which blur animal/human boundaries. What problems does a text pose when it presents the "human as *animal rationale*"? Does the text reinforce human/animal boundaries, or does it blur those boundaries? If so, how so? And to what end? How does the text portray the consequences of maintaining or questioning animal/human boundaries? Is it still true that "sameness, not difference, provokes our greatest anxiety (and our greatest fascination)" (3) when the text represents animals? For example, filmmakers anthropomorphize animals all the time, animated or not, yet those animals do not threaten or menace, or do they? Consider representations of animals that do, in fact, menace, and explore the source of our anxiety. What boundaries or borders do they cross?

WORKS CITED

Barash, David. "Who Are We?" *The Chronicle Review*, vol. 55, no. 11, 7 November 2008, p. B18.
Bennett, Andrew and Nicholas Royle. *An Introduction to Literature, Criticism and Theory*, 4th ed., Pearson/Longman, 2009.
Bhabha, Homi K. *The Location of Culture*. 1994. Routledge, 2012.
Blade Runner. Directed by Ridley Scott, Warner, 1982.
Bowser, J. Dallas. "Take up the Black Man's Burden." *Colored American*, 8 April 1899.
Douglass, Frederick. *Narrative of the Life of Frederick Douglass, an American Slave. The Frederick Douglass Papers. Series Two: Autobiographical Writings. Volume 1: Narrative*, edited by John W. Blassingame, et al., Yale UP, 1999.
Fuss, Diana, editor. *Human, All Too Human*. Routledge, 2013.
Johnson, H. T. "The Black Man's Burden: A Response to Kipling." *Christian Recorder*, 1899.
Kipling, Rudyard. "The White Man's Burden: The United States and the Philippine Islands." *McClure's*, vol. 12. no. 4, 12 February 1899.
Labouchère, Henry. "The Brown Man's Burden." *Truth*, February 1899.
Rossetti, Christina. *Speaking Likenesses*. Macmillan, 1874.
Shelley, Mary. *Frankenstein*, 3rd ed., edited by Johanna M. Smith, Bedford/St. Martin's, 2016.

CHAPTER 19

Historicizing and contextualizing

A full cultural analysis will need to push beyond the boundaries of the text, to establish links between the text and values, institutions, and practices elsewhere in the culture.

(Stephen Greenblatt "Culture" 226)

PROBLEMS, PUZZLES, AND QUESTIONS

In 1939, Metro-Goldwyn-Mayer produced *The Wizard of Oz*, an adaptation based on L. Frank Baum's 1900 novel *The Wonderful Wizard of Oz*. Adaptations always differ from the original, and one key change is the color of Dorothy's slippers from silver to red. Apparently, MGM wanted to capitalize on technicolor technology, but the more interesting question is, "Why were the shoes silver in the novel?" Some scholars argue that the tale is a populist allegory, and the silver shoes dancing upon a golden road foreground the debate between "silverites" and "goldbugs" during the 1896 and 1900 political campaigns.

Joyce Carol Oates published "Where Are You Going? Where Have You Been?" in 1966. The story depicts a young woman named Connie who is lured into leaving her home with the stranger Arnold Friend. Oates readily explains that she based her story on the real-life Charles Schmid who killed a number of young women in Tucson in 1966. Bob Dylan's "It's All Over Now, Baby Blue" prompts the dedication, "For Bob Dylan."

Robert Herrick's 1648 poem "Delight in Disorder" describes the merits of an imperfectly dressed woman. As he praises an "erring lace" (5), a "cuff neglectful" (7), a "tempestuous petticoat" (10), and a "careless shoestring" (11), Herrick employs a number of oxymorons like "sweet disorder" (1) and "fine distraction" (4) concluding that all result in a "wild civility" (12) that "bewitch[es]" (13) the narrator.

All three texts address their relationship with history differently. Baum writes *The Wonderful Wizard of Oz* in the context of debates about monetary policy. A real-life murderer and a song inspire Oates' story, but her story is not historical fiction. Herrick's poem seems more detached from its time period, at least at first glance, but the poem speaks to the larger culture's interest in order, aesthetics, and morality. What is the relationship between a text and its context? Is there such a thing as a "proper" or "appropriate" context? Is a text independent of its historical situation, an autonomous artifact that transcends its time? Does the text mirror its time period, suggesting that a poem, story, play, or film reflects reality? Is the text void of accurate meaning if we are unaware of the historical background that informs the work? Does the context explain the literary text, or does the text describe the context? Or, does the text play a more active role?

KEY PASSAGES

The turn toward placing a work in its historical context as a way to understand literature began in the 1930s and 1940s, but intensely re-examined in the early 1980s when Stephen Greenblatt edited a special issue of the academic journal *Genre* that addressed the relationship between a literary text and its context, questioning, for example, a text's autonomy or a work's ability to reflect a time period's worldview. This issue of *Genre* led to wide-ranging discussions and spawned what we now know as "New Historicism." This chapter is not interested in New Historicism *per se,* and despite a legion of books and articles that describe New Historical protocols, Greenblatt insists that New Historicism is not "a repeatable methodology or a literary critical program" (*Practicing* 19). On the other hand, Greenblatt does encourage us to question common assumptions we may have about the role representations play. In an essay entitled "Culture" that appears in Frank Lentricchia and Thomas McLaughlin's *Critical Terms for Literary Study* (1995), Greenblatt helps us rethink the relationship between texts and contexts:

> Western literature over a very long period of time has been one of the great institutions for the enforcement of cultural boundaries through praise and blame.
>
> (226)
>
> A full cultural analysis will need to push beyond the boundaries of the text, to establish links between the text and values, institutions, and practices elsewhere in the culture.
>
> (226)
>
> Cultural analysis must be opposed on principle to the rigid distinction between that which is within a text and that which lies outside.
>
> (227)
>
> They [novels] do not merely passively reflect the prevailing ratio of mobility and constraint; they help to shape, articulate, and reproduce it through their own improvisatory intelligence. This means that, despite our romantic cult of originality, most artists are themselves gifted creators of variations upon received themes.
>
> (229)
>
> It remains essential to study the ways in which these materials are formally put together and articulated in order to understand the cultural work that the text accomplishes.
>
> (230)

These five passages encourage us to approach literary works as active players in a larger socioeconomic system, but the claims deserve closer attention.

DISCUSSION

First, Greenblatt rejects the formalist position that we can ignore context and focus instead on how literary devices convey themes. Second, Greenblatt discourages us from separating literature and history or embracing the idea that history provides a stable background to analyze literary texts. Instead, by asserting that representations both "shape, articulate, and reproduce" (229) the collections of beliefs and practices that constrain us as well as provide room for improvisation and critique, Greenblatt reminds us that cultural representations are not passive or neutral mirrors of reality but active participants in a larger cultural debate or conversation. A literary work advocates, during a particular time and place, for a set of values and practices, and the text shapes our perceptions about people, places, events, attitudes, values, and hierarchies. As Robert Scholes clarifies, "We are not talking about rigid structures, of course, but about lines of filiation, cultural pathways by which an individual, in abandoning one view or attitude, would be led toward one or another of a limited set of alternatives" (31–32).

And one way that representations lead us down a cultural pathway or enforce cultural boundaries is through a process of "praise and blame," the way a work associates a particular network of attitudes, values, and hierarchies—an ideology, really—with a set of appealing or unappealing consequences. For example, in "The Birthmark," Nathanial Hawthorne portrays Alymer as a scientist who strives to perfect the flawed natural world. This desire leads to an experiment to remove a birthmark that blemishes his beautiful wife Georgiana, but the "cure" kills her. By laying out this cause–effect relationship, Hawthorne critiques science's impulse to control nature. He praises imperfect humanity while blaming science's desire for perfection.

However, understanding the way a text celebrates or subverts is just the first step. Greenblatt encourages us to think of a text as part of a larger network of institutions, practices, and beliefs. In other words, Greenblatt blurs the boundaries between text and context. Greenblatt wants to "push beyond the boundaries of the text, to establish links between the text and values, institutions, and practices elsewhere in the culture" (226), and he opposes "the rigid distinction between that which is within a text and that which lies outside" (227). For example, Hawthorne's celebration of Nature and the "natural" and his critique of science and the artificial echo the pathways we see in 19th-century America. One of the oppositions organizing values and choices occurred between a suspicion of empiricism and qualities such as reason, order, restraint, balance, and clarity on the one hand, and privileging subjective experience, imagination, and the individual on the other hand. If one rejects the notion that reality is external, only to be discovered by the cold eye of science, then one is likely to turn inward and locate reality in the self. Or, questioning subjective experience leads one to find truth in external quantifiable systems. In short, Greenblatt encourages us to erase the boundary between the "literary" and "historical backdrop," for every document and practice is a "text" that shares a number of value systems and hierarchies.

Notice the shift from making claims about what a text "says" to making claims about what a work "does" in a particular time and place. This way of thinking about literature's active role is one of the most important changes we have seen in the literary criticism. And when Greenblatt suggests that literary texts are active participants in a cultural debate, he notes that, "despite our romantic cult of originality, most artists are themselves gifted creators of variations upon received themes" (229). In other words, writers and artists convey their "personal" views, but they work within a preexisting context that offers and limits the cultural codes, networks, and values they can employ. Any "personal" view is actually very public and social as well. We often say a text "negotiates" with its context, and as with all negotiations, one works within a particular network—what some call a "discourse"—of people, languages, practices, values, and goals that determine who has power and who does not. To put it yet another way, writers and artists have agency, but the agency is limited by the available ways of thinking, speaking, writing, and being. This network or discourse enables and empowers us, but it also limits and constrains us.

And what do we gain? After you have placed a work within its cultural context and explored how the work uses cultural materials to contribute to a contemporary debate, the result is "a heightened understanding of a work of literature produced within that culture" as well as "a heightened understanding of the culture within which it was produced" (227). Because literary texts mesh so thoroughly with the "values, institutions, and practices elsewhere in the culture" (226), learning about the one will inevitably teach us about the other. In short, we are less of a "literary" critic and more of a "cultural" critic because Greenblatt does not want us to separate the literary from the cultural.

POTENTIAL PROJECTS

Greenblatt maintains that we should view a text as evidence of a negotiation with the culture that produced it, and as a result, we should connect a text's value system with the culture's beliefs, hierarchies, and institutions. However, it is not enough to establish a link between a text and its cultural moment, implying that the work merely reflects the values, debates, and preoccupations of its day. Instead, assume that texts are shaping forces, acts of improvisation within a system of constraints and opportunities. Texts take an active role in trying to encourage readers to adopt certain identities, and they affirm or critique (praise and blame) specific practices, values, hierarchies, and attitudes. Texts are never neutral; they always (knowingly or not) have a point of view that they advocate. Consider the following ambitious project:

Identify constraints and improvisations within a particular context

Begin by situating a text in a particular social and cultural context. The goal is to "reconstruct the situation in which [the text is] produced" (227). This move requires historical research. Reconstructing a text's context may seem like a daunting task, especially if you are not a trained historian, but it may help to think of a context as a conversation or debate about the same issues that your text addresses. What are people, at the time the author is working, saying about those issues? Use primary texts and archival materials from the period. And as you read these documents, trace and foreground the arguments, reasons, and language they use to frame the debate.

Then, turn your attention to your particular literary text, film, or work of art and ask, "What kinds of behavior, what models of practice, does this work seem to enforce?" (226). Identify the values, attitudes, and beliefs the text celebrates and critiques. How does a narrative's cause–effect relationships suggest that one value system benefits one segment of society while harming another? Does the text's language privilege certain forms of order over another? What social hierarchies does the text naturalize or critique? Following Greenblatt, connect the literary text to the social text by examining what links exist "between the text and values, institutions, and practices elsewhere in the culture" (226) and ask, "What are the larger social structures with which these particular acts of praise or blame might be connected?" (226). In short, you are identifying connections between a text's and a culture's value systems and social structure, *not* in the name of using a novel, poem, or film as a mirror to reflect the cultural moment, but with a desire to understand how your chosen text enforces or challenges cultural boundaries.

Finally, simultaneous with asking what the text praises and blames, Greenblatt reminds us that, "it remains essential to study the ways in which these materials are formally put together and articulated in order to understand the cultural work that the text accomplishes" (230).

In other words, you not only need to answer, *What* does the text do? but you also need to answer, *How* does the text do what it does? You still need to be a close reader of texts by looking at the underlying structure, literary devices, juxtapositions, cause–effect relationships, and other strategies the author uses to craft a text, and then explain *how* the writer uses these tools to reinforce or critique cultural boundaries.

For example, to make sense of the King Louie scene in Disney's *The Jungle Book* (1967), we place the film in the context of the Civil Rights Movement and ask, How do the competing discourses of power, race, identity, and equality enable and constrain what *The Jungle Book* suggests about race? "What kinds of behavior, what models of practice, does this work seem to enforce" (226)? How, as well, does the film use characterization and cause–effect relationships to encourage us to identify with Baloo and Bagheera and the values and social order they represent? To understand *A Narrative of the Captivity and Restoration of Mrs. Mary Rowlandson* (1682), we situate her narrative among the debates during the King Phillip's War, and we examine how Christian and colonial discourses provide a "repertoire of models" to define Anglo–Native relationships. How, for example, does Rowlandson use biblical passages and the generic conventions of the captivity narrative and the jeremiad to justify both colonization and preservation of Native Americans? Bharati Mukherjee's "A Wife's Story" (1988) requires us to learn more about the conflicts and tensions Indian immigrants experienced during the 1980s in the United States, and then explore how discourses of gender, race, and nationality simultaneously legitimize and limit what Mukherjee conveys about female Indian immigrants. To grasp Art Spiegelman's *Maus* (1991), we need to identify the discussions addressing Holocaust survivors and their children, as well the disagreements among scholars about memory, trauma, and representation. We examine how the graphic novel and its use of cat and mice metaphors transmit particular cultural beliefs while also unsettling conventional values, practices, and patterns.

In every case, we examine how the available ways of thinking, speaking, and writing in that particular context both enable and empower but also limit and constrain these writers, and we explore the links "between the text and values, institutions, and practices elsewhere in the culture" (226). We constantly identify the ways that these texts enforce "cultural boundaries through praise and blame" (226), and we always ask, "What are the larger social structures with which these particular acts of praise or blame might be connected" (226)? In short, a text and a context belong to what Greenblatt calls a "particular network of negotiations" (229), and our task is to describe these interactions and collaborations created by a culture's desire to set, reinforce, and patrol boundaries and by an artist's ability to unsettle, question, and push against those same cultural boundaries using available linguistic, aesthetic, and cultural tools.

WORKS CITED

Greenblatt, Stephen. "Culture." *Critical Terms for Literary Studies*, 2nd ed., edited by Frank Lentricchia and Thomas McLaughlin, U of Chicago P, 1995, pp. 225–232.

Greenblatt, Stephen and Catherine Gallagher. *Practicing New Historicism.* U of Chicago P, 2000.

Herrick, Robert. "Delight in Disorder." *The Longman Anthology of British Literature: The Early Modern Period*, 3rd ed., edited by Constance Jordan and Clare Carroll, Pearson/Longman, 2006, p. 1707.

Scholes, Robert. *Protocols of Reading.* Yale UP, 1989.

CHAPTER 20

Signifying through time

It seems that on a just view of the matter the books we call classics possess intrinsic qualities that endure, but possess also an openness to accommodation which keeps them alive under endlessly varying dispositions.

(Frank Kermode 44)

PROBLEMS, PUZZLES, AND QUESTIONS

Traditionally attributed to Homer, the *Iliad* dates to 8th century BCE in Greece, and the work collapses the ten-year siege of Troy to a 15,693-line narrative. Over the years, students have read these stories in ancient Greece, Italy, and other cosmopolitan centers, and the stories surface in medieval Europe, the Renaissance, and contemporary culture. Films, art, drama, novels, and even comic books return time and again to these narratives. But why? What is it about the *Iliad* that speaks across time and space?

When I was an undergraduate, I recall the option of taking an entire course on Edmund Spenser who is most famous for writing the epic poem and elaborate allegory *The Faerie Queene* (1590) that features the Spenserian stanza. In terms of literary history, Spenser is a heavy weight. However, does your university dedicate an entire course to Spenser? When was the last time you read *The Faerie Queene*? Can you identify any adaptations, remakes, or even any allusions to Spenser's work? I suspect the answer to all those questions is mostly no. How do we explain the silence? How can an author who some claim is one of the greatest English language poets just fade away like that?

Admittedly, many forces are at work when we ask why a text remains or disappears from the public eye: editors, publishers, retail outlets, teachers, book reviewers, and consumers all play a role. Plus, filmmakers, artists, musicians, and social media make some works more visible than others. While these external forces certainly have a hand in a work's longevity, it still seems fair to ask whether there is something about the text itself that helps it endure. How can readers who span centuries and embrace different cultures, values, and practices return to the same text while simultaneously ignoring other works that impressed his or her contemporary readers? Or, put more broadly, why do some works live and others pass away? Do enduring works contain qualities that others do not?

KEY PASSAGES

In 1973, the University of Kent invited Frank Kermode to deliver the T. S. Eliot Memorial Lectures, an honor given to eminent scholars and poets. Eliot's own "What is a Classic?" prompts Kermode to explore the question in his lectures which become *The Classic: Literary Images of Permanence and Change* (1975). Kermode questions Eliot's demand that readers make the effort "to speak to the classic in *its* time" (43), lest we overestimate the importance of our own time. For Eliot, "a just perception of the permanent relations of the Enduring and the Changing should ... make us realize our own time in better proportion to times past and times to come" (qtd. in Kermode, 43). In other words, Eliot insists that readers should evaluate their culture, value, and literary works in light of past civilizations. We adjust to the past, not ask the past to adjust to us, for we are "transient" while the past is "Eternal." For Kermode, however, Eliot misunderstands the correlation. Kermode wants to rethink the relationship between permanence and change, and he offers us a more nuanced reason why we continue to read "old books."

> And this means that over and over again in time, those old books are accommodated to the sense of readers whose language and culture is different. Here, we deal in dispositions, not essences. The paradox—that there is an identity but that it changes—is made more difficult by the certainty it can in some measure be redeemed from change, by an effort of interpretation rather than of simple accommodation, the establishment of "relevance." It seems that on a just view of the matter the books we call classics possess intrinsic qualities that endure, but possess also an openness to accommodation which keeps them alive under endlessly varying dispositions.
> (43–44)

> I think there is a substance that prevails, however powerful the agents of change; that *King Lear*, underlying a thousand dispositions, subsists in change, prevails, by being patient of interpretation.
>
> (134)
>
> To put this in a different way, one may speak of the text as a system of signifiers which always shows a surplus after meeting any particular restricted reading.
>
> (135)
>
> The survival of the classic must therefore depend upon its possession of a surplus of signifier; as in *King Lear* or *Wuthering Heights* this may expose them to the charge of confusion, for they must always signify more than is needed by any one interpreter or any one generation of interpreters.
>
> (140)

While many assert that "classics" are "beyond time, beyond vernacular corruption and change" (141), Kermode claims that "all we need do is bring [the classics] down to earth" (141), and this metaphor suggests that works that reach centuries of readers are actually rooted to time and place, a paradox we need to clarify.

DISCUSSION

A key problem when we discuss literary value is avoiding a kind of relativistic, "beauty is in the eye of the beholder" approach as well as dismissing the view that value is completely objective and external to the reader. Phrased as a question, is value external or internal? Kermode threads this needle by talking about texts in terms of "accommodation." One sense of accommodation refers to an ability to make room or space for someone, but the word also refers to a capacity to "fit in." But what does a text "accommodate" when Kermode writes that "openness to accommodation ... keeps them alive under endlessly varying dispositions" (44)? Kermode acknowledges that readers from different time periods, cultures, practices, and value systems read "old books," so when a text accommodates these readers, it allows them ways to construct meaning and relate to seemingly remote characters, settings, and choices. A classic continues to speak to readers, despite the fact that, say, the Sage Vyasa composes the *Bhagavad Gita* in southeast Asia sometime between the 5th century to the 2nd century BCE, Virgil writes the *Aeneid* around 29–19 BCE Rome, Hawthorne crafts *The Scarlet Letter* in 19th-century America, and Virginia Woolf's *To the Lighthouse* appears in early 20th-century Britain. The text's ability to be "patient of interpretation" (134) allows a text to accommodate, to speak simultaneously to, a wide range of readers.

But what does it mean to be "patient of interpretation" (134) or open to "endlessly varying dispositions" (44)? Kermode relies, in part, on a container metaphor: "one may speak of the text as a system of signifiers which always shows a surplus after meeting any particular restricted reading" (135). We can imagine a collection of toy blocks that we use to build skyscrapers, bridges, houses, and farms. Kermode suggests that no matter how many structures—or interpretations—we build, extra blocks always remain because we can never integrate every block within a single coherent structure, and those extra blocks allow other builders the freedom to add to and take away what we have built, but no one can quite use all the blocks. Put in literary terms, a text accommodates a vast number of readers across time and place because the text, due to its "intrinsic qualities" (44), is so complex, rich, and indeterminate that readers can construct meaning that addresses their particular needs. The work is designed in such a way that these elements—its structure, language, intertextual connections, images, themes, etc.—resonate and signify in a variety of ways and can even be "possibly enlarged by the action of time" (134). In short, the work is never quite comprehensible. It fails "to give a definitive account of itself" (114). We privilege no particular interpretation, for the classic revels in pluralism.

Kermode never describes a classic's opposite, but his language suggests that a lesser work does not offer enough complexity to resonate across time and place. The work may depend too much on contextual information, wed itself too closely to a particular time and place, or limit its relationships to other texts and events. The work is "closed" (74) in the sense that one can more easily account for all the details we encounter. There is no "surplus" (135) of meaning.

Yet another way to summarize the difference between works that endure and those that fade is Kermode's contrast between an "old classic" and a "modern classic": "Unlike the old classic, which was expected to provide answers, this one poses a virtually infinite set of questions" (114). In short, it is the difference between a closed and open system, a determinate and indeterminate text.

POTENTIAL PROJECTS

Kermode does not offer us a way to *make sense* of texts as much as he investigates the relationship between the old and the new: "It is a question of how the works of the past may retain identity in change, of the mode in which the ancient presents itself to the modern" (16). While this question does not really state that he is discussing quality *per se*, the unstated assumption is that Kermode offers us a method to determine value. Longevity implies quality, and quality suggests an ability to accommodate centuries of readers and interpretations.

Evaluate a text's ability to endure

First, complete some preliminary research by comparing old and new literary anthologies. What works endure? What works are now absent? Ask teachers about their syllabi. Are there literary works they no longer teach and texts they have always taught? Gloss curriculum catalogs and notice which courses, particularly courses dedicated to single authors, persist or have faded away. Look as well at the catalogs of Library of America, Everyman's Library, or Oxford's World Classics.

Then, test Kermode's theory by asking, "Why have some of these works endured and others have not?" The critical move is thinking and writing in Kermode's terms: What allows texts to "accommodate" (40) a wide variety of interpretations or remain "patient of interpretation" (134)? What are the "intrinsic qualities" (44) that provide an "openness to accommodation" (44)? What is it about the text that always provides a "surplus of signifier" (140), and an ability to pose a "virtually infinite set of questions" (114)? And what do other texts lack? Why are they more closed? In what sense are enduring texts more open?

Accommodate critical vocabularies

In their introduction to literary theory, Andrew Bennett and Nicholas Royle remind us that

> critical vocabularies change over time while always being in any case somewhat porous, unstable, contentious. In the eighteenth century, the vocabulary of value included ideas of proportion, probability and propriety; the Romantics developed a vocabulary of the sublime, imagination and originality; while nearer to our time, the New Critics valued complexity, paradox, irony and tension in poems, and postmodern critics valorize disjunction, fragmentation, heteroglossia, aporia, decentring.
> (48)

This project is a variation of the first, but Bennett and Royle give us a useful list of qualities to discuss. Admittedly, grasping all those terms may require some research, but once you feel comfortable with those concepts, you can explain how an "old book" accommodates, or not, those competing critical vocabularies. What is it about, say, Shakespeare's *Hamlet* that allows Neoclassical, Romantic, New Critics, and postmodern critics to relate to and find relevant? But why does not every Shakespeare or English Renaissance syllabus include *Coriolanus*, *Cymbeline*, or *Titus Andronicus*? Or, why does Thoreau's *Walden* appeal to Romantics, as well as modernists and postmodernists? Or does it? Does a "surplus of signifier" remain after Romantics and modernists have interpreted Thoreau's account of his time in the woods?

CONNECT AND THEORIZE

In a discussion about the potential for infinite interpretations, Kermode refers to Roland Barthes who also revisits the definition of a "classic":

> Curiously enough, Barthes reserves the terms 'classic' for texts in which they more or less succeed, thus limiting plurality and offering the reader, save as accident prevents him, merely a product, a consumable. In fact what Barthes calls 'modern' is very close to what I am calling 'classic', and what he calls 'classic' is very close to what I call 'dead'.
>
> (136)

Read this textbook's chapter on Roland Barthes who coins the terms "readerly" and "writerly" to describe different roles a work may ask readers to play. Compare and contrast Barthes' theory of readerly and writerly texts with Kermode's theory of accommodation. Do writerly texts endure and readerly texts disappear? What similarities exist between a text that is open to accommodation and one that makes the reader "no longer a consumer, but a producer of the text" (Barthes, 4)?

WORKS CITED

Barthes, Roland. *S/Z*. Translated by Richard Miller. 1970. Hill, 1974.
Bennett, Andrew and Nicholas Royle. *An Introduction to Literature, Criticism and Theory*, 4th ed., Pearson/Longman, 2009.
Kermode, Frank. *The Classic: Literary Images of Permanence and Change*. Viking, 1975.

CHAPTER 21

Thinking ecologically

> The individuality of an organism is not definable except through its interactions with its environment, through its interdependencies.
>
> (Karl Kroeber 7)

PROBLEMS, PUZZLES, AND QUESTIONS

A mix of memoir, natural history, and philosophy, *Walden* (1854) describes Henry David Thoreau's experience living in a small cabin near Walden Pond in Massachusetts. The pond and surrounding area frames Thoreau's reflections:

> In the silicious matter which the water deposits is perhaps the bony system, and in the still finer soil and organic matter the fleshy fibre or cellular tissue. What is man but a mass of thawing clay? The ball of the human finger is but a drop congealed. The fingers and toes flow to their extent from the thawing mass of the body. Who knows what the human body would expand and flow out to under a more genial heaven? Is not the hand a spreading *palm* leaf with its lobes and veins? The ear may be regarded, fancifully, as a lichen, *umbilicaria*, on the side of the head, with its lobe or drop. The lip (*labium* from *labor* (?)) laps or lapses from the sides of the cavernous mouth. The nose is a manifest congealed drop or stalactite. The chin is a still larger drop, the confluent dripping of the face.
>
> (307–308)

We can admire the sensory detail and unconventional comparisons, but does the passage blur the boundary between human and nature or simply anthropomorphize what Thoreau encounters in the woods? Does he celebrate a natural process or objectify it, turning the pond into a convenient metaphor to convey his ideas about renewal? How would we describe the relationship between human and nonhuman, and what are the consequences of comparing a human body to a bit of clay, a drop congealed, a palm leaf, a bit of lichen, and a stalactite?

Nearly a century later in "The Fish" (1946), Elizabeth Bishop describes the act of catching a "tremendous fish" (1). She meticulously records the details: "his brown skin hung in strips / like ancient wallpaper" (10–11). She notes that he was "speckled with barnacles, / fine rosettes of lime, / and infested / with tiny white sea-lice" (16–19). The narrator draws attention to the remnants of fishing line:

> and then I saw / that from his lower lip / —if you could call it a lip— / grim, wet, and weaponlike, / hung five old pieces of fish-line, / or four and a wire leader / with the swivel still attached, / with all their five big hooks / grown firmly in his mouth.
>
> (47–55)

The narrator notices "where oil had spread a rainbow" (69). She suddenly releases the fish. What is the effect of anthropomorphizing the fish, of portraying the broken fishing lines as "medals with their ribbons" (44)? Does the narrator recognize herself in the fish, or does the fish become an object, an *Other* she cannot understand? Is the poem about the fish, the narrator, or the relationship between humans and animals? What are the implications of each answer?

What is striking about these examples is the close interaction characters have with the natural world. Thoreau reflects on the muddy pond beneath his feet. Bishop's narrator encounters a fish. Admittedly, the narratives are about characters and relationships, but they also foreground our relationship with the environment, prompting us to ask, What is our relationship with nonhuman nature? Does nature even exist independently from human supervision? Where should we direct our critical eye?

KEY PASSAGES

Karl Kroeber published *Ecological Literary Criticism: Romantic Imagining and the Biology of Mind* (1994) in response to what he describes as an "esoteric abstractness that afflicts current theorizing about literature" (1). By "esoteric abstractness," Kroeber asserts that literary theorists in the 1980s and early 1990s developed literary theories that did not engage the "opportunities offered by recent biological research to make humanistic studies more socially responsible" (1). He wants literary criticism to "contribute to the practical resolution of social and political conflicts that rend our society" (1). By doing so, Kroeber offers a useful way to think about the "linkages between natural and cultural processes" (1) as well as what he describes as the "sensory, emotional, and imaginative aspects of art" (2) that restore a physical presence to what others describe too abstractly or as a social construct.

> Contemporary biological thinking ... no longer identifies individuality with autonomy and separation. For leading contemporary biologists, the individuality of an organism is not definable except through its interactions with its environment, through its interdependencies. An organism's uniqueness consists in "intersubjective" connections and is determined not by separation but by "attunement," participation in "communities" (both inside itself and in the external environment) defined by historically individualized mutualities of need and desire.
> (7)

> An ecological view of the world, even a proto-ecological one, must be fundamentally materialistic, since its basic premise is that human beings are appropriately situated here on earth. How nature appears to be ordered, the romantics realized, is largely shaped by our internalized cultural presuppositions. To judge these, to reinforce or revise them, we must estimate how congruent they in fact are to the materiality of the physical universe that we experience every moment of our lives.
> (9)

A familiar thread that runs through many of the concepts we explore in this textbook is the focus on relationships and connections, and Kroeber echoes the trend in a more sociobiological context: nothing is isolated or autonomous; one thing connects with another, and things, as ecologists know, cannot exist without other things. The difference here is the relationship between individuals and their environment, between the human and nonhuman, divisions Kroeber asks us to question.

DISCUSSION

Kroeber's insights apply to a wide range of texts, but it is useful to remember that he focuses on British Romantic poets whom he describes as "forerunners of a new biological, materialistic understanding of humanity's place in the natural cosmos" (2), yet another reminder of his attention to the deep interrelationship between humans and the natural world. This connection, Kroeber asserts, is a source of pleasure for Romantics because "humankind *belonged* in, could and should be at home within, the world of natural processes" (5). This attention to human/nonhuman relationships is a key to understanding Kroeber, and for those interested in mapping how humans and their environment interrelate, these key passages remind us that we need to think more scientifically when we read and watch portrayals of nature.

When Kroeber claims that "contemporary biological thinking" (7) has moved beyond the idea that individuals are autonomous and separate, he is referring to work represented by Nobel laureate biologist Gerald Edelman who maintains that our nervous system generates unique neural networks that respond to external stimuli. Particular neural pathways survive if they respond effectively to what we encounter, while under used or weak networks disappear, and the variations in response shape our identity and individuality. In short, we use neural pathways to adapt to our surroundings, or we lose them. Edelman's research focuses on the deep processes of the brain, but Kroeber builds on the idea that this constant interaction with the environment creates our individual identities. In other words, Kroeber extends Edelman's work by suggesting that the process that traces nearly invisible neural networks also describes our relationship with our environment. We and our environment are interdependent in the sense that what we encounter shapes who we are, and then we act on the environment which, in turn, responds to us. We are not autonomous and separate, but interdependent and interconnected.

By using the terms "attunement" and "intersubjective connections," Kroeber echoes the work of a number of feminist scholars who blur the boundary between mind and nature, subject and object, and knower and known. For example, Jessica Benjamin explains that

> this intersubjective perspective envisions a more complex world than the realm of lifeless objects created by the radical separation of subject and object, self and other. By investing

> one's full attention in the object, one allows it to emerge as real and whole, so that the self is not lost but heightened through pleasure in the object.
>
> (192)

To put it another way, Benjamin and others redefine learning about the environment as an act of communion, not conquest (192). We are "attuned" to our environment in the sense that we empathize, adapt, assimilate, and recognize our mutual interdependence. The opposite, of course, would require us to separate ourselves, focus on differences, and insist on the environment's otherness. "Intersubjective connections" suggest the blurring of identities. Benjamin, for example, cites scientist Barbara McClintock who describes her research with chromosomes:

> When I was really working with them I wasn't outside, I was down there. I was part of the system. ... It surprised me, because I actually felt as if I was right down there and these were my friends. ... As you look at these things, they become part of you. And you forget yourself.
>
> (qtd. in Benjamin, 192)

Her observations suggest a sharing of consciousness. One is not merely observing. One is becoming part of the environment one is studying.

When Kroeber writes, "an ecological view of the world, even a proto-ecological one, must be fundamentally materialistic, since its basic premise is that human beings are appropriately situated here on earth" (9), he is resisting those who separate humans from nature by transforming natural processes into abstractions, celebrating a metaphysical or spiritual reality that transcends our material existence, or privileging humans and objectifying nature. In other words, a materialistic view maintains that we *belong* in the world, that we are part of nature.

And when he writes, "How nature appears to be ordered, the romantics realized, is largely shaped by our internalized cultural presuppositions. To judge these, to reinforce or revise them, we must estimate how congruent they in fact are to the materiality of the physical universe that we experience every moment of our lives" (9), Kroeber argues that we impose order on nature, but he wants us to test those presuppositions, those preexisting ideas or assumptions, by experiencing the natural world. We invent "nature" in the sense that our intellectual frameworks define what nature is (and is *not*), and determine its value and significance. However, we still bump into rocks, suffocate if we cannot breathe, and enjoy the warmth of the sun. By looking at, smelling, touching, tasting, and listening to what we encounter, we use our bodies to judge whether or not our "cultural presuppositions" are accurate. By learning about our environment, we learn about ourselves, for we are part of the environment, and we enjoy an intersubjective connection and interdependence.

POTENTIAL PROJECTS

Kroeber's core concepts offer us a flexible and interdisciplinary approach to make sense of how writers, filmmakers, and artists portray nonhuman nature. As you explore these representations in word and image, keep in mind the key ideas: Kroeber is interested in blurring the boundaries between species, examining how we interact with our nonhuman environment, describing the various ways that human and nonhuman elements are interdependent, and thinking in terms of systems and interactions. Draw as well on key phrases: "linkages between natural and cultural processes," "interactions with its environment," "interdependencies," "intersubjective connections," and "attunement." Following Kroeber, read with an eye on developing "mutually enriching interconnections between humanistic and scientific modes of understanding humankind, the earth we inhabit, and their reciprocal interdependencies" (140). Cultural representations should "strengthen and reinforce our participative engagements with our natural environment" (138). In short, Kroeber encourages an activist, socially responsible form of reading. Finally, note that Kroeber's insights apply to works entirely dedicated to reflecting on nature like, say, a Wordsworth poem or particular passages or images in longer works. However, any work offers opportunities to apply Kroeber's insights. Do not limit yourself to "nature writing."

Assess a sense of belonging

Does a literary text, film, or work of art identify "individuality with autonomy and separation" (7), or does the work establish a character's individuality based on "interactions with [the] environment, through its interdependencies" (7)? Do characters separate themselves from their nonhuman environment or attune themselves to nature? And how does the text reject, embrace, or complicate these "intersubjective' connections"? What cause and effect relationships does the work associate with attunement or separation?

For example, Pixar's *WALL-E* (2008) invites us to reflect on our relationship with our environment and ponder the consequences of separation and autonomy by portraying a trash compactor robot who finds himself in a sterile wasteland, a probe named EVE who seeks life on the abandoned planet, and a spaceship full of obese and weak humans. Werner Herzog's *Grizzly Man* (2005) documents Timothy Treadwell's relationship with grizzly bears in Alaska, and the film prompts us to examine how Herzog portrays notions of "interdependencies," "intersubjective connections," and "attunement" with animals. Does *Grizzly Man* promote "mutually enriching interconnections between humanistic and scientific modes of understanding humankind, the earth we inhabit, and their reciprocal interdependencies" (140)? How does *Grizzly Man* help us explore the ways people displace their own desires and fears onto their environment?

Identify the essential

Many works pay keen attention to setting and the environment, often using fine sensory detail to describe plants, animals, weather, and geology. However, does the work present these nonhuman elements as the focus of our attention or as mere props, settings, metaphors, and symbols? Does the work reframe nature in human terms by anthropomorphizing flora and fauna, or does the author present nature as the focus of our attention? Even more importantly, does the work use the "materiality of the physical universe that we experience every moment of our lives" (9) to assess our cultural presuppositions and intellectual frameworks? For example, Jonathan Edwards' "Personal Narrative" (1765) describes a moment of spiritual union:

> And scarce anything, among all the works of nature, was so sweet me as thunder and lightning. Formerly, nothing had been so terrible to me. I used to be a person uncommonly terrified with thunder: and it used to strike me with terror, when I saw a thunderstorm rising. But now, on the contrary, it rejoiced me. I felt God at first appearance of a thunderstorm. And used to take the opportunity at such times, to fix myself to view the clouds, and see the lightnings play, and hear the majestic and awful voice of God's thunder....
>
> (794)

Edwards associates thunderstorms with the divine, but does this connection reduce a storm to a symbol, or does the passage exemplify "linkages between natural and cultural processes" (1)? Does the physical world alter Edwards' cultural assumptions, or does his faith in God humanize or even deify a thunderstorm? Theologically, what happens when Edwards feels God's presence in a thunderstorm instead of a church? What happens when the natural world replaces a holy space like a chapel?

Consider as well texts like Sylvia Plath's "Stings" (1962), a poem that describes the relationship between bees and beekeepers. Plath certainly uses the image of the beekeeper, the bees, and the hive to comment on heterosexual relationships: "I stand in a column / Of winged, unmiraculous women, / Honey-drudgers. / I am no drudge" (20–23). However, with an eye on portrayals of nature, we should ask whether or not Plath turns natural processes into an abstract concept about gender relations, or does she suggest that we are part of nature? What, in fact, do we learn about bees, and does Plath's observations "strengthen and reinforce our participative engagements with our natural environment" (Kroeber 138)?

WORKS CITED

Benjamin, Jessica. *The Bonds of Love: Psychoanalysis, Feminism, & the Problem of Domination*. Pantheon, 1988.
Bishop, Elizabeth. "The Fish." *Poems: Elizabeth Bishop*, edited by Saskia Hamilton, Farrar, 2011, pp. 43–44.
Edwards, Jonathan. "Personal Narrative." *Jonathan Edwards: Letters and Personal Writings*, edited by George S. Claghorn, Yale UP, 1998, pp. 790–804.
Kroeber, Karl. *Ecological Literary Criticism: Romantic Imagining and the Biology of Mind*. Columbia UP, 1994.
Plath, Sylvia. "Stings." *The Collected Poems*, edited by Ted Hughes, Perennial, 1981, pp. 214–215.
Thoreau, Henry David. *Walden*, edited by J. Lyndon Shanley, Princeton UP, 2016.

CHAPTER 22

Recognizing conceptual metaphors

Our ordinary conceptual system, in terms of which we both think and act, is fundamentally metaphorical in nature.

(George Lakoff and Mark Johnson 3)

PROBLEMS, PUZZLES, AND QUESTIONS

We usually encounter metaphor when we read novels, short stories, and poems. For example, Terry Tempest Williams' "An Unspoken Hunger" (1994) uses metaphorical language in a prose poem to describe a relationship:

> It is an unspoken hunger we deflect with knives—one avocado between us, cut neatly in half, twisted then separated from the large wooden pit. With the green fleshy boats in hand, we slice vertical strips from one end to the other. Vegetable planks. We smother the avocado with salsa, hot chilies at noon in the desert. We look at each other and smile, eating avocados with the sharp silver blades, risking the blood of our tongues repeatedly.
>
> (79)

Much of the language is not literal. We deflect hunger. Avocados are fleshy boats. Avocado slices are akin to long thin flat pieces of lumber. At a more subtle level, the images of tropical fruit, salsa, chilies, noon, and a desert setting suggest lightly repressed lust and desire. We expect literature to work indirectly like this, more suggestive and allusive than literal and direct.

We praise Abraham Lincoln for his eloquence in his "Gettysburg Address" (1863): "Four score and seven years ago our fathers brought forth, upon this continent, a new nation, conceived in liberty, and dedicated to the proposition that 'all men are created equal'." Lincoln's speech is no less metaphorical, but the words do not draw as much attention to themselves. His use of "our fathers" and "conceived in liberty" are no more literal than deflecting hunger with knives, but do we recognize the metaphors as metaphors?

Or consider President Richard Nixon's announcement of the National Cancer Act of 1971:

> The effort to mobilize a concerted national campaign against cancer has continued to make significant progress since those proposals were submitted. One of the most important steps was the approval by the Congress of the additional $100 million I requested to support an expanded attack on cancer. ... Now this year of preparation for an all-out assault on cancer comes to a climax with the signing of the National Cancer Act. The new organizational structure which this legislation establishes will enable us to mobilize far more effectively both our human and our financial resources in the fight against this dread disease.

Notice his use of *mobilize, campaign, attack, assault*, and *fight*. The words are certainly metaphorical, but few of us believe that Nixon is waxing poetic as he describes a new initiative to cure cancer. "Fighting cancer" is just the way we talk when we describe medical treatments.

Finally, in *Shady Characters: The Secret Life of Punctuation, Symbols, and Other Typographical Marks* (2013), Keith Houston describes his research process: "I hunted down the symbol in my copy of the *Typographic Desk Reference*" (ix). "This curt description invited more questions than it answered" (ix). "What were the roots of its pithy, half-familiar name?" (x). "A web search yielded a list of books to read and sites to browse" (x). "In February 2009, my meandering note-taking and browsing snapped sharply into focus" (x). "This book is here to bring them into the light of day, and I can only hope to do justice to Penny Speckter and all the others who have helped me on the way here" (x). Houston is writing a history of typography, not a novel, but he still describes the process figuratively. Note his word choice: "hunted down," "this curt question invited," "What were the roots," "A web search yielded," "my meandering note-taking," "snapped sharply into focus," "bring them into the light of day," "do justice," and "on the way here." Does

Houston merely produce nonfiction, or does his use of metaphorical language differ from Williams' narration?

All these passages interest us because these writers use language in nonliteral ways, but the degree to which the language draws attention to itself varies. We cannot help but notice that Williams talks about desire and passion in terms of hunger. On the other hand, asking if someone has lost her battle with cancer does not strike us as literary language, just as Houston's description of his research as a hunt does not make us pause and linger on his word choice. So, is metaphor a form of extraordinary or ordinary language? Can metaphor shape the very way we think about politics, education, love, relationships, and every aspect of our life? Is metaphor as alive in the boardroom as it is in the classroom?

KEY PASSAGES

It is not strange to believe that we have ideas, and then we search for the right words to express those ideas. As English writer Samuel Johnson phrases it, "Language is the dress of thought" (48). A more contemporary version is, "I know what I want to say, but I just cannot find the words to say it." In this case, metaphor is merely a literary device used to convey a preexisting idea. However, George Lakoff and Mark Johnson question the premise of this relationship in *Metaphors We Live By* (1980), a work that combines philosophy with cognitive linguistics. Instead of viewing metaphor merely as a linguistic construction, Lakoff and Johnson assert that metaphors are primarily conceptual. This shift from metaphor as ornament to metaphor as concept revises cause-effect relationships and expands our notion of metaphor's effect and value.

> Metaphor is for most people a device of the poetic imagination and the rhetorical flourish—a matter of extraordinary rather than ordinary language. Moreover, metaphor is typically viewed as characteristic of language alone, a matter of words rather than thought or action. For this reason, most people think they can get along perfectly well without metaphor. We have found, on the contrary, that metaphor is pervasive in everyday life, not just in language but in thought and action. Our ordinary conceptual system, in terms of which we both think and act, is fundamentally metaphorical in nature.
>
> (3)

> The concepts that govern our thought are not just matters of the intellect. They also govern our everyday functioning, down to the most mundane details. Our concepts structure what we perceive, how we get around in the world, and how we relate to other people. Our conceptual system thus plays a central role in defining our everyday realities. If we are right in suggesting that our conceptual system is largely metaphorical, then the way we think, what we experience, and what we do every day is very much a matter of metaphor.
>
> (3)

Lakoff and Johnson's work blurs the boundary of the literary and everyday life, and this overlapping of worlds is what makes their work particularly useful and interesting.

DISCUSSION

Metaphorical language substitutes one thing for another. As Lakoff and Johnson assert, *"the essence of metaphor is understanding and experiencing one kind of thing in terms of another"* (5). This idea is familiar territory. For example, when Wilfred Owen writes, "Dim, through the misty panes and thick green light, / As under a green sea, I saw him drowning" (13–14), he helps us understand a chemical gas attack, an experience few of us have endured, to the more common feeling of gasping for air as we sink in water. The comparison is never perfect, but a close approximation helps us understand events beyond our experience.

Lakoff and Johnson extend metaphor's ability to help us understand one thing in terms of another to the way we think about and even experience what we encounter every day. In other words, the key move is to recategorize metaphor: "extraordinary language" is actually "ordinary language." What seems like specialized use of poetic speech is actually rather common, so common, in fact, that we do not recognize its presence or influence.

More precisely, Lakoff and Johnson focus on metaphor's role in our conceptual systems: "our ordinary conceptual system, in terms of which we both think and act, is fundamentally metaphorical in nature" (3). And by saying that our conceptual systems play a "central role in defining our everyday realities" (3), Lakoff and Johnson maintain that we do not encounter reality as it is, but reality in terms of something else. They offer many useful examples. The most famous is "Argument is war." They point out that when we talk about arguments, we use phrases like "Your claims are *indefensible*. He *attacked every weak point* in my argument. His criticisms were *right on target*. I *demolished* his argument. I've never *won* an argument with him" (4), and so on. They point out that "It is important to see that we don't just *talk* about arguments in terms of war. We can actually win or lose arguments. We see the person we are arguing with as an opponent" (4). They remind us that talking about arguments in terms of war would not strike us as being poetic or eloquent. Instead, "this is the *ordinary* way of having an argument and talking about one" (5). They add that

> the metaphor is not merely in the words we use—it is in our very concept of an argument. The language of argument is not poetic, fanciful, or rhetorical; it is literal. We talk about arguments that way because we conceive of them that way— and we act according to the way we conceive of things.
>
> (5)

To put it another way, although the conceptual systems are metaphorical, we experience them as literal. Words like "indefensible, attack, on target, demolished" have lost their metaphorical effect in the same way that the phrases "Your introduction is rough," "Your writing is clear," and "Your ideas need more support" do not strike my students as particularly poetic. That is just the way we discuss writing. And yet, those conceptual metaphors not only imply qualities of good writing, but they define writing itself.

Consider one final illustration. This textbook's introduction describes universities as communities, often populated by "foreign language speakers" who speak the language of physics, psychology, kinesiology, or literary theory. That conceptual metaphor encourages us to think of discussions, not as debates that we win or lose, but as conversations that require give and take. Our classmates are not opponents, but conversation partners, a relationship that implies a particular ethical code. And the translation metaphor encourages us to think of explanations as close approximations, never one-to-one correspondences. Plus, we need to extend ourselves by learning a new language so that we can converse with others. Note, too, that other theory textbooks encourage students to think of theory as a "lens," a conceptual metaphor that foregrounds different ways of seeing, while "toolbox" metaphors draw attention to theory as a device or implement we use to complete a task. Each conceptual metaphor—theory as foreign language, lens, tool—defines theory, describes our roles and relationships, and implies a purpose.

POTENTIAL PROJECTS

Lakoff and Johnson's contribution extends well beyond linguistics. The theory is flexible because their argument pays attention to how we derive meaning from everyday language and thought, and scholars have used the idea of conceptual metaphors to discuss everything from literature, film, TV shows, historical sites, and video games to education, psychology, neuroscience, criminal law, and geo-engineering. Consider a few options:

Identify implications

Follow Lakoff and Johnson's lead by embracing the premise that "metaphor is pervasive in everyday life, not just in language but in thought and action. Our ordinary conceptual system, in terms of which we both think and act, is fundamentally metaphorical in nature" (3).

Choose a nonliterary piece of writing you may encounter every day: a travel essay, a medical brochure, corporate documents, political speeches, marketing material for a university, an editorial, a biology textbook, etc. Then, identify the conceptual metaphor(s) the author uses, and, more importantly, explore how these metaphors "structure what we perceive, how we get around in the world, and how we relate to other people" (3). Examine how these conceptual metaphors influence "the way we think, what we experience, and what we do" (3). In other words, focus on the effect or function of these conceptual metaphors. While Susan Sontag does not reference Lakoff and Johnson, her short books *Illness as Metaphor* (1978) and *AIDS and Its Metaphors* (1989) offer very good examples of how conceptual metaphors shape the way we think of disease.

Critique conceptual metaphors

This option extends the first project. As described above, assume that our conceptual systems are metaphorical in nature, and that they shape "the way we think, what we experience, and what we do" (3). Note, however, that Lakoff and Johnson remind us that we use parts of conceptual metaphors, but not every part. For example, they point out that the conceptual metaphor "theories are buildings" foregrounds "foundations, support, form, and framework," and we talk in terms of theories "standing, falling, and collapsing." On the other hand,

> the roof, internal rooms staircases, and hallway are parts of a building not used as part of the concept THEORY. Thus

> the metaphor THEORIES ARE BUILDINGS has a 'used' part (foundation and outer shell) and an 'unused' part (rooms, staircases, etc.).
>
> (52)

Your project is to explore ways that the "unused" parts of the conceptual metaphor undermine or problematize the used parts. For example, if a medical brochure uses war metaphors (i.e. mobilize, campaign, attack, assault, and fight) to describe our response to disease, then you can identify the unused parts of that metaphor (peace negotiation, treaty, truce, retreat, surrender, etc.) to question the war metaphor itself and its accompanying treatments. Notice that this project moves you beyond analysis to critique and response.

Theorize reading metaphors

Consider the implications of common conceptual metaphors we use to define reading: dissect, dig, construct, explore, digest, and unravel. How else do teachers define the reading process? How do these metaphors define what a text is, describe our role, suggest how to read, and distinguish between a compelling or inadequate interpretation? If you plan to teach literature, how does your choice of reading metaphors determine your pedagogy? What are the gains and limitations of each reading metaphor? How can we rethink these metaphors if we, as described above, focus on the unused parts?

WORKS CITED

Houston, Keith. *Shady Characters: The Secret Life of Punctuation, Symbols, and Other Typographical Marks*. Norton, 2013.

Johnson, Samuel. *The Lives of the Poets: A Selection*. Oxford UP, 2009.

Lakoff, George and Mark Johnson. 1980. *Metaphors We Live By*. U of Chicago P, 2003.

Lincoln, Abraham. "The Gettysburg Address." *Our Documents*, www.urdocuments.gov/doc.php?flash=false&doc=36&page=transcript. Accessed 11 January 2018.

Nixon, Richard. "Statement about the National Cancer Act of 1971." *The American Presidency Project*, www.presidency.ucsb.edu/ws/?pid=3276. Accessed 11 January 2018.

Owen, Wilfred. "Dulce Et Decorum Est." *The Collected Poems of Wilfred Owen*, edited by C. Day Lewis, New Directions, 1965.

Williams, Terry Tempest. *An Unspoken Hunger: Stories from the Field*. Vintage, 1994.

CHAPTER 23

Representing disability

> To prostheticize, in this sense, is to institute a notion of the body within a regime of tolerable deviance.
>
> (David T. Mitchell and Sharon L. Snyder 6–7)

PROBLEMS, PUZZLES, AND QUESTIONS

In "Good Country People" (1955), Flannery O'Connor describes Joy Hopewell, a 32-year with a weak heart who sports glasses and wears a prosthetic leg because of a hunting accident when she was ten. Joy repudiates her mother's upbringing, earning a Ph.D. in philosophy, declaring herself an atheist, and changing her legal name to Hulga. A Bible salesman arrives, a man Joy's mother declares is an example of "good country people." Joy and the salesman eventually find their way to a loft where, after some flirting, he removes her glasses and artificial leg. After a brief argument, the salesman slips through the hole in the loft, with her leg in his briefcase, declaring that "'I've gotten a lot of interesting things,' he said. 'One time I got a woman's glass eye this way'" (291). He leaves her sitting alone in the straw. Is O'Connor interested in portraying life with disabilities, or are these prostheses and impairments—an artificial limb, prescriptive lenses, a glass eye, a weak heart—little more than literary devices used to suggest something about "good country people" and naïve young women?

Raymond Carver's "Cathedral" (1981) describes a man who is irritated by his wife's announcement that her blind friend Robert needs to spend the night at their home. The narrator is candid: "And his being blind bothered me. My idea of blindness came from the movies. In the movies, the blind moved slowly and never laughed. Sometimes they were led by seeing-eye dogs" (514). The three of them spend the evening together, the wife eventually nodding off. The narrator begins to watch a documentary about cathedrals. He describes what he sees to Robert who suggests that the narrator draw a cathedral, and his hand will follow along. At one point, Robert tells the narrator to close his eyes:

> His fingers rode my fingers as my hand went over the paper. It was like nothing else in my life up to now.
> Then he said, 'I think that's it. I think you got it,' he said. 'Take a look. What do you think?'
> But I had my eyes closed. I thought I'd keep them that way for a little longer. I thought it was something I ought to do.
> 'Well?' he said. 'Are you looking?'
> My eyes were still closed. I was in my house. I knew that. But I didn't feel like I was inside anything.
> 'It's really something,' I said.
>
> (528–529)

Carver represents blindness positively and even conventionally. Literature and film often portray blind characters who can "see" better than others, and they often serve as guides and mentors. But is Carver's portrait an example of "transgressive reappropriation," a celebration of being an outsider, or does Carver merely use blindness as a metaphor in an effort to illustrate the difference between "looking" and "seeing," numbness and sensitivity? And why do many narratives present blindness as a gift, but describe other impairments negatively?

The King's Speech (2010) dramatizes the story of Prince Albert, Duke of York, who later becomes King George VI. Prince Albert struggles with a profound stutter, a trait that limits his ability to present himself as a modern monarch whose voice needs to reach all of England and the Empire. Prince Albert agrees to work with speech therapist Lionel Logue who not only prescribes physical exercises, but also explores Prince Albert's psychological baggage. With Logue's help, the Prince is able to deliver his 1939 address announcing that Britain is at war with Germany. The film ends with a title card that explains that Logue and the Prince remained friends for the rest of their lives. While the film offers a sympathetic portrayal of disability, we can still ask, Is the film about disability, an odd-couple friendship, an obstacle that a character needs to overcome, or what Lennard Davis calls "enforced normalcy"?

These are only a few examples of how film and literature have portrayed the disabled, but in addition to the questions above, representations of the disabled also invite us to ask: Why do disabilities pique our curiosity? Does the construction of normalcy go hand in hand with the construction of disability? Is disability a subject or a literary device?

KEY PASSAGES

The American Disabilities Act of 1990 defines "disabled" as a physical or mental impairment that "substantially limits one or more major life activities." Given its ability to impact every human, disability crosses race, sexuality, gender, and any other kind of social group. Plus, the category is fluid. Some are born with impairments, while others become disabled due to accident, disease, or age. If we live long enough, odds are we will join the group. Acknowledging disability's instability as an identity category provides us with new opportunities. As Lennard Davis explains, "when we start conceiving of disability as a descriptive term and not as an absolute category, then we can begin to think in theoretical and political ways about this category" (8). In *Narrative Prosthesis: Disability and the Dependencies of Discourse*, David T. Mitchell and Sharon L. Snyder build on Davis' work by trying to understand "the difference that disability makes. Where did disability fit on a map of marginality and identity?" (x). On the one hand, we encounter the disabled every day, in life and art, perhaps even in the mirror. On the other hand, disability does not often enter the conversation when we discuss social categories. As a result, Mitchell and Snyder assert that "disability studies challenges the common ascription of inferior lives to persons with physical and cognitive differences" (2). They are keenly interested in how writers, artists, and filmmakers use disability to serve aesthetic, cultural, and political interests, and they provide several productive insights:

> Our phrase *narrative prosthesis* is meant to indicate that disability has been used throughout history as a crutch upon which literary narratives lean for their representational power, disruptive potentiality, and analytical insight. Bodies show up in stories as dynamic entities that resist or refuse the cultural scripts assigned to them.
> (49)
>
> The narration of the disabled body allows a textual body to *mean* through its long-standing historical representation as an overdetermined symbolic surface; the disabled body

> also offers narrative the illusion of grounding abstract knowledge within a bodily materiality. *If the body is the Other of text, then textual representation seeks access to that which it is least able to grasp.* If the nondysfunctional body proves too uninteresting to narrate, the disabled body becomes a paramount device of characterization.
>
> (64)
>
> The need to restore a disabled body to some semblance of an originary wholeness is the key to a false recognition: that disabilities extract one from a social norm or average of bodies and their corresponding (social) expectations. To prostheticize, in this sense, is to institute a notion of the body within a regime of tolerable deviance. If disability falls too far from an acceptable norm, a prosthetic intervention seeks to accomplish an erasure of difference all together; yet, failing that, as is always the case with prosthesis, the minimal goal is to return one to an acceptable degree of difference.
>
> (6–7)

These passages remind us of the importance of representation, and Mitchell and Snyder draw attention to disability's capacity to question normalcy, human boundaries, and cultural meaning, key relationships we need to address in greater detail.

DISCUSSION

Let us begin by exploring what Mitchell and Snyder mean by "narrative prosthesis" (49). A prosthesis is an artificial device that replaces or augments a body part: a tooth implant, silicone breast, artificial limb, hearing aid, etc. For Mitchell and Snyder, a *narrative* prosthesis refers to the act of using disability as a literary device in three ways. First, disability calls a story into being because "something has gone amiss with the known world" (53), and the narrative needs to address the "abnormality." In other words, the disabled, whose bodies "resist or refuse the cultural scripts assigned to them" (49), are stock characters that invite our attention. What caused the disability? What impact does it have? Can the character overcome or compensate? If so, how so? If not, why not? The character's deviation from the norm justifies the telling of the story, and the narrative promises insight and understanding. The disabled, then, serve as a "crutch" for storytellers because disability generates a reason to tell a story, particularly a story that seeks to rescue, correct, or resolve a deviation.

Second, disability also functions as a prosthesis by serving as a literary and cultural metaphor. When Mitchell and Snyder refer to disability as an "overdetermined symbolic surface" (64), and when they assert that "the disabled body also offers narrative the illusion of grounding abstract knowledge within a bodily materiality" (64), they point out that the disabled body has long served as a physical marker of interior qualities and character. For example, they remind us that Richard III's hunchback, Ahab's peg leg, or Oedipus' hobble suggest something problematic about who they are on the inside. On the other hand, the disabilities evident in William Faulkner's Benjy, Charles Dickens' Tiny Tim, and Winston Groom's Forrest Gump mark an astute perception and moral goodness. Or as Mitchell and Snyder phrase it, "To give an abstraction a body allows the idea to simulate a foothold in the material world that it would otherwise fail to procure" (62–63). Narratives are about particular people, places, things, and actions, but those tangible and visible elements signify abstract themes, values, attitudes, politics, and identities.

Third, while disability acts as a prosthesis in the sense that narratives lean on disability to justify the telling of a story, the relationship works the other way as well. A narrative acts as a prosthesis by bringing "the body's unruliness under control" (6). In other words, a disabled body deviates from an idealized version of wholeness and health. The disabled character is no longer part of the community. The disabled are, as Mitchell and Snyder write, extracted "from a social norm or average of bodies and their corresponding (social) expectations" (6). Narrative's role, therefore, is to portray disability in such a way that the "deviation" falls within "an acceptable norm," just as a prosthesis fills in a gap or restores an ability. The ultimate goal, however, is to "accomplish an erasure of difference all together" (7). And how does a narrative do that? As Mitchell and Snyder explain,

> the repair of deviance may involve an obliteration of the difference through a 'cure,' the rescue of the despised object from social censure, the extermination of the deviant as a purification of the social body, or the revaluation of an alternative mode of being.
>
> (53–54)

They discuss, for example, the Victorian tale of "The Steadfast Tin Soldier" that describes the adventures of a one-legged toy soldier who endures an arduous adventure—a fall, a storm, an involuntary boat ride, an encounter with a rat, a belly of a fish, an oven, and unrequited love—that minimizes his outsider status, but he is eventually tossed in the fireplace and melts. The tin soldier is still blemished, unable to fit the norm, so go he must.

In short, disability draws attention to itself, thus calling a story into being. The narrative then uses disability as a metaphor to convey meaning and character, all while it tries to rescue, repair, or purge the disability.

POTENTIAL PROJECTS

As Mitchell and Snyder remind us, literature and cultural representations are *commentaries* on disability, and as such, they do not offer us truth as much as imaginative responses to bodies that differ from others. Disability's challenges have affinities with other minority discourses, and it may be beneficial to explore other chapters in this textbook that address representations of identity.

Identify narrative coding

How does a narrative or image portray the disabled? Negative stereotypes abound. For example, Mitchell and Snyder cite Paul Longmore who identifies three common images: "disability is a punishment for evil; disabled people are embittered by their 'fate'; disabled people resent the nondisabled and would, if they could, destroy them" (18). Mitchell and Snyder add several common tropes: "the passively suffering angel of the house, the overcompensating supercrip, the tragically innocent disabled child, the malignant disabled avenger, and the angry war veteran" (25). How do these narratives bring "the body's unruliness under control" (6)? How does the representation of disability fit or resist these portrayals?

On the other hand, explore positive representations. But what counts as a "positive" portrayal? Do narratives and representations find ways to celebrate those with disabilities? Beware, however, of romanticized images of the disabled or what some call "disabled heroism" (23). What purpose does a romanticized portrayal serve?

Shift your attention

Rather than focusing on disabled characters, focus on representations of disabled lives. Are portrayals of disability accurate or misleading?

What was left out in the name of convenience or a trim narrative? Mitchell and Snyder remind us that

> a literal representation of disability would capture the myriad negotiations of a fraught social environment, obstacles would prove themselves of societal making rather than individual limitation, and technology previously hidden in the corners of homes and institutions would take center stage in the drama of disability as a lived experience.
>
> (24)

Consider the effect, significance, and politics of narratives that (un)realistically portray disabled lives.

Explore subversive inversions

Social movements often resignify disparaging terms like *queer*, *girl*, *bitch*, and *nigga* in an effort to deflate the term's power. Disability groups have made a similar move with *cripple* and *gimp*. Mitchell and Snyder note that "the power of transgression always originates at the moment when the derided object embraces its deviance as value" (35). In other words, resignification exposes the term as derogatory, shaming "the dominant culture into a recognition of its own dehumanizing precepts" (35–36), and recodes the meaning in positive ways. Mitchell and Snyder offer a useful example in their discussion of madness which is often associated with truth and revelation. Emily Dickinson's recoding of madness offers a useful example:

> Much Madness is divinest Sense –
> To a discerning Eye –
> Much Sense – the starkest Madness –
> 'Tis the Majority
> In this, as All, prevail –
> Assent – and you are sane –
> Demur – you're straightway dangerous –
> And handled with a Chain –
>
> (101)

Therefore, discuss how particular representations of disability subvert attempts to exclude and dehumanize by resignifying terms and privileging outsider status. Explore how being "abnormal" liberates the disabled from oppressive normalcy.

WORKS CITED

The American Disabilities Act. *U.S. Equal Employment Opportunity Commission*, www.eeoc.gov/laws/statutes/adaaa.cfm.

Carver, Raymond. "Cathedral." *Collected Stories*, edited by William L. Stull and Maureen Patricia. Carroll, Library of America, 2009, pp. 514–529.

Davis, Lennard J. *Enforcing Normalcy: Disability, Deafness, and the Body*. Verso, 1995.

Dickinson, Emily. "Much Madness Is Divinest Sense." *Final Harvest: Emily Dickinson's Poems*, edited by Thomas Herbert Johnson, Little, 1961, p. 101.

The King's Speech, Directed by Tom Hooper. Momentum, 2010.

Mitchell, David T. and Sharon L. Snyder. *Narrative Prosthesis: Disability and the Dependencies of Discourse*. U of Michigan P, 2000.

O'Connor, Flannery. "Good Country People." *The Complete Stories*. Noonday, 1991, pp. 271–291.

CHAPTER 24

Losing and recovering our sovereignty

> What has taken place is a radical loss of sovereignty.
>
> (Walker Percy 54)

PROBLEMS, PUZZLES, AND QUESTIONS

Before *Star Wars: The Last Jedi* (2017) even arrived in theaters, we encountered countless trailers, advertisements, late-show commentaries, guest appearances, and other forms of promotion. Before we even took that first bite of popcorn, we probably had a good sense of the conflicts, characters, settings, and potential plot points. Watching the film itself may have become a game of "Who was right, and who was wrong?" Does the hype spoil the experience? How do all those intermediaries shape what you see when you watch the film?

We should not forget the filters that come between us and a novel, poem, play, and other texts we encounter. For example, when your 20th-century American literature professor assigns Robert Frost's "The Road Not Taken" (1916), you may recognize the poem from high school or maybe even a funeral, wedding, or graduation ceremony. Odds are the poem is part of a literature anthology. You will, for example, find Robert Frost in the "Toward the Modern Age" section of the seventh edition of the *Heath Anthology of American Literature* and after "World War I and Its Aftermath" in the ninth edition of *The Norton Anthology of American Literature*. The editors situate Robert Frost between María Cristina Mena and Sherwood Anderson in the *Heath* and between Gertrude Stein and Susan Glaspell in the *Norton*. The poem itself comes after a short explanation of biographical, historical, and literary contexts. A professor probably frames your reading experience by placing Frost's poem within a syllabus and initiating discussion topics before you even encounter the poem on your own. Is all this apparatus helpful or just clutter? Are you grateful for the support, or do you wish you could read the poem without all the scaffolding?

In *Presenting Shakespeare: 1,100 Posters from Around the World* (2015), we see examples of how illustrators have visually interpreted Shakespeare's plays. An 1894 poster portrays Hamlet from the side wearing a simple black Renaissance gown on a beige background, isolated and contemplative as he stares at a skull. Another poster foregrounds violence and regicide by portraying a lightly outlined Hamlet impaled on a bed-sized crown. A clown nose attached to a skull in another poster combines the tragic with the comic, perhaps mocking the earnest "To be or not to be" monologue. Do the posters help or hinder? Are they tangential to reading *Hamlet* or a useful supplement? Are they superfluous or necessary? Do they misdirect or interfere?

These examples remind us that we live in a mediated world. We struggle to have what some might call an "authentic" experience, a moment that allows us to encounter, say, a story without any preconceived notion about what we are about to read. Another way to pose the question is to ask, where does the text begin and end? Is the cover of *Hamlet* part of the play? Does the footnote in the *Heath Anthology* that tells us that Jonathan Edwards is "said to have been one of the quietest, least spectacular of preachers in his own day" (723) actually become part of "Sinners in the Hands of an Angry God?" And do these questions matter? Should we care?

KEY PASSAGES

Walker Percy asserts emphatically that, yes, those questions do matter, and we should worry about the way our culture and institutions mediate, filter, and package representations and experiences. In "The Loss of the Creature," a chapter in his book *The Message in the Bottle: How Queer Man Is, How Queer Language Is, and What One Has to Do with the Other* (1975), Percy focuses on loss, particularly the loss of sovereignty or the ability to be in control of what one perceives. He argues that media surround or come between us and the object or event and shape the way we perceive the experience, just as I am influencing your interpretation of Percy's essay right now. In other words, our culture mediates our experience, so we never have a direct or authentic relationship with what we encounter. While we should certainly question the possibility of having an authentic, unfiltered experience, Percy's observations on the effect of mediation encourage us to at least investigate the effects of this framing. Percy offers us several key concepts we can use:

> I refer to the general situation in which sovereignty is surrendered to a class of privileged knowers, whether these be theorists or artists. A reader may surrender sovereignty over that which has been written about, just as a consumer may surrender sovereignty over a thing which has been theorized about. The consumer is content to receive an experience just as it has been presented to him by theorists and planners. The reader may also be content to judge life by whether it has or has not been formulated by those who know and write about life.
> (54–55)
>
> There is a double deprivation. First, the thing is lost through its packaging. The very means by which the thing is presented for consumption, the very techniques by which the thing is made available as an item of need-satisfaction, these very means operate to remove the thing from the sovereignty of the knower.
> (61–62)
>
> The second loss is the spoliation of the thing, the tree, the rock, the swallow, by the layman's misunderstanding of scientific theory. He believes that the thing is *disposed of* by theory, that it stands in the Platonic relation of being a *specimen of* such and such an underlying principle. In the transmission of scientific theory from theorist to layman, the expectation of the theorist is reversed. Instead of the marvels of the universe being made available to the public, the universe is disposed of by theory. The loss of sovereignty takes this form: As a result of the science of botany, trees are not made available to every man. On the contrary, the tree loses its proper density and mystery as a concrete existent and, as merely another *specimen of* a species, becomes itself nugatory.
> (62–63)

> The highest role of the educator is the maieutic role of Socrates: to help the student come to himself not as a consumer of experience but as a sovereign individual.
>
> (63)

Notice his diction: symbolic packaging, spoliation, deprivation, specimen, sovereignty, sovereign knower, consumer. These terms are key to understanding how Percy thinks about our relationship with texts and experiences, and they deserve close attention.

DISCUSSION

Percy complicates the definition of what a "text" is. We often think that we are merely reading a poem, play, or story. We are just watching a film, listening to a song, or examining a painting. Percy reminds us that the "text" includes all the words, images, and guides that surround the narrative or image.

Symbolic packaging

Symbolic packaging refers to the material that surrounds the text, site, film, painting, song, event, etc. "Packaging" implies that this material encloses, but is not essential to the experience. We have to work our way through these extraneous materials to reach what we really want. A package also implies that the materials are grouped and networked in intricate ways. "Symbolic" suggests that this packaged network conveys meaning. Most importantly, this packaging shapes the very way we perceive and process our experience.

Note that some scholars call these extraneous materials "paratexts," and paratexts usually refer to the "verbal frames" or additions that include "names and pseudonyms, titles and subtitles, cover notes, blurbs, dedications, notes, prefaces and postfaces, epigraphs and 'epitexts'" (Maclean 273). Percy would agree, but he expands the notion of paratext to refer to all the material and people who come between us and an experience, and that may include guides, visual displays, teachers, theories, assignments, translations, signs, etc.

Spoliation/deprivation

"Spoliation" and "deprivation" refer to the moment when symbolic packaging interferes and deprives the knower of a direct encounter.

Percy clarifies, "'Unspoiled' does not mean only that a place is left physically intact; it means also that it is not encrusted by renown and by the familiar... that it has not been discovered by others" (51). In literary terms, we can imagine encountering a story written by no one we know, a story that has invited no critical attention.

But Percy also singles out a particular form of spoiling:

> It is the mistaking of an idea, a principle, an abstraction, for the real. As a consequence of the shift, the "specimen" is seen as less real than the theory of the specimen. As Kierkegaard said, once a person is seen as a specimen of a race or a species, at that very moment he ceases to be an individual. Then there are no more individuals but only specimens.
>
> (58)

As Percy explains earlier, "marvels" and "mystery" populate the world, but theory replaces particular and concrete instances with abstractions and ideals: "The phrase *specimen of* expresses in the most succinct way imaginable the radical character of the loss of being which has occurred under his very nose" (59). In other words, the moment we declare that James Joyce's "Araby" (1914) exemplifies a *Bildungsroman*, Virginia Woolf's *To the Lighthouse* (1927) represents a stream of consciousness narrative, or Harriet Jacobs' *Incidents in the Life of a Slave Girl* (1861) epitomizes a slave narrative, we have transformed the individual text into a mere specimen, and in the process, an abstraction, an idealized version, has usurped the original text.

Sovereignty/sovereign individual

"Sovereignty" refers to the power to act independently and without interference because a sovereign is the supreme power or authority. Therefore, when Percy writes that "these very means operate to remove the thing from the sovereignty of the knower" (62) or "What has taken place is a radical loss of sovereignty" (54), Percy is saying that the reader, viewer, tourist, listener, or patron of the arts is not acting independently. They are mere "consumers" who have surrendered their power to an authority and who submit to experiences that the "expert and planner" have prepared for them. In contrast to the consumer, the "sovereign knower confronts the thing to be known" (47), without any intermediary, without any preconceived notions, or at least on their own terms.

Are we doomed to be consumers? No. Percy offers a few solutions that are rooted in the idea of subverting the planner's efforts: "leaving the beaten track" (48), immersing oneself in total familiarity, encountering accidents or disasters, decontextualizing, exerting great effort, or learning from a teacher who, following Socrates' tradition, will step outside the system and serve as a midwife and tease out the sovereign knower's latent ideas or help the student become a sovereign knower. Admittedly, Percy often faults teachers for spoiling a student's experience, but his celebration of "the maieutic role of Socrates" (63) suggests that intermediaries are not the problem as much as the role they serve.

POTENTIAL PROJECTS

Percy's argument has two main points: Symbolic packages in various forms deprive us of our authority as sovereign knowers, and we need to work to recover what is lost. Admittedly, Percy seems to have too much faith in our ability to have an authentic experience that allows us to restore, without mediating influences, the "thing itself." And no doubt, there are degrees of sovereignty, not a simple choice between becoming a sovereign knower or a consumer. Nevertheless, the insight that we encounter symbolic packages and paratexts that often include editors, teachers, biographies, book covers, prefaces, trailers, rating systems, awards, theories, assignments, among other seemingly endless forms of filters, frames, and lenses, long before we encounter the poem, music, or painting, encourages us to explore the specific methods and effects of these symbolic packages. Consider these projects and questions:

Redirect your focus

Instead of focusing on a particular poem, story, or play, direct your attention to the effects of the "packaging" that surrounds those works. In other words, don't make sense of Jane Austen's *Pride and Prejudice* (1813). Instead, pay attention to the book cover, the advertising blurbs, editorial footnotes, and introduction that precede the novel. Or, compare and contrast, say, how Penguin Books, Dover Thrift Editions, or Amazon Digital Editions transform readers into "consumers of a prepared experience." Plus, how might book reviews ask us to surrender our sovereignty, predisposing us to notice particular aspects of style or content?

Phrased differently, follow Percy's lead by exploring how the symbolic packaging takes away readers' sovereignty. Explain, perhaps, how the package "spoils" the text by turning a reader into a "consumer of a prepared experience." Discuss how the paratexts shape readers' perceptions, interpretations, and attitude. You may want to draw attention to what the symbolic packaging neglects. What would readers miss by submitting to the "expert and the planner"? What interpretations does the symbolic complex deny us? This path requires that you understand the text well enough to know what the "experts and planners" ignore.

Extend the insight

Instead of focusing on literature, consider the "symbolic packages" that surround a painting in a museum, a new film, a national park, an exhibit, or a song. As with the project described above, you need to explain how the packaging shapes our experience of the text, object, image, site, or experience. Note the particular way the symbolic packaging reduces what we see to a mere specimen, a mere example of an abstract principle, theory, concept, or movement. In other words, how does the symbolic package remove an object's uniqueness and mystery, becoming merely "an example of" some abstract category?

Evaluate pedagogies

Use Percy's essay to discuss the gains and limitations of specific teaching styles. On the one hand, you can explain how particular ways of teaching merely function as symbolic packages that come between students and a sovereign relationship with the subject matter. Describe how particular pedagogies transform students into "consumers of prepared experiences." On the other hand, Percy celebrates the "maieutic role of Socrates" which suggests that some pedagogies are more effective than others. Your task, then, is to explain how a particular teaching style can "help the student come to himself not as a consumer of experience but as a sovereign individual" (63). In other words, what techniques do "sovereignty-stealing" teachers use, and what techniques do "sovereignty-restoring" teachers use?

WORKS CITED

Lauter, Paul, general editor. *Heath Anthology of American Literature: Volume A*, 7th ed., Wadsworth, 2014.
Maclean, Marie. "Pretexts and Paratexts: The Art of the Peripheral." *New Literary History*, vol. 22, no. 2, 1991, pp. 273–279.
Percy, Walker. *The Message in the Bottle: How Queer Man Is, How Queer Language Is, and What One Has to Do with the Other*. Farrar, 1975.

CHAPTER 25

Resisting the dominant culture

> Autoethnography, transculturation, critique, collaboration, bilingualism, mediation, parody, denunciation, imaginary dialogue, vernacular expression—these are some of the literate arts of the contact zone.
>
> (Mary Louise Pratt 37)

PROBLEMS, PUZZLES, AND QUESTIONS

Based on the fiction of Sherman Alexie, the 1998 film *Smoke Signals*, directed by Chris Eyre, portrays Thomas Builds-the-Fire and Victor, Coeur d'Alene Native Americans, trying to hitch a ride with two young native women, Velma and Lucy. Velma asks, "Need a ride?" then follows up with, "What are you going to trade for it? Remember... We're Indians; we barter." Thomas trades a story for a ride, and after Thomas finishes his dramatic narrative that blurs truth and fiction, Lucy asks, "So whaddya think?" Velma replies, "Well, I think it's a fine example of the oral tradition." They laugh and make room for Victor and Thomas. How do we make sense of this exchange? What is the effect when Native American characters echo the academic discourse anthropologists, historians, and literary theorists use to describe Native culture?

William Apess was born in 1798 in Massachusetts to a mother who may have been a slave and a father who descended from Pequot Indians. In "An Indian's Looking-Glass for the White Man," a chapter in a life history published around 1833, Apess critiques the mistreatment Indians endure. Like many essays written by Native Americans, Apess' work points out Anglo-European hypocrisy, especially the failure to act on Christian principles as they brutalize Native Americans. His rhetoric is worthy of attention. He points out that the settlers' principles are only "skin deep." He poses many questions:

> Now let me ask you, white man, if it is a disgrace for to eat, drink, and sleep with the images of God, or sit, or walk and talk with them. Or have you the folly to think that the white man, being one in fifteen or sixteen, are the only beloved images of God?
>
> (97)

"Now, if they who teach are not essentially affected with pure love, the love of God, how can they teach as they ought?" (98). "Did you ever hear or read of Christ teaching his disciples that they ought to despise one because his skin was different from theirs?" (98). One of the most interesting strategies is a kind of identity reversal:

> Jesus Christ being a Jew, and those of his Apostles certainly were not whites—and did not he who completed the plan of salvation complete it for the whites as well as for the Jews, and others? And were not the whites the most degraded people on the earth at that time? And none were more so, for they sacrificed their children to dumb idols!
>
> (98)

Invoking biblical language, Apess draws attention to the ethnicity of Jesus and his apostles while recoding whites as godless uncivilized heathens.

Finally, consider the "History of the Miraculous Apparition of the Virgin of Guadalupe." Initially, an oral narrative told around 1531, the story describes how the lowly Indian Juan Diego encounters the Virgin Mary who asks him to send a message to the Spanish bishop, telling him to build a church honoring her. What is noteworthy is the particular way the story merges cultures. The Virgin identifies with the colonized group: "Am I not of your kind?" (47). An image of the Virgin appears on Diego's mantle which is made of *ayate*, a "course fabric made of cactus fibre, rather like homespun" (51). The location of the future church is a hilltop covered in *"thorns, cactuses, caves and mezquites"* (50), traditionally a ritual site associated with a female fertility goddess Tonantzin.

What we should notice in these examples is the particular way the marginalized use the language, values, and cultural codes of the colonizer. The colonized have apparently adopted the invader's language and beliefs, even their sacred texts, but not completely. Lucy and Velma sound like university professors, William Apess speaks like a well-seasoned Christian minister, and the Virgin Mary is a brown Indian fertility goddess. What is going on here?

KEY PASSAGES

We often think of "community" as a close-knit group. Members know each other, and they even identify with each other. Whether it is a church congregation or a nation-state, we feel like we are part of the same group. Mary Louise Pratt explains that "languages [are] seen as living in 'speech communities,' and these tended to be theorized as discrete, self-defined, coherent entities, held together by a homogeneous competence or grammar shared identically and equally among all the members" (37). We often think that "principles of cooperation and shared understanding are normally in effect" (38). In other words, we assume we are all friends playing the same game and obeying the same rules. Pratt reminds us, however, that groups, especially groups that come from different classes and cultures, may not be playing the same game or striving to achieve the same goals. As a result, Pratt points out, when we study the failure to communicate, we fault the ruler breaker: "usually only legitimate moves are actually named as part of the system, where legitimacy is defined from the point of view of the party in authority" (38). In fact, these rule-breaking moves, or uses of language that do not conform to the established grammar, become invisible or incomprehensible. They do not count.

And herein lies our interest. How do we make sense of texts that lie outside of convention, outside of assumed language rules? How do we reclaim what Pratt describes as "miscomprehension, incomprehension, dead letters, unread masterpieces, absolute heterogeneity of meaning" (37)? Pratt offers us several useful insights we can use to answer these questions:

> I use this term [contact zone] to refer to social spaces where cultures meet, clash, and grapple with each other, often in contexts of highly asymmetrical relations of power, such as colonialism, slavery, or their aftermaths as they are lived out in many parts of the world today.
>
> (34)

> Guaman Poma's *New Chronicle* is an instance of what I have proposed to call an autoethnographic text, by which I mean a text in which people undertake to describe themselves in ways that engage with representations others have made of them. Thus, if ethnographic texts are those in which European metropolitan subjects represent to themselves their others (usually their conquered others) autoethnographic texts are representations that the so-defined others construct in response to or in dialogue with those texts.
>
> (35)
>
> Ethnographers have used the term *transculturation* to describe processes whereby members of subordinated or marginal groups select and invent from materials transmitted by a dominant or metropolitan culture.... While subordinate peoples do not usually control what emanates from the dominant culture, they do determine to varying extents what gets absorbed into their own and what it gets used for. Transculturation, like autoethnography, is a phenomenon of the contact zone.
>
> (36)

Contact zones, autoethnography, and transculturation—how are these terms connected, and how do they help us understand how marginalized groups resist those in positions of power and authority?

DISCUSSION

Pratt originally read her essay as a keynote speaker at the Modern Language Association's literacy conference in 1990, a time when interest in colonized and marginalized groups was exploding thanks to seminal works by Franz Fanon in the 1960s and Edward Said's *Orientalism* in 1978, among other scholarly contributions. A revised version of this essay became the introduction to her book *Imperial Eyes: Studies in Travel Writing and Transculturation* (1992). Pratt is particularly interested in 18th- and 19th-century travel writing and the ways in which Europeans represent the "other" that they encounter, but she is equally interested in how these "newly discovered" groups respond. Of course, Pratt's project is part of the larger interest in colonial and postcolonial studies which focus on the interaction between colonists and indigenous groups. Pratt encourages us to ask, "How do colonized and marginalized groups respond to their invaders and oppressors?" Let's return to those passages.

First, Pratt uses the term "contact zone" to complicate the traditional notion of "community." Instead of thinking of group members as similar, equal, and friendly, Pratt encourages us to focus on the moments when people may share the same space but disagree, largely because members do not share the same levels of power, authority, and status. She draws our attention to slavery and colonialism, but her essay reminds us that an elementary school pupil also enters a contact zone. In fact, all of us enter contact zones every day, sometimes from a position of privilege and sometimes as a subordinate. She maintains that a contact perspective reminds us that we form our identities by how we define our relations to others. In other words, encountering others shapes, even forms, our identity because we notice differences, and those differences matter when it comes to explaining ourselves to ourselves. To be us, we need others who are not us.

Second, although she lists many "arts" or strategies disenfranchised group members may use (critique, collaboration, bilingualism, mediation, parody, denunciation, imaginary dialogue, vernacular expression) to gain power, authority, and status, two strategies are especially useful: autoethnography and transculturation.

Pratt refers to Guaman Poma's *New Chronicle*, a verbal-visual text written between 1600 and 1615 by the Andean Guaman Poma, as an "autoethnography." The "auto" of "autoethnography" refers to the "self" and "ethnography" refers to the act of describing another's culture. Therefore, an "autoethnographic" text is a kind of self-study. What is important, however, is that group members produce these self-studies in order to respond to "representations others have made of them" (35). In other words, authors are keenly aware that someone else has portrayed them to others, tried to make sense of them, most likely in their own language and frame of reference. As Pratt notes, the Europeans produced ethnographies whose purpose is to "represent to themselves their others" (35). We could think of an "autoethnographic text" then, as part of a conversation, a dialogue that seeks to engage, even correct, those ethnographies that the invaders created. Above all, writers do not produce autoethnographies just for themselves; they produce them for those in positions of power and authority. As a result, they involve "a selective collaboration" (35) with those in authority. For example, sent to King Philip III of Spain, Guaman Poma's *New Chronicle* critiques colonial rule and offers an alternative to direct Spanish governance. There are traces of multiple languages and frames of reference used by groups involved in the contact zone, thus producing a kind of hybrid text that may confuse readers.

An autoethnography is related to the process of "transculturation" which is one way to describe these hybrid texts. When Pratt writes that transculturation describes "processes whereby members of subordinated or marginal groups select and invent from materials transmitted by a dominant or metropolitan culture" (36), she maintains that those groups have a degree of agency, an ability to choose, redefine, and recode cultural practices, languages, values, and beliefs colonizers have imposed. In other words, group members can use the "master's tools" to dismantle the master's house. The traditional example is Caliban from Shakespeare's *The Tempest*. Miranda addresses Caliban, a slave, and declares, "One thing or other. When thou didst not, savage, / Know thine own meaning, but wouldst gabble like / A thing most brutish, I endow'd thy purposes / With words that made them known" (1.2.356–59). But Caliban replies: "You taught me language, and my profit on't / Is, I know how to curse. / The red-plague rid you / For learning me your language!" (1.2.363–65). We see how Caliban, a subordinated and marginalized member of the group, is able to "select and invent from the materials transmitted by a dominate or metropolitan culture" (36) to critique the colonial power. Caliban uses language Miranda taught him to curse Prospero and Miranda.

If we return to the key question, "How do we make sense of texts that lie outside of convention, outside of the assumed language rules?" we can answer by exploring the ways these texts respond to and subvert "authorized" genres, languages, cultural practices, and values by engaging in autoethnography and transculturation.

POTENTIAL PROJECTS

Choose a work by a writer who belongs to a marginalized, disenfranchised, or colonized group, not merely a sympathizer or advocate of that group. This writer, filmmaker, or artist may be from a historically marginalized ethnic group, or the writer identifies with a minority group defined by gender, class, sexuality, religion, age, disability, geography, or education level, among all the many sources of discrimination. Once you have an appropriate text in mind, consider these projects and questions:

Redefine a text as autoethnography/transculturation

Embrace Pratt's premise that your chosen author, filmmaker, or artist is part of a contact zone, and as a result, she engages with other groups who are more powerful and dominant. She does not share the same levels of power, authority, privilege, and status. Help us understand this socioeconomic context. Using *Smoke Signals* as an example, I would not only recount the fraught history between Native and non-native groups, but I would also describe the contemporary relationship between the Coeur d'Alene tribe and the federal government. I would also explain that the non-natives have produced "ethnographies" of the subordinate group, and these representations may take the form of narratives in print, on the screen, or on the web. For example, I may describe what historians, anthropologists, and literary critics have said about Native populations, but I would also reference how films, TV shows, advertisements, toy makers, Halloween costume designers, and artists have portrayed Native Americans, often as noble savages, conquered rebels, a vanished group, or as alcoholic poor people living on god-forsaken reservations.

The next step, the core of the analysis, is to explain how the text's creator crafts an "autoethnography" to respond to the dominant group's representations and/or engages in transculturation. You need to identify the various ways the writer responds to or engages representations others have made of that group and explore how the writer "constructs his text by appropriating and adapting pieces of the representational repertoire of the invaders" (36) or dominant group. This "representational repertoire" refers to not only language, but also value systems, customs, structures, genres, cultural codes, social practices, images, or figures. How does the marginalized writer appropriate the imposed language and value system to respond to resist, reverse, critique, or mock those who colonize, oppress, marginalize, or disenfranchise? For example, my brief discussions of "History of the Miraculous Apparition of the Virgin of Guadalupe" and William Apess' narrative suggest how writers appropriate a Christian framework that soldiers, missionaries, and settlers imposed, but then recode that framework in ways that reference these representations and images, then ridicules, subverts, and reverses them. They are able to "select and invent from the materials" they have received. Juan Diego uses those materials to transform the Virgin Mary into a fellow Indian while Apess recasts white settlers as sinners who need redemption from a brown Jesus.

Extend the insight

Pratt focuses on colonized groups, but she also describes her son's elementary school experience in terms of a contact zone. You can follow her lead and explore any situation or context "when speakers are from different classes or cultures, or one party is exercising authority and another is submitting to it or questioning it" (38). Situations may include classrooms, bureaucratic institutions, businesses, sport organizations, government agencies, in short, any relationship that involves an uneven balance in power and privilege. Your task is to discuss how the subordinate groups produce autoethnographies or engage in forms of transculturation to respond to and resist powerful groups or individuals. How do these autoethnographies respond to representations others have made of them, and how do they reappropriate, recode, and subvert texts, institutions, and value systems imposed upon them?

WORKS CITED

Apess, William. "An Indian's Looking Glass for the White Man." *A Son of the Forest and Other Writings by William Apess, a Pequot*, edited by Barry O'Connell, U of Massachusetts P, 1997, pp. 155–161.

Lazo de la Vega, Luis. "The Miraculous Apparition of the Beloved Virgin Mary, Our Lady of Guadalupe, at Tepeyacac, near Mexico City." *The Dark Virgin: The Book of Our Lady of Guadalupe*, edited by Donald Demarest and Coley Taylor, Coley Taylor, 1956, pp. 39–53.

Pratt, Mary Louise. "Arts of the Contact Zone." *Profession*, 1991, pp. 33–40.

Shakespeare, William. *The Tempest. The Riverside Shakespeare*, 2nd ed., Houghton, 1997.

Smoke Signals. Directed by Chris Eyre, Miramax, 1998.

CHAPTER 26

Adapting and appropriating

> Adaptation is, however, frequently a highly specific process involving the transition from one genre to another.
>
> (Julie Sanders 24)

PROBLEMS, PUZZLES, AND QUESTIONS

Nathaniel Hawthorne's "Rappaccini's Daughter" (1844) describes an old scientist who creates an enclosed garden tended by his daughter Beatrice who eventually meets a young man named Giovanni Guasconti. Dr. Rappaccini has transformed the garden into a toxic playground, for every plant and drop of water is poisonous. Rappaccini's nemesis Professor Pietro Baglioni provides an antidote for the young couple, but instead of becoming healthy, Beatrice dies. The knowing reader will recognize the Garden of Eden plot, but the tale recodes the roles. The malicious scientist Rappaccini stands in for God. Beatrice is more Adam than Eve, and Baglioni undermines Rappaccini's project, but with a desire to help the two lovers rather than destroy them. Hawthorne adapts the Genesis creation story, but to what end? What is the role of adaptations and appropriations? Hawthorne's version does not faithfully reproduce the original story (which is, in fact, an adaptation of an even older creation myth), but is that a strength or a weakness? Should adaptations respect originals in theme even as they alter the form, or do they serve a different purpose?

In its prime, *The Simpsons* adapted and appropriated cultural texts so often that fans created websites that identified the countless references, from an iconic Stanley Kubrick framing of Maggie sporting Alex DeLarge's eyelashes, hat, and cane from *A Clockwork Orange*, a graphic match of a drain cross-dissolving into Homer's eye as we see in *Psycho*, and Bart and Milhouse dancing like Gene Kelly and Frank Sinatra in *On The Town*, to "archival footage" of *Steamboat Itchy*, Abe and Mrs. Bouvier sitting in the back of the bus as Benjamin and Elaine do in *The Graduate*, and Mr. Burns' lamenting a lost bear reminiscent of young Kane's forgotten sled in Orson Welles' *Citizen Kane*. No doubt we experience a degree of pleasure when we recognize the images, but how might these appropriations actually undermine the textual authority of their precursors, especially when viewers encounter *The Simpsons* long before they ever encounter the originals? Does this reversal signal a new relationship based on networks and webs rather than linear sequence? Can the adaptation usurp the precursor?

In March 2017, the Whitney Museum displayed "Open Casket," a rather abstract painting of Emmett Till who was lynched in 1955. Controversy followed, but the disagreement had less to do with the image than the artist, Dana Schutz, a white woman who based her painting on photographs of Emmett published in *Jet* magazine and *The Chicago Defender*. As reported by Randy Kennedy of the *New York Times*, protesters insisted that the museum remove and destroy the painting. Hannah Black, for example, insists that "The subject matter is not Schutz's." She adds, "I feel like she doesn't have the privilege to speak for black people as a whole or for Emmett Till's family." Schutz responds by insisting that

> I don't know what it is like to be black in America but I do know what it is like to be a mother. Emmett was Mamie Till's only son. The thought of anything happening to your child is beyond comprehension. Their pain is your pain. My engagement with this image was through empathy with his mother.

The argument poses a number of questions: Are adaptations or appropriations neutral? Are there limits to what we can adapt or appropriate? Are there multiple ways to lay claim to or identify with a source text? Do some groups have more of a right to a precursor or original than others?

These questions prompt us to ask about the role, purpose, originality, authorship, and value of adaptations and appropriations, and we can also ask if *The Simpsons*, "Rappaccini's Daughter," or "Open Casket" actually differ from every other kind of literary work or cultural representation, for are not all texts and works of art acts of rewriting and revision, products of intertextuality, transtextuality, and transgeneric practices?

KEY PASSAGES

Adaptations invite us to compare texts, tempting us to ask if an adaptation is "faithful" to the original. For example, despite the relocation in time, place, and culture, does Baz Luhrmann's film *Romeo + Juliet* (1996) accurately capture in theme and form what Shakespeare's play initially expressed? Following the lead of many other scholars, Julie Sanders' *Adaptation and Appropriation* (2006) reminds us that fidelity is the wrong question to ask for a number of reasons. Fidelity is not even possible. Forms differ in strength and weakness, tools, techniques, and resources for expression. We cannot even agree on what constitutes the "essential" theme and form. Instead of offering moralistic judgments, Sanders encourages us to rethink the value and purpose of adaptations, for "it is at the very point of infidelity or departure that the most creative acts of adaptation take place" (24). Her celebration of difference and contrast pushes us into more interesting territory, for betrayal sparks our attention more than fidelity. She prompts us to ask different questions, particularly about the "specific impulses and ideologies, personal and historical, at play in various adaptations" (23), and that is where we now focus our attention.

> Adaptation is, however, frequently a highly specific process involving the transition from one genre to another: novels into film; drama into musical; the dramatization of prose narrative and prose fiction; or the inverse movement of making drama into prose narrative. It can also involve the making of computer games or graphic novels or be dispersed into modes such as music or dance.
>
> (24)
>
> We can easily continue the linguistic riff, adding into the mix: variation, version, interpretation, imitation, proximation, supplement, increment, improvisation, prequel, sequel, continuation, afterlife, addition, paratext, hypertext, palimpsest, graft, rewriting, reworking, refashioning, re-vision, re-evaluation. And new digital cultures and technologies have further expanded the lexicon with concepts such as remediation and specific concepts such as the mash-up, remix, hack, and sample.
>
> (5)

> Adaptation studies throws up a rich lexicon of terms: version, variation, interpretation, continuation, transformation, imitation, pastiche, parody, forgery, travesty, transposition, revaluation, revision, rewriting, echo.
>
> (22)
>
> Adaptation can be a transpositional practice, casting a specific genre into another generic mode, an act of re-vision in itself. It can parallel editorial practice in some respects, indulging in the exercise of trimming and pruning: yet it can also be an amplificatory procedure engaged in addition, expansion, accretion and interpolation.... Adaptation is nevertheless frequently involved in offering commentary on a source text. This is achieved most often by offering a revised point of view from the "original," adding hypothetical motivation or voicing what the text silences or marginalizes. Yet adaptation can also continue a simpler attempt to make texts "relevant" or easily comprehensible to new audiences and readerships via the processes of proximation and updating. This might, for example, be aimed at engaging with youth audiences or, through translation in its broadest sense, linguistic and interpretative, in global, intercultural contexts.
>
> (22–23)
>
> Appropriation carries out the same sustained engagement of adaptation but frequently adopts a posture of critique, overt commentary and even sometimes assault or attack.
>
> (6)
>
> In appropriations the intertextual relationship may be less explicit, more embedded, but what is often inescapable is the fact that a political or ethical commitment shapes a writer's, director's or performer's decision to reinterpret a source text.
>
> (3)

Adaptation is familiar territory, and even the specialized terms pose few problems. However, there are nuances to discuss, and the subtle differences encourage us to think more critically as we compare and contrast adaptations and their source texts.

DISCUSSION

Sanders writes that adaptation involves "the transition from one genre to another" (24), but she is really referring to forms and modes, not genre in the narrow sense. Yes, novels and plays become films, and presidential debates become comic sketches, but sometimes the changes are even more dramatic. As Sanders points out, written texts become computer games, songs, and dances, or even *Disney on Ice*. Images and poems inspire each other as well. William Carlos Williams transforms Bruegel the Elder's painting "Landscape with the Fall of Icarus" into poetry, and Williams' poem "The Great Figure" prompts Charles Demuth to render "I Saw the Figure 5 in Gold" in paint. We may benefit by thinking of "transition" as "translation in its broadest sense, linguistic and interpretive" (23). When we adapt a text, we first interpret or make sense of the source text, then we translate it into a different language and value system. What we might gain in clarity, we may lose in beauty. What we lose in simplicity, we gain in nuance.

Why adapt? Why not create something new, or at least choose not to foreground the explicit relationship with other texts? Sanders catalogs a few purposes and methods. Adaptations may recontextualize older narratives to make them more relevant and understandable to contemporary audiences. Relocating a story can also comment on specific events, thus serving as an interpreter or critic. Adaptations trim and prune or add and expand. They can change point of view, add new points of view, and fill in gaps, silences, and repressed voices and identities. Adaptations may pay respectful homage, or destabilize, undermine, or parody the authority and cultural power of a source text. Sanders sympathetically cites Adrienne Rich and her notion of revision: "We need to know the writing of the past and know it differently than we have ever known it; not to pass on tradition but to break its hold over us" (qtd. in Sanders 12). In short, adaptations can perpetuate the values, hierarchies, and aesthetics of the source text, or they can break the spell and offer a counter-interpretation and help us see the original anew.

The long list of terms Sanders provides to discuss adaption, from *variation*, *version*, and *proximation* to *revision*, *rewriting*, and *echo* shed additional light on adaptation's various relationships and purposes. Each term offers an implicit theory that defines an adaptation's purpose and relationship a work may have with its precursor. For example, calling an adaptation an "interpretation" suggests a desire to decipher, clarify, and search for meaning in the source text. A "palimpsest" portrays an adaptation as a trace of barely visible previous texts, layers of partially erased memory. A "graft" suggests a new offshoot that derives its nourishment from the original. A "parody" implies a mocking imitation with an eye on reform. "Sampling" recontextualizes and recodes parts of preexisting work. A "forgery" implies a deceptive imitation. In other words, adaptation serves as an umbrella term for different relationships and goals. It matters a great deal whether we say that a film or painting is a "supplement," "improvisation," or "mash-up" because the terms contain a set of assumptions about an adaptation's relationship with the source text. The various terms are not synonyms. Instead, they offer a nuanced understanding of the adaptation's form and goal.

Sanders acknowledges that appropriation is a form of adaptation, but why does she differentiate between the two? Although Sanders always moderates her claims, evident in words like "tend," "often," "may," and "frequently," she maintains that appropriation adopts a critical edge, "a posture of critique, overt commentary and even sometimes assault or attack" (6). This attention to appropriation's subversive potential (without denying that "mere" adaptions can subvert as well) is particularly useful when we discuss groups that differ in hierarchies and power. However, as an act of borrowing without the owner's permission, appropriation cuts both ways. Groups in power may appropriate, repurpose, and exploit an oppressed or colonized culture's identity, customs, practices, and aesthetics, but marginalized groups can appropriate imposed narratives, customs, values, languages, and practices as a way to respond to and critique those in power. In short, in terms of power dynamics, appropriation can "punch up" or "punch down," so we should be attentive to the consequences and politics of this cultural poaching because "a political or ethical commitment shapes a writer's, director's or performer's decision to reinterpret a source text" (3). Recontextualizing a precursor is not a neutral act because redefining the relationship between texts signals a desire to address relations of power.

We often think of adaptations as derivative, a kind of parasite on the original. That is unfortunate. Instead, adaptations are creative works in their own right, and they differ little from other cultural representations because all cultural representations and practices respond to and build upon precursors. The difference is that adaptations and appropriations foreground that relationship. As Sanders explains, "these are not belated and unoriginal practices but rather vitally creative ones, ones that provide new cultural content in an increasingly diverse range of contexts and communities" (212).

POTENTIAL PROJECTS

While all texts and cultural practices are intertextual in that they "invoke and rework other texts in a rich and ever-evolving cultural mosaic" (21), adaptations draw attention to their source text in a more open and self-conscious way. Remember as well that our goal is not to pass judgment on an adaptation's faithfulness to the original. Instead, we search for differences and interrogate their effects. As we often ask in this textbook, "What does the adaptation do, and how does it do what it does?"

Identify the effect, purpose, or result

With an eye on an adaptation and its source texts, explore roles and effects. Does the adaptation recontextualize the narrative in time and place, and if so, to what end? For example, what is the significance of recasting Othello as a tier-one basketball player on a college campus who falls for the dean's daughter? For Sanders, "by exploring contemporary US issues via the filtering lens of a Shakespearean tragedy," Blake Nelson's *O* "exposes the class rivalries and racism embedded in the US education system" (65). What is the result of re-situating Joseph Conrad's *Heart of Darkness* (1899) during the Vietnam War in *Apocalypse Now* (1979)? Perhaps Francis Ford Coppola uses Conrad's narrative to frame the war as a descent into barbarity and madness. And what is the significance of Jane Smiley relocating *King Lear* to an Iowa farm in *A Thousand Acres* (1991)?

Or, does the adaptation comment on, clarify, or interpret the source text? For example, Tim Burton's *Charlie and the Chocolate Factory* (2005) addresses Willy Wonka's prehistory in an attempt to root Willy's eccentricities in a flawed father-son relationship. Consider other questions as well: Does the adaptation pay homage to precursors as we see in the respectful remakes of John Steinbeck's *The Grapes of Wrath* (1939) or parody the authority and cultural power of J.R.R. Tolkien's *The Hobbit* (1937), as we read in A.R.R.R. Roberts' *The Soddit or Let's Cash in Again* (2003). Or, does the adaptation critique the original, evident in Alice Randall's *The Wind Done Gone* (2001) and Jean Rhys' *Wide Sargasso Sea* (1966)? Or, does the adaptation extend and amplify the narrative? For example, Sanders points out that Patricia Rozema's film *Mansfield Park* (1999) draws attention to British colonialism and slavery, elements that Jane Austen largely hides in the novel. What is the effect or purpose of this addition? In short, when reading and watching adaptations, identify what the work adds, deletes, and modifies, and always ask, "To what end? What is the effect, purpose, or result?"

Recognize relationships and purpose

Adaptation is always about relationships among texts, and Sanders' catalog of terms encourages more nuanced analysis when we describe these relationships: variation, version, interpretation, imitation, proximation, supplement, increment, improvisation, prequel, sequel, continuation, afterlife, addition, paratext, hypertext, palimpsest, graft, rewriting, reworking, refashioning, revision, re-evaluation, remediation, mash-up, remix, hack and sample, transformation, pastiche, parody, forgery, travesty, transposition, revaluation, revision, and echo.

Instead of talking in terms of "adaptation," identify the text's specific relationship with its source text by choosing one of those terms. Then, theorize what the term implies, and use the definition to describe the text's form and purpose. How does the term help us understand the adaptation in a new way? What do we learn about an adaptation's form, purpose, and politics by calling, say, the musical *Les Misérables* (1980) an echo instead of a supplement, improvisation, version, or a mere adaptation? What do we learn about *Blade Runner 2049* (2017) by claiming it is a palimpsest or graft instead of a sequel?

Examine acts of appropriation

No doubt acts of appropriation can exploit an oppressed or colonized culture's customs, practices, and aesthetics, from Picasso's Africanized prostitutes in *Les Demoiselles d'Avignon* (1907) to sexy Pocahontas Halloween costumes. However, for this project, we will follow Sanders' lead and insist that, as a form of adaptation, appropriation embraces a "political or ethical commitment" (3) that adopts "a posture of critique, overt commentary and even sometimes assault or attack" (6). Therefore, explore how a text appropriates another text or parts of another text, and identify the effect, purpose, and consequences. Does the appropriation subvert the values, hierarchies, and social relationships of the source text? Does the work destabilize the authority of the original or undermine common assumptions and values? And in every case, ask, "How so?" What are the devices and strategies that the appropriation uses to critique a source text?

For example, what is the significance of Barbara Kruger's collages that appropriate black and white images and add text? We see an image of a little girl looking at a boy flex his bicep, but the words "We don't need another hero" is superimposed on the image. In "latero story" (1988), what does Puerto Rican-American poet Tato Laviera gain by appropriating the narrative of the American Dream and the self-made entrepreneur to describe how a "twentieth-century welfare recipient" grows rich picking up the trash produced by Americans addicted to consumerism and other pathologies? Or, what is the significance of an anonymous poet writing soon after the American Revolution who uses the tune of "God Save America," already an appropriation of "God Save the King," for her poem-song "Rights of Women" (1795) that begins, "God save each Female's right, / Show to her ravish'd sight / Woman is Free" (1–3)? In short, identify the ways that writers, filmmakers, and artists selectively borrow and repurpose texts or parts of texts as a way to serve a larger "political or ethical commitment" (Sanders 3).

WORKS CITED

Anonymous. "Rights of Women." *The Heath Anthology of American Literature. Volume A*, 7th ed., edited by Paul Lauter, Wadsworth, 2014, pp. 1163–1165.

Kennedy, Randy. "White Artist's Painting of Emmett Till at Whitney Biennial Draws Protests." *The New York Times*, www.nytimes.com/2017/03/21/arts/design/painting-of-emmett-till-at-whitney-biennial-draws-protests.html. Accessed 20 January 2018.

Laviera, Tato. "Latero Story." *Bendición: The Complete Poetry of Tato Laviera*, Arte Público, 2014, pp. 141–142.

Sanders, Julie. *Adaptation and Appropriation*. Routledge, 2006.

CHAPTER 27

Describing homosocial relationships

'Homosocial desire,' to begin with, is a kind of oxymoron.

(Eve Sedgwick 1)

PROBLEMS, PUZZLES, AND QUESTIONS

In a 1989 Levi Strauss ad, we see an old blue pickup truck ambling down a country road, eventually stopping to help a stranded couple whose car broke down. We hear the Ronettes sing "Be My Baby" as a rugged country beau, clad in a red bandana and blue denim jacket and jeans, twists open the radiator cap as the other man—part boyfriend and part father—can only stand idly by as radiator fluid soaks his shoes. We then watch the good Samaritan slowly pull his pants off, showing off his bright white underwear. He ties his pants to truck and car, mimicking the iconic Levi jeans stretched between two horses, then motions for the woman to join him. As they drive up the hill, shifting into second gear dislodges his bumper, freeing himself of the other driver and his disabled car. The words "Separates the Men from the Boys" is superimposed on the screen. The men are clearly rivals, but what role does the woman play? Does she express her own sexual desires by abandoning her date? Is she a prize the loser passes onto the winner? Or, does she indirectly help the men bond? And what does, in fact, separate the men from the boys?

First published in the *South-Carolina Gazette* in 1743, "Verses Written by a Young Lady, on Women Born to be Controll'd" declares, "How wretched is a woman's fate, / No happy change her fortune knows, / Subject to man in every state. / How can she then be free from woes?" (1–4). The poem catalogs the problems: "In youth a father's stern command, / And jealous eyes control her will; / A lordly brother watchful stands, / To keep her closer captive still. / The tyrant husband next appears, / With awful and contracted brow" (5–10). What role does the woman play as father and brother pass her to "tyrant husband"? Can the woman escape this patriarchal chain?

Starved for attention, poets describe tender moments in the trenches of WWI. In "Louse Hunting," Isaac Rosenberg describes soldiers, "Nudes—stark aglisten," who pick lice from their fellow soldiers: "Dug in supreme flesh / To smutch the supreme littleness" (19–20). Rupert Brooke's "Fragment" draws attention to the body's beauty: "Pride in their strength and in the weight and firmness / And link'd beauty of bodies, and pity that / This gay machine of splendour 'ld soon be broken" (9–11). In "Casualty," Robert Nichols' persona addresses a fellow soldier: "My comrade that you could rest / Your tired body on mine" (10–11). He stresses the life-saving relationship: "That your body might drink / Warmth from my body, strength from my veins, / Life from my heart that monstrously beats" (16–18). In what ways do these tender and moving passages blur the boundaries between brotherhood and eroticism? Are these expressions of deep friendship or something more? What do we learn about male desire in the context of war?

KEY PASSAGES

Eve Sedgwick published *Between Men: English Literature and Male Homosocial Desire* (1985) as part of the Gender and Culture series, edited by Carolyn Heilburn and Nancy Miller. In the Preface to the revised 1993 edition, Sedgwick explains that "I intended *Between Men* very pointedly as a complicating, antiseparatist, and antihomophobic contribution to a feminist movement" (viii), but her work helps foreground a queer turn in the way we discuss gender, sexuality, patriarchy, and desire. We find Sedgwick's insights especially useful because her discussion is as much about men's relationships with women as they are with men. What is between men? Women. Sedgwick offers an innovative way to discuss male homosocial desire, homophobia, patriarchy, and misogyny.

> "Male homosocial desire": the phrase in the title of this study is intended to mark both discriminations and paradoxes. "Homosocial desire," to begin with, is a kind of oxymoron. "Homosocial" is a word occasionally used in

history and the social sciences, where it describes social bonds between persons of the same sex; it is a neologism, obviously formed by analogy with "homosexual," and just as obviously meant to be distinguished from "homosexual." In fact, it is applied to such activities as "male bonding," which may, as in our society, be characterized by intense homophobia, fear and hatred of homosexuality.

(1)

The emerging pattern of male friendship, mentorship, entitlement, rivalry, and hetero- and homosexuality was in an intimate and shifting relation to class; and that no element of that pattern can be understood outside of its relation to women and the gender system as a whole.

(1)

In any male-dominated society, there is a special relationship between male homosocial (*including* homosexual) desire and the structures for maintaining and transmitting patriarchal power: a relationship founded on an inherent and potentially active structural congruence.

(25)

In any erotic rivalry, the bond that links the two rivals is as intense and potent as the bond that links either of the rivals to the beloved: that the bonds of "rivalry" and "love," differently as they are experienced, are equally powerful and in many senses equivalent.

(21)

Patriarchal heterosexuality can best be discussed in terms of one or another form of the traffic in women: it is the use of women as exchangeable, perhaps symbolic, property for the primary purpose of cementing the bonds of men with men.

(25–26)

For a man to be a man's man is separated only by an invisible, carefully blurred, always-already-crossed line from being "interested in men."

(89)

As Sedgwick explains, "The present study is concerned, not distinctively with homosexual experience, but with the shape of the entire male homosocial spectrum, and its effects on women" (90). What interests Sedgwick is how men use women to form bonds with each other, even though they may be rivals, lovers, siblings, role models, friends, and colleagues. She explores the fine line between homosocial relationships and heterosexuality, a tangle we will now discuss.

DISCUSSION

Desire is the key word because desire does not mark an emotion as much as an "affective or social force, the glue, even when its manifestation is hostility or hatred or something less emotively charged, that shapes an important relationship" (2). In other words, the focus of inquiry is not erotic feelings, but a particular kind of social arrangement. The argument is less about personal psychology than it is about how men and women relate to each other.

Sedgwick defines male homosocial desire, but note the paradox. On the one hand, homosocial desire describes how men seek the company of other men and promote their interests. Homosocial behavior can even include a degree of emotional intimacy and physical affection, evident, for example, in sports when men hug, slap a bum, or bump chests after a teammate scores a goal. On the other hand, homophobia marks these male bonding experiences. Men can be interested in other men, but not *too* interested. Homophobic comments police the boundaries by encouraging men to repress any homosexual desire they may have. More importantly, Sedgwick reminds us that homophobic boundary patrolling goes well beyond harassing homosexual men: "it is analytically important to remember that the domination offered by this strategy is not only over a minority population, but over the bonds that structure all social form" (87). Homophobia regulates the many by oppressing the few, but the line between homosocial and homosexual is often fuzzy and even invisible. As Sedgwick points out, being "interested in men" (89) automatically blurs the lines. The vague boundary and tension between homosocial and homosexual behavior invite us to examine that paradoxical arrangement.

Note, too, that the coding of male homosocial desire does not stay the same. Class structure shapes the pattern and social arrangement. Sedgwick reminds us, for example, that homosocial desire among ancient Greeks, organized by lines of class and age, differs from, say, Shakespearian

London and Victorian social patterns. Plus, homosocial behavior becomes meaningful only in "its relation to women and the gender system as a whole" (1). In other words, we cannot discuss homosocial behavior without talking about men's relationships with women. Why?

Sedgwick argues that "In any male-dominated society, there is a special relationship between male homosocial (*including* homosexual) desire and the structures for maintaining and transmitting patriarchal power: a relationship founded on an inherent and potentially active structural congruence" (25). In other words, patriarchy requires men to maintain social bonds with each other in order to dominate women, so it makes sense that male homosocial desire is "congruent" with patriarchy in the sense that male bonding aligns well with a social arrangement that privileges men. Sedgwick's key contribution is to suggest that women are part of male homosocial relationships.

How so? Sedgwick argues that we can understand these homosocial relationships by recognizing a triangular structure—a triangle of desire—that positions women as mediators between rival men, mentors and novices, or even fathers and sons. Heterosexual romance most often marks these rivalries, for two men vie for the same woman, or the woman is the pretext for the men to meet. The intense relationship—the social bond—between the two men is what counts. Following René Girard's work on erotic triangles, Sedgwick echoes the idea that "the choice of the beloved is determined in the first place, not by the qualities of the beloved, but by the beloved's already being the choice of the person who has been chosen as a rival" (21). In other words, we desire what others desire, and that reciprocal relationship is part of the social bond between men. The result is that men can "consolidate partnership with authoritative males in and through the bodies of females" (38), and this triangle allows men to bond with other men in the context of heterosexuality which reinforces the boundaries between being homosocial and homosexual. In short, women serve as a tool or vehicle for male bonding, and those relationships empower men while simultaneously obscuring or masking the intense homosocial relationship.

Another way to understand this relationship is to consider how Sedgwick works within theories of gender economies. Building on Gayle Rubin's work, Sedgwick explains that

> patriarchal heterosexuality can best be discussed in terms of one or another form of the traffic in women: it is the use of women as exchangeable, perhaps symbolic, property for the primary purpose of cementing the bonds of men with men.
> (25–26)

For Rubin, "if it is women who are being transacted, then it is the men who give and take them who are linked, the woman being a conduit of a relationship rather than a partner to it" ("Traffic" 174). The result is that women do not benefit, but by exchanging women, men "exchange sexual access, genealogical statuses, lineage names and ancestors, rights and *people*—men, women, and children—in concrete systems of social relationships" (177). Although Sedgwick focuses less on the actual physical exchange of women, she points out that homosocial relationships among men erase female identity even as they use women as a "conduit of a relationship" (174) that solidifies their social position.

In short, the phrase "between men" in the title of her book suggests that men develop paradoxical homosocial relationships with other men, marked by both intimacy and repulsion, and the phrase also reminds us that women serve as conduits and mediators between men as they develop beneficial relationships with other men at the expense of women.

POTENTIAL PROJECTS

Following Sedgwick's lead means we need to focus first, and foremost, on male desire, especially the particular way men develop homosocial bonds in the context of a triangular relationship with male rivals and women. As she explains, "the present study is concerned, not distinctively with homosexual experience, but with the shape of the entire male homosocial spectrum, and its effects on women" (90). We can articulate the ways cultural representations portray how male homosocial desire, homophobia, patriarchy, and misogyny relate to each other. As a result, we turn our attention to how male bonding operates within so-called heterosexual writing, as well as exploring the fuzzy line between homosocial and homosexual relationships.

Identify what is between men

First, focus on narratives that represent "male friendship, mentorship, entitlement, rivalry" (1), particularly relationships where women are involved. Countless texts come to mind, from *Star Wars*, *Hamlet*, and *Wuthering Heights* to *Harry Potter*, *Gone with the Wind*, *The Lord of the Rings*, and *The Great Gatsby*. Second, how does the story portray these relationships in ways that define male roles? How do women play a mediating role? How might they affirm heterosexuality in the face of potential homosexuality? How does the narrative allay homosexual anxiety? How does the narrative define masculinity? In short, your task is to not only examine how men respond to other men, but also pay attention to the particular way women serve as "exchangeable, perhaps symbolic, property for the primary purpose of cementing the bonds of men with men" (25–26). How do men use women to reinforce a patriarchal social order, even as men strive to subdue other men?

Interrogate boundaries

As your premise, use Sedgwick's observation that "For a man to be a man's man is separated only by an invisible, carefully blurred, always-already-crossed line from being 'interested in men'" (89). Explore how narratives play with this line. Road films, buddy films, bromances, and war films are fertile territory as you examine how men navigate the "invisible, carefully blurred, always-already-crossed line" that supposedly separates men. From *The 40-Year-Old Virgin*, *The Hangover*, and *Pulp Fiction* to Darcy and Bingley in *Pride and Prejudice*, Holmes and Watson in *Sherlock Holmes*, and Art and Arthur in *The Mysteries of Pittsburgh*, these stories portray homosocial relationships. As you examine these kinds of narratives, discuss how they both define and blur the boundaries of what it means to be "a man's man." How does a particular story reinforce "intense homophobia, fear and hatred of homosexuality" (1), even as the narrative blurs and erases that hostility by promoting male relationships and interests? Or as Sedgwick phrases it, "another phenomenon that begins to make sense in a new way is the tendency toward important correspondences and similarities between the most sanctioned forms of male-homosocial bonding, and the most reprobated expressions male homosexual sociality" (89). When do those forbidden practices appear more like homosocial expressions of solidarity, and when does masculine affection seem like homosexual desire?

Extend the insight

Build on Sedgwick's idea that a triangle of desire positions women as mediators between rival men by exploring ways that technology—guns, machines, cars, robots, computers, etc.—plays the same role as women. In other words, examine how nonhuman objects allow men to develop homosocial relationships and simultaneously preserve their masculinity and heterosexuality. Just as a man's desire for a woman may shape a rival's desire for the same woman, a man's celebration of a particular technology can bring men together. And just as "the use of women as exchangeable, perhaps symbolic, property" (25–26) cements male bonds, so, too, can a form of technology serve as a pretext for male attachment and intimacy. Similar to what we asked above, how does the story portray these relationships in ways that define male roles? Do men feminize these forms of technology? How does the role of technology allay homosexual anxiety? How do men use technology to reinforce a patriarchal social order, even as they strive to subdue another man?

WORKS CITED

Anonymous. "Verses Written by a Young Lady, on Women Born to Be Controll'd." *The Heath Anthology of American Literature*. Volume A, 7th ed., edited by Paul Lauter et al. Wadsworth, 2014, p. 858.

Brooke, Rupert. "Fragment." *The Complete Poems of Rupert Brooke*, Sidgwick & Jackson, 1932, p. 150.

Nichols, Robert. "Casualty." *Valour and Vision: Poems of the War 1914–1918*, edited by Jacqueline T. Trotter, Longman, 1920, pp. 107–108.

Rosenberg, Isaac. "Louse Hunting." *Isaac Rosenberg*, edited by Vivien Noakes, Oxford UP, 2008.

Rubin, Gayle. "The Traffic in Women: Notes on the 'Political Economy' of Sex." *Toward an Anthropology of Women*, edited by Rayna R. Reiter, Monthly Review, 1975, pp. 157–210.

Sedgwick, Eve Kosofsky. *Between Men: English Literature and Male Homosocial Desire*. Columbia UP, 1985.

CHAPTER 28

Defamiliarizing the familiar

And art exists that one may recover the sensation of life; it exists to make one feel things, to make the stone *stony*.

(Viktor Shklovsky 778)

PROBLEMS, PUZZLES, AND QUESTIONS

James Joyce's *Finnegans Wake* (1939) challenges us in ways other works do not.

> —I apologuise, Shaun began, but I would rather spinooze you one from the grimmgests of Jacko and Esaup, fable one, feeble too. Let us here consider the casus, my dear little cousis (husstenhasstencaffincoffintussemtossemdamandamnacosaghcusaghhobixhatouxpeswchbechoscashlcarcarcaract) of the Ondt and the Gracehoper.
>
> (414)

Why does Joyce combine words (apologuise and spinooze), playfully allude to the Bible (Jacko and Esaup), pun on an Aesop fable (the Ondt and the Gracehopper), and combine words to create a cacophonous mishmash? Why torture language in this way?

E. E. Cummings' poem "anyone lived in a pretty how town" (1940) vexes us in a different way. We recognize the words, but not the syntax: "anyone lived in a pretty how town / (with up so floating many bells down) / spring summer autumn winter / he sang his didn't he danced his did" (1–4). Is "anyone" a pronoun or a noun? Is "how" an adverb, interrogative adverb, or an adjective? Are "didn't" and "did" verbs or nouns?

An excerpt from Gertrude Stein's self-described portrait "Cezanne" (1923) is fairly simple in terms of vocabulary and syntax:

> The Irish lady can say, that to-day is every day. Caesar can say that every day is to-day and they say that every day is as they say.
> In this way we have a place to stay and he was not met because he was settled to stay. When I said settled I meant settled to stay. When I said settled to stay I meant settled to stay Saturday. In this way a mouth is a mouth. In this way if in as a mouth if in as a mouth where, if in as a mouth where and there. Believe they have water too.
>
> (329)

However, while individual sentences make sense most of the time, they do not cohere. The cumulative effect is nonsense. She does not even seem to use words to convey meaning. Does she have another goal in mind?

We encounter challenging literature and art from this period, works that do not always use language to represent something we can recognize and easily interpret. But modernists are not alone. From unusual ancient metaphors to postmodern inventions, many writers challenge assumptions, innovate forms, and experiment with language. But why frustrate, even alienate readers? Why are we, at the same time, often drawn toward these difficult works? How do we make sense of prose and poetry that resists our familiar reading strategies?

KEY PASSAGES

Around the period of the Russian Revolution in 1917, a group of intellectuals, later called the "Russian Formalists," theorized the function of the "literary." Two schools of thought formed, and Viktor Shklovsky helped found the Society for the Study of Poetic Language, a collection of scholars who focused on form and technique. The timing of the group's formation is important, for as M. A. R. Habib points out, these formalists perceived "their opposition to traditional art as a political gesture" (197). Note, however, that they were not puppets of the revolution. They trained as literary scholars, and the Stalinist regime later suppressed them because their methods were not in line with totalitarian aims.

In "Art as Technique" (1917), Shklovsky argues against the notion that there are literary or poetic themes and subjects, and he asserts instead that what makes a work "literary" or even aesthetic is not the content, but the devices, procedures, and techniques a writer uses. He shifts our attention from *content* (what is represented) to *form* (how it is represented). The "literary" uses language in ways that other language does not. However, understanding *why* writers and artists produce works that draw our attention to form is essential. Shklovsky's redefinition of art's purpose will help us understand literary and artistic experiments that challenge our assumptions and conventional reading practices. Consider Shklovsky's iconic passage:

> Habitualization devours works, clothes, furniture, one's wife, and the fear of war. "If the whole complex lives of many people go on unconsciously, then such lives are as if they had never been." And art exists that one may recover the sensation of life; it exists to make one feel things, to make the stone *stony*. The purpose of art is to impart the sensation of things as they are perceived and not as they are known. The technique of art is to make objects "unfamiliar," to make forms difficult, to increase the difficulty and length of perception because the process of perception is an aesthetic end in itself and must be prolonged. *Art is a way of experiencing the artfulness of an object: the object is not important.*
>
> (778)

Shklovsky offers a theory of art that connects psychology, physiology, and aesthetics, and this combination requires some unpacking.

DISCUSSION

Shklovsky first identifies a problem: "Habitualization devours work, clothes, furniture, one's wife, and the fear of war. 'If the whole complex lives of many people go on unconsciously, then such lives are as if they had never been'" (778). He clarifies,

> If we start to examine the general laws of perception, we see that as perception becomes habitual, it becomes automatic. Thus, for example, all of our habits retreat into the area of the unconsciously automatic; if one remembers the sensations of holding a pen or of speaking in a foreign language for the first time and compares that with his feeling at performing the action for the ten thousandth time, he will agree with us.
>
> (778)

Our actions and perceptions have become mindless habits. What was once exciting and new passes without notice. We have grown numb and blind: "After we see an object several times, we begin to recognize it" (779). Recognition in this context is a liability, not a virtue. Why? Shklovsky insists that "the object is in front of us and we know about it, but we do not see it" (779). We may "recognize" an apple, but that just means we know it superficially.

He then offers a solution: art and the "literary" wake us up: "Art exists that one may recover the sensation of life; it exists to make one feel things, to make the stone *stony*" (778). Art helps us reexperience the person, place, object, and event. The verb "recover" is important, for it implies that we have lost what we once had, and what escapes us now is a keen awareness of those daily experiences, the effect they used to have on us. For example, over time a "stone" becomes abstract, a mere idea, because it has grown too familiar. However, art makes that "stone" tangible, as palpable as it was when we picked it up for the first time and sensed its texture, color, and heft.

Consider how Ezra Pound wakes us up in his short poem "In a Station of the Metro": "The apparition of these faces in the crowd; / Petals on a wet, black bough." What could be more ordinary than countless faces in a subway? But Pound helps us recover the sensation of seeing these subway riders for the first time. He draws our attention to the ethereal, almost ghostlike quality of their faces. They are, perhaps, a flash of color in a dreary place. By equating faces with petals, the familiar scene on a metro becomes unfamiliar. Invisible qualities and attributes suddenly appear.

Just as art helps us recognize the beauty of ordinary experiences or even regain the "fear of war," Shklovsky shifts the focus to perception itself, to the experience of reading and viewing:

> **The purpose of art is to impart the sensation of things as they are perceived and not as they are known. The technique of art is to make objects 'unfamiliar,' to make forms difficult, to increase the difficulty and length of perception because the process of perception is an aesthetic end in itself and must be prolonged.**
>
> (778)

How does art help the reader experience the *process* of encountering the object or experience? For Shklovsky, art draws our attention to the means and manner of a sentence (or a painting, work of sculpture, or bar of music). Art makes us slow down and work because "the language of poetry is, then, a difficult, roughened, impeded language" (783). The difficult forms and labor-intensive language encourage us to pause and ponder and feel. Note that the purpose of reading literature or viewing art is not to learn something. Shklovsky divorces the aesthetic experience from utilitarian or pragmatic concerns. Instead, art's purpose is to engage us in the very act of exploring, pondering, feeling, questioning, and thinking. The means have become the ends, and that is why he concludes that, "art is a way of experiencing the artfulness of an object; the object is not important" (778). The process and pleasure of discerning, perceiving, and looking at the object count more than the object itself.

For example, when we think of a root cellar, the image that may come to mind has grown vague and abstract. But when we read these lines, another process takes place: "Nothing would sleep in that cellar, dank as a ditch, / Bulbs broke out of boxes hunting for chinks in the dark" (Roethke 1–2). What makes these lines "literary" is that they "impart the sensation of things as they are perceived" (Shklovsky 778). How so? Roethke's use of alliteration not only draws attention to the words as words, but words as sounds: The repetition of the "d," "b," and "k" does not just convey information; they transform reading into a sensory experience, an aesthetic event. Or let us return to that short passage from *Finnagans Wake*. Instead of using the word "apologize," Joyce writes, "I apologuise" to draw our attention to the way that saying "sorry" is a kind of mask or evasion. We are hiding something when we express regret. Deciphering the word—discovering the art and craft of the diction—is an aesthetic experience. Plus, the phrase "I apologuise" makes us aware of words as words. We become conscious of the sounds of words in the same way an abstract painting might make us aware of line, color, texture, and shape. Pushing the concept to the extreme, asserting that "the object is not important" suggests that the meaning of "I apologuise" may not even be relevant. Instead, recognizing the artfulness of combining those two words, taking time to figure out its meaning, and noting the pleasure of just saying "I apologuise" may be enough because this process prolongs the time we spend on the words.

In short, literary language can "defamiliarize" or "make strange" ordinary objects and experiences. Literary devices draw our attention to the workings of language as language. Art changes the very way that we perceive the world around us and prolongs the experience of reading and watching.

POTENTIAL PROJECTS

As we have seen, Shklovsky encourages us to explain how a text estranges and defamiliarizes the familiar and ordinary. Shklovsky wants us to focus on *how* a text conveys meaning instead of merely trying to summarize *what* a text suggests or implies. Uri Margolin highlights this attention to specific literary strategies:

> Natural language is defamiliarized through figures of sound and sense, such as meter and wordplay, and worn-out literary conventions through depriving them of their motivation, 'laying them bare,' so to speak, and parodying them. Our habitual perception of reality is disrupted through distorting the temporal and causal order of events and the logical order of information and by seeing the familiar from a nonstandard perspective such as that of an outsider, a child, or a deranged person. Works of art are assemblages of materials and devices, writers are craftsmen using devices to create certain effects, and scholars should single out the devices and explain their structure and aesthetic functioning.

In other words, when we discuss a text, we explain how its figures of speech, narrative structure, point of view, genre, and literary devices that include imagery, diction, syntax, rhythm, meter, rhyme, allusion, character, and setting make the familiar strange, the ordinary new, and the unconscious conscious. Always ask, "How do literary devices help us experience the person, place, object, or event differently or as if for the first time?" Consider these projects, uses, and questions:

Make sense of experimental literature

Shklovsky's theory grows out of European modernism, a movement that is often defined by radical experiments with language and form. As we have seen, authors like James Joyce, E. E. Cummings, and Gertrude Stein, as well as their fellow travelers like William Faulkner, Virginia Woolf, T. S. Eliot, Wallace Stevens, Marianne Moore, H. D. Franz Kafka, John Dos Passos, Ernest Hemingway, Eugene O'Neill, Marcel Proust, among so many more, offer ample opportunities to discuss texts that estrange and defamiliarize. Note, too, that experimentation did not end (or even begin) with the modernists. Late 20th-century and contemporary literature and pop culture often seek to jolt us awake by playing with form.

A useful first step is to explain that the writer's subject matter is not particularly exotic: a tea party, a christening, a bench on a train platform, a pastry. Then explain how the author uses literary devices to "recover the sensation" of that experience, "impart the sensation of things as they are perceived," make the object or experience unfamiliar, increase "the difficulty and length of perception," help us experience "*the artfulness of an object*," or uncover the beauty of the ordinary.

For example, while far less ordinary than subway passengers or a moth flying toward the moon, many fear that representations of the Holocaust have become routine and familiar. We have grown too comfortable with black and white images of orphaned children, rail coaches with pleading faces, and bodies stacked like cord wood. In this context, Art Spiegelman's *Maus I* and *Maus II* use cats and mice as proxies for Nazis and Jews in graphic novels that disrupt our habitual ways of thinking about Jews, Germans, survivors, victims, artists, and their roles and relationships in the Holocaust. The form itself—graphic novel, animal metaphors, self-reflexive commentary—forces us out of our conventional ways of understanding the Holocaust, and the work encourages us to reflect on the means and manner of representation. The shock of drawings in sequenced boxes and dialogue bubbles sensitize us to several important questions: How should one represent the Holocaust? Should images of the Holocaust provide aesthetic pleasure? What does it mean to survive the Holocaust? As you analyze a text you have chosen, make the same critical moves: Draw attention to the literary devices the writer uses to defamiliarize the ordinary, recover lost sensations, and prolong the aesthetic experience.

Extend an insight

Scholars often extend an insight or apply an observation to another field. For example, even though Shklovsky focuses on literary texts, you can apply Shklovsky's notion of defamiliarizing to the visual arts, architecture, film, dance, sculpture, and theater. Echoing a question we used before, how does the painting, building, film, dance, sculpture, or play help us experience a person, place, object, or experience differently or as if for the first time? What strategies do these works of art employ in order to estrange or defamiliarize what has grown boring and mundane?

For example, how does the Pompidou Center in Paris encourage us to rethink the fundamental assumptions of what a building is supposed to look like? How does Cy Twombly's painting "Leda and the Swan" "impart the sensation of things as they are perceived and not as they are known" (778)? How does Constantin Brâncuşi's "Bird in Space" help us experience anew the beauty of a bird in flight? How does Luis Buñuel's *Un Chien Andalou* "increase the difficulty and length of perception" (778)? Of course, you will need to speak the language of the discipline when you discuss art, film, architecture, theater, etc. but in every case you will explain how those artistic devices, techniques, and strategies defamiliarize and estrange what has become common and habitual.

WORKS CITED

Cummings, E. E. "Anyone Lived in a Pretty How Town." *Complete Poems: 1904–1962*, edited by George J. Firmage, Liveright, 1991, p. 515.

Habib, M. A. R. *Literary Criticism from Plato to the Present: An Introduction.* Wiley-Blackwell, 2011.

Joyce, James. *Finnegans Wake.* Penguin, 1999.

Margolin, Uri. "Russian Formalism." *The Online Johns Hopkins Guide to Literary Theory and Criticism*, 2nd ed., edited by Michael Groden, Martin Kreiswirth, and Imre Szeman, Johns Hopkins UP, 2012.

Pound, Ezra. "In a Station of the Metro." *Personae: The Collected Poems of Ezra Pound*, Liveright, 1926, p. 109.

Roethke, Theodore. "Root Cellar." *The Collected Poems of Theodore Roethke*, Anchor, 1975, p. 36.

Shklovsky, Viktor. "Art as Technique." *The Critical Tradition: Classic Texts and Contemporary Trends*, edited by David H. Richter, Bedford/St. Martin's, 2007, pp. 775–784.

Stein, Gertrude. "Cezanne." *Selected Writings of Gertrude Stein*, edited by Carl Van Vechten, Vintage, 1990, p. 329.

CHAPTER 29

Questioning gender binaries

> For what makes a woman is a specific social relation to a man, a relation that we have previously called servitude.
>
> (Monique Wittig 20)

PROBLEMS, PUZZLES, AND QUESTIONS

In Ursula Le Guin's sci-fi novel *The Left Hand of Darkness* (1969), Genly Ai is a male emissary who travels to the planet Gethen to invite the inhabitants to join a coalition. He struggles understanding the culture, for they are ambisexual. Sex is fluid. Inhabitants are sexually "inactive" and androgynous until a period called "kemmer" occurs, at which point hormones temporarily decide one's sex. Gethenians "do not know whether they will be the male or the female, and have no choice in the matter" (91). The absence of fixed gender not only leads to a more peaceful existence, but epistemologically speaking, these ambisexuals know more than those who are strictly male or female. In fact, Genly Ai's masculine ways of thinking and acting prevent useful communication. It is only after time spent with the native Estraven that Ai learns to navigate and form loving relationships with the Gethenians. Although groundbreaking in the way that the narrative explores the effects of gender coding and roles, the novel invites us to ask whether or not Le Guin escapes binary notions of gender by celebrating ambisexuality. Does ambisexuality offer a third category or merely "menwomen," a blend of masculinity and femininity?

Anne Garréta's *Sphinx* (1986) describes a memory of a love story between two characters, a young theology student and an exotic dancer who meet at a nightclub. We only know them by "I" (*je* in French) and "A★★★." What is remarkable is the fact that Garréta composes the narrative without coherent and consistent gender markers, no mean feat in a language like French whose gender agreements permeate every aspect of the language. Garréta plays as well with pronouns, and the narrator will alternate gender markers when describing the same noun. At no point do we learn each character's sex, and we discern little of outward appearance beyond learning that one character is black and the other white. The novel encourages us to ponder how we make sense of relationships when we are free of gender strictures, and the narrative compels us to interrogate our gender assumptions. What do we conclude when we read *je*'s narration?

> I would spend my nights waiting for A★★★ to appear on the stage of the Eden, a cabaret on the Left Bank. And who wouldn't have been enamored of that svelte frame, that musculature seemingly sculpted by Michelangelo, that satiny skin far superior to anything I had ever known?
>
> (1–2)

Where is our evidence that A★★★ is male or female? Do we learn any more when they have sex the first time: "Crotches crossed and sexes mixed, I no longer knew how to distinguish anything" (55)?

Note as well the popularization of transgender literature. Recent book lists draw attention to fiction and memoirs that focus on transgender identities: Severo Sarduy's *Cobra* (1972), Leslie Feinberg's *Stone Butch Blues* (1993), Kate Bornstein's *Gender Outlaw* (1994), K. M. Szpara's *Transcendent: The Year's Best Transgender Speculative Fiction* (2016), Alex Gino's *George* (2015), and Meredith Russo's *If I Was Your Girl* (2016), among many more. Do these works subvert binary notions of gender, or do they gain their identity by presenting themselves as the new oppositional term that confronts heterosexuality? Do they foreground the constructed nature of gender and sex, or do they embrace an essentialist notion of identity? Is identity a matter of self-realization, self-fashioning, or social construction?

All these examples foreground the various ways we discuss sexual and gender identity. We recognize the earnest attempts to question binary ways of thinking about identity, yet oppositional pairs creep in. We look for a third way in form and content, but others want to undermine the entire way we discuss sexual relationships. While some want to multiply identity categories, others want to erase them.

KEY PASSAGES

Initially, a lecture delivered at the "30th Anniversary Conference of the Second Sex" held at New York University, Monique Wittig's "One Is Not Born a Woman" (1979) commemorates Simone de Beauvoir's claim that "One is not born, but becomes a woman. No biological, psychological, or economic fate determines the figure that the human female presents in society; it is civilization as a whole that produces this creature, intermediate between male and eunuch, which is described as feminine" (qtd. in Wittig 10). That is, there are no essential or permanent qualities attached to being a man or a woman. Wittig builds on de Beauvoir's idea that our culture constructs what it means to be a "woman" and a "man," extending her argument to suggest that we need to undermine the very categories of sex and gender. Identity results less from essential biological qualities than social relationships, and this shift to a socially constructed identity is especially useful when we encounter texts that seek to escape identity categories all together.

> A materialist feminist approach to women's oppression destroys the idea that women are a "natural group."
>
> (9)
>
> Thus it is our historical task, and only ours, to define what we call oppression in materialist terms, to make it evident that women are a class, which is to say that the category "woman" as well as the category "man" are political and economic categories not eternal ones. Our fight aims to suppress men as a class, not through a genocidal, but a political struggle. Once the class "men" disappears, "women" as a class will disappear as well, for there are no slaves without masters. Our first task, it seems, is to always thoroughly dissociate "women" (the class within which we fight) and "woman," the myth. For "woman" does not exist for us: it is only an imaginary formation, while "women" is the product of a social relationship.
>
> (15)
>
> Without class and class consciousness there are no real subjects, only alienated individuals. For women to answer the question of the individual subject in materialist terms is first to show, as the lesbians and feminists did, that

> supposedly "subjective," "individual," "private" problems are in fact social problems, class problems; that sexuality is not for women an individual and subjective expression, but a social institution of violence. But once we have shown that all so-called personal problems are in fact class problems, we will still be left with the question of the subject of each singular woman—not the myth, but each one of us.
>
> (19)
>
> For what makes a woman is a specific social relation to a man, a relation that we have previously called servitude, a relation which implies personal and physical obligation as well as economic obligation.
>
> (20)
>
> At this point, let us say that a new personal and subjective definition for all humankind can only be found beyond the categories of sex (woman and man) and that the advent of individual subjects demands first destroying the categories of sex, ending the use of them.
>
> (19–20)
>
> Lesbian is the only concept I know of which is beyond the categories of sex (woman and man), because the designated subject (lesbian) is *not* a woman, either economically, or politically, or ideologically.
>
> (20)

Wittig asks us to explore the relationship that women have with other women, men, and social systems. She encourages us to ask whether it matters if we conceive of women as individuals or members of a class, a natural group or a political category, a myth or a reality. And if gender and sexual oppositions oppress, then what is the solution?

DISCUSSION

When Wittig argues that "a materialist feminist approach to women's oppression destroys the idea that women are a 'natural group'" (9), she asks us to process two ideas. First, by referencing "materialist feminist," Wittig rejects the argument that biology, metaphysical forces, or personal choice, what we might call "non-materialist" approaches, determine gender differences. Instead, a "material feminist" insists that material conditions—social arrangements, hierarchies, cultural practices, institutions, modes of production, language, etc.—construct our identity and define our relationships with others. In short, gender and sex are social constructions, not givens. And by "natural group," Wittig is referring to the idea popularized by many feminists in the 1970s that women connect with each other in ways that transcend context, that women share inherent and enviable qualities, particularly associated with the female body. Wittig questions this essentialist idea that women have an innate and intrinsic connection with one another that cuts across time and space. For Wittig, our culture invents and defines the categories "woman" and "man" because the web of economic, legal, and social institutions constructs gender and sexual identity. Our particular sociohistorical context shapes how we conceive of "man" and "woman."

While women are not a natural group, Wittig insists they are a class. What is the difference? As noted above, when we say that women are a "natural group," we are saying that all women share some essential qualities. When we say that women are a "class," we are asserting that their identity depends on a social relationship that could change. Therefore, when Wittig says that "what makes a woman is a specific social relation to a man, a relation that we have previously called servitude" (20), she contends that a person is a "woman" because she is in the position of servitude. Conversely, a person is a "man" when that person is in a position of power who can demand certain personal, physical, and economic obligations. In short, our social position determines whether or not we are a "man" or a "woman" in the same way people are upper middle class, middle class, or working class. If men and women are political and economic categories of people, then it follows that our goal is to "suppress men as a class, not through a genocidal, but a political struggle. Once the class 'men' disappears, 'women' as a class will disappear as well, for there are no slaves without masters" (15).

But how do we eliminate "men" as a category? First, Wittig insists that "Our first task, it seems, is to always thoroughly dissociate 'women' (the class within which we fight) and 'woman,' the myth" (15). In other words, "woman" refers an idealized person who has certain essential qualities, what Wittig calls "an imaginary formation" (15). On the other hand, "women" refers to those who are subservient to others. When Wittig maintains that "'woman' is there to confuse us, to hide the reality 'women' (16), she is saying that we need to resist the idea that individual women share innate qualities with other women, but we *do* need to preserve the idea that women are "women" because they share the same material conditions and subservient relationship to men. In sum, eliminate the mythic and essentialist "woman," but keep the politically and socially constructed category "women."

The second task is to recognize one's social position. The moment women recognize that relationships, institutions, language, cultural practices, etc. subjugate them, the moment when women realize that "supposedly 'subjective,' 'individual,' 'private' problems are in fact social problems, class problems" (19), women become "real subjects" in the sense that they are active agents. This change in thinking, from conceiving of sex and gender as "an individual and subjective expression" (19) to framing sex and gender as a "social institution of violence" (19) allows women to align themselves with other women at the level of shared social conditions in particular contexts and actively work to alter the relationships. But Wittig is not asking women to join forces and argue from a position of a disenfranchised class. She is not interested in positioning women against men in a fight for equal rights, more freedom, and more opportunities. Such a move will merely reinforce the opposition. She has something more radical in mind.

Wittig's solution is to eliminate the social categories of men and women that support the very idea of heterosexuality:

> Let us say that a new personal and subjective definition for all humankind can only be found beyond the categories of sex (woman and man) and that the advent of individual subjects demands first destroying the categories of sex, ending the use of them.
>
> (19–20)

In other words, as long as we talk in terms of "man" and "woman," we cannot escape a heterosexual framework which, for Wittig, is the source of oppression because heterosexuality "produces the doctrine of the difference between the sexes to justify this oppression" (20). Instead, she is encouraging us to think beyond binary relationships and categories of opposition. It is less a matter of reversing the binary structure of sex and gender than it is dispensing with the binaries themselves.

What would destroying the categories of sex look like? Wittig offers one idea: "Lesbian is the only concept I know of which is beyond the categories of sex (woman and man), because the designated subject (lesbian) is *not* a woman, either economically, or politically, or ideologically" (20). However, Wittig is not asking us all to become literal lesbians. Rather, she is speaking of lesbianism as a concept as well as a social and political category that escapes the logic of heterosexuality because to be lesbian is not to be "man" or "woman." While lesbianism is one concept, there may be others that function in the same way. By analogy, let us return to the concept of zombies (discussed in the chapter on alterity). As I explain there, zombies escape the logic of *either/or* by being both dead and alive while simultaneously being neither dead nor alive. They are *undecidable*, and as a result, they disrupt the conceptual order. The category "lesbian" works the same way. The lesbian escapes the logic of *either/or*, and as a result, lesbianism subverts heterosexuality. Are there other identity categories that function the same way?

In sum, Wittig rejects the notion that we are inherently "man" and "woman," and she encourages us to view the issue of sexual difference as a class struggle. To resolve this conflict, we must destroy the very categories of "man" and "woman," and if we succeed, then heterosexuality as an institution and practice loses its justification and force, and women are free of personal, economic, and physical obligations.

POTENTIAL PROJECTS

Wittig's project is ambitious, even utopian. We have to admit as well that literature, film, and other cultural productions cannot by themselves eliminate heterosexuality or directly alter the social system. Therefore, as readers and viewers of literature, film, and art, how can we use Wittig's theory? Because Wittig is interested in conceiving of identities "beyond the categories of sex" (19–20), literature and cultural representations can help us imagine what those alternatives might be.

Dissociate women from woman

Wittig asserts that our first task is to "always thoroughly dissociate 'women' (the class within which we fight) and 'woman,' the myth" (15). In other words, Wittig describes at least two ways to think about portrayals of women: as a "natural group" or as a social class. Therefore, explore how a literary work or cultural representation presents men and women. Even if the text celebrates women and, say, a capacity for empathy, cooperation, or alternative epistemologies, does the work suggest that biology, metaphysical forces, or personal choice determine those qualities? Or, does the text embrace a materialist approach and root sexual and gender differences in material conditions—social arrangements, hierarchies, cultural practices, institutions, modes of production, language, etc.? And what is the effect of those portrayals? Does the text reinforce gender difference and binary ways of thinking of sex, or does the work subvert heterosexuality and the social systems that render women as servants to men? Put more simply, does the work encourage us to put quotation marks around women and men, naturalize the categories, or offer yet another alternative?

Identify an identity beyond traditional categories

Wittig notes that "Lesbian is the only concept I know of which is beyond the categories of sex (woman and man), because the designated subject (lesbian) is *not* a woman, either economically, or politically, or ideologically" (20). As we discussed above, Wittig does not want us to become literal lesbians as much as she wants alternatives to binary thinking. Your task is to find texts that offer alternative identities. Discuss texts that redefine the "social relation" that women have with men or even destroy "heterosexuality as a social system which is based on the oppression of women by men and which produces the doctrine of the difference between the sexes to justify this oppression" (20). As we noticed in my examples in the PPQ section and as Wittig's own creative work suggests, we should consider form as well as content. For example, in *Les Guérillères*, Wittig employs the feminine plural pronoun *elles* to "universalize the point of view of *elles*. The goal of this approach is not to feminize the world but to make the categories of sex obsolete in language. I, therefore, set up *elles* in the text as the absolute subject of the world" (85). And in *The Opoponax*, Wittig uses the impersonal French pronoun *on* "that is neither gendered nor numbered," to "locate the characters outside of the social division by sexes and annul it for the duration of the book" (83). Therefore, pay particular attention to *how* a work plays with form to imagine identities "beyond the categories of sex" (20).

WORKS CITED

Garréta, Anne. *Sphinx*. 1986. Translated by Emma Ramadan, Deep Vellum, 2015.
Le Guin, Ursula. *The Left Hand of Darkness*. 1969, Ace, 2000.
Wittig, Monique. *The Straight Mind and Other Essays*, Beacon, 1992.

CHAPTER 30

Building on another's work
Identifying key concepts

> There is then creative reading as well as creative writing. When the mind is braced by labor and invention, the page of whatever book we read becomes luminous with manifold allusion.
>
> (Ralph Waldo Emerson 90)

WHAT IS CREATIVE READING?

You have encountered twenty-nine chapters that describe how to use key passages to make sense of literature, film, art, performances, and daily experiences, but those chapters just invite you to learn more. The more concepts and terms you collect—the more languages you learn to speak—the more prepared you are to understand what you read, watch, and experience. The next step is for you to identify, clarify, and apply concepts you find useful, interesting, insightful, and productive. This chapter describes how to recognize "productive passages" that allow you to be a creative reader so that, as Emerson declares, "the page of whatever book we read becomes luminous with manifold allusion" (90).

WHAT IS A PRODUCTIVE PASSAGE?

What makes one passage more "productive" than another? What qualities does a passage have that allows us to use it as a lens, framework, system, or method? Consider two passages found in Eva Hoffman's "The New Nomads" (1998). If our task is to understand the immigrant's experience, make sense of those in exile, or understand a migrant's situation, then which passage below helps us the most? Hoffman argues that

> The new nomadism is different from other Diasporas. It exists in a decentered world, one in which the wanderers no longer trace and retrace a given territory or look to any one symbolic locus of meaning.
>
> (57)

She also asserts that

> At the same time, we need a conception of a shared world, a world in which we exist by virtue of shared interests rather than mutual alienation, to which we can bring our chosen commitments and hopes.
>
> (62)

What can we *do* with each paragraph? What language offers us a lens, a way of seeing, or a method to understand those who wander?

I hope you chose the first passage. Why? Admittedly, the second passage encourages us to theorize, to think of ways that we can connect with other people in a positive way, but Hoffman does not offer us a theory or a concept, only a desire or plea. We might accept her invitation to conceive of a shared world, and we might be able to discuss how a work promotes "shared interests rather than mutual alienation," but this passage is not "productive" in the sense that she presents an interpretive framework or lens that we can use to make sense of another's experience or text.

On the other hand, the first passage defines a term. We learn what a "new nomad" is, and she describes its qualities. A number of projects come to mind: we can compare new nomads with old nomads. We can better understand the situation these nomads face. We can make sense of an immigration narrative by using terms like "decentered" to describe immigrants who no longer have a home or stable way to interpret their own experience. In fact, Hoffman helps us understand what a "decentered world" even means: "one in which the wanderers no longer trace and retrace a given territory or look to any one symbolic locus of meaning" (57). In short, she offers us a theory of nomadism—definitions, categories, frameworks—and she presents specialized vocabulary to describe her theory.

Consider another passage in Slavoj Žižek's *Looking Awry* (1991):

> What the fantasy stages is not a scene in which our desire is fulfilled, fully satisfied, but on the contrary, a scene that realizes, stages, the desire as such. The fundamental point of psychoanalysis is that desire is not something given in

> advance, but something that has to be constructed—and it is precisely the role of fantasy to give the coordinates of the subject's desire, to specify its object, to locate the position the subject assumes in it. It is only through fantasy that the subject is constituted as desiring: *through fantasy, we learn how to desire*.
>
> (6)

This passage is productive because Žižek defines fantasy and psychoanalysis' foundational premise, describes how fantasy functions, and articulates particular mechanisms. These acts—defining a concept, describing a function or method, delineating a process—enable us to apply his claims to any number of texts and experiences.

For example, if our desires are constructed, not found, and if fantasy is a framework that creates desire itself as Žižek asserts, then consider the role of advertising. Advertisements do not respond to our fantasies; they produce them. They give "the coordinates of the subject's desire, to specify its object, to locate the position the subject assumes in it" (6). An advertisement for Asiana Airlines alternately portrays a man and woman sitting in a first-class lounge chair atop a flowing piece of blue, red, yellow, and white fabric that meanders over iconic world sites. A female Korean flight attendant prepares a lavish spread of smoked salmon, cheese, and stuffed olives on crisp white linens. Another pair of attendants throw magic dust into the night sky. Yet another woman tucks a man in bed and smiles approvingly. This advertisement gives "coordinates of the subject's desire" by focusing on mobility, food, a particular kind of beauty, and the quest to be the center of another's attention. The advertisement locates "the position the subject assumes in it" by inviting us to imagine being pampered by gorgeous and caring maternal figures. Using Žižek's concepts, we may conclude that this advertisement does not respond to our orientalist fantasies but constructs and defines them. Literary narratives function in the same way, as do, at a subtler level, the assumptions we have about gender, race, class, sexuality, behavior, values, social order, etc. In short, elements outside ourselves construct fantasies, preexisting social frameworks, that teach us what and how to desire, thus blurring internal and external forces. Žižek's productive passage enables these interpretive acts by defining fantasy and desire and describing how the process of fantasy works. His definitions help us make sense of how advertisements work on us.

Passages are productive so long as they supply us with a way to understand the meaning, significance, function, workings, relationships, and value of another text or experience. A theory can be as simple as a metaphor that one of Edwidge Danticat's characters employs: "When you write, it's like braiding your hair. Taking a handful of coarse unruly strands and attempting to bring them unity" (220). Or, our theory may come from a book-length work like Karl Marx's *Capital* that describes in complex detail the limitations of a particular economic system. I am not suggesting that one sentence is equal to a book-length treatise, but both offer a way to see anew what we read, watch, and experience. They only differ in degree and explanatory power.

WHAT IS THE NEXT STEP?

First, choose a "theory text." The most obvious sources are theory anthologies like *The Norton Anthology of Theory and Criticism* (2018), *Literary Theory: An Anthology* (2017), *The Critical Tradition* (2006), or *Modern Literary Theory: A Reader* (2001), but we encounter theories in stand-alone essays, critical monographs, and even literary texts themselves. You need not limit yourself to literary theory. Nearly every discipline, from psychology, sociology, and philosophy to biology, physics, and economics, offers concepts that we can use to make sense of or evaluate cultural representations.

Second, read with an eye on productive passages. Instead of merely learning what an author suggests about people, places, things, emotions, psychic processes, identity, power, cultural practices, beauty, form, relationships, etc. ask instead, "How can I *use* a particular explanation, concept, or definition to interpret or judge the value of another text or experience?" Read pragmatically. A passage's value relates to its ability to help us see with new eyes and understanding.

Third, follow my lead and produce your own "theory chapter":

- Identify problems, puzzles, and questions we need to solve or answer.
- Introduce and contextualize the key passages. Help us understand the passages' source and the larger conversation the work addresses.
- Clarify the passages in detail, almost line by line. Remember, you are not describing a school of criticism, an entire work, or everything a particular theorist believes. Instead, you are making a particular concept or framework intelligible for a wider audience.
- Describe a few sample projects. As noted above, "How can we use this explanation, concept, or definition to make sense of particular texts, cultural practices, or experiences?" Craft assignments for your classmates.

If we return to our foreign language metaphor, recall that we read with a desire to learn a new language, join a different conversation and community that require us to think, read, write, and speak differently. We connect to texts, contexts, and other readers in new ways, and in the process, we enrich our experience of what we read, watch, and encounter.

WORKS CITED

Asiana Airlines Global TV Commercial 2011. www.youtube.com/watch?v=jRV7-nH_maE. Accessed 29 April 2018.

Danticat, Edwidge. *Krik? Krak!* Vintage, 1996.

Emerson, Ralph Waldo. "The American Scholar." *Selected Essays*, edited by Larzer Ziff, Penguin, 1987, pp. 83–106.

Hoffman, Eva. "The New Nomads." *Letters of Transit*, edited by André Aciman, New, 1999, pp. 35–63.

Žižek, Slavoj. *Looking Awry: An Introduction to Jacques Lacan through Popular Culture.* MIT, 1993.

Index

accommodation 161–5
adaptation 204–11
alterity 95–6, 98–100
Althusser, Louis 15–21
American Disabilities Act 183
Anzaldua, Gloria 24, 68, 136
Appiah, Kwame Anthony 22–8
appropriation/re-appropriation 97, 104, 106, 148, 201–2, 204–7, 209, 211; *see also* transculturation
arborescent systems 110–11, 114–15
Arnold, Matthew 3
attunement 168–9
Austin, J. L. 31–6, 73
autoethnographic text 199–200

Bakhtin, Mikhail 40–5
Barthes, Roland 47–52, 165
Bartholomae, David 3, 7
Baudrillard, Jean 53–60
belatedness 80, 82–3; *see also* trauma
believing game 11–12
Bentham, Jeremy 131–4; *see also* Panopticon
Bhabha, Homi 63–8, 148
binary relations: binary logic and liminality 67; gender binaries 71, 75, 100, 229–30, 234; binary systems 110–12, 114–15; disrupting human/nonhuman binaries 145–8; 168–71

Bloom, Harold 3
boundaries/borders: subversion of social boundaries 44–5, reality and representations 57–9; between identities 64–8; consumer and producer 104–5; subversive potential of shock 128; fantasy and reality 139–42; human and nonhuman 146–51, 167–72; text and context 154–5; sexuality 216–19
Butler, Judith 71–6

carnival/carnivalesque 38–45; *see also* grotesque realism
Caruth, Cathy 78–83
class: unofficial culture 41, 44; as conceptual category 63; and race 88–91; as producers 103–5; homosocial relations 215–16; women as a class 231–5
classic 43, 48–9, 161–3, 165
clôtural reading 95–9
community 7–8, 45, 63–5, 133, 198, 200
compoundedness 87, 89–91; *see also* intersectionality
concept: role of theory 3–6; value to scholars 9–12; effect of 177–80; as subversive strategy 234
conceptual metaphor 176–80

conceptual order and framework: disruptions of 81, 93, 235
consciousness: false consciousness 11, 15–16, 55, 120; formation of *mestiza* consciousness 68; trauma 79–80; double consciousness 117–22; shock 124–6; the uncanny 139–40
constative 31–2, 34, 73; *see also* performative
consumer: reader as consumer 47, 49, 51; consumer as poacher 102–3, 105–6; consumer of prepared experience 191–5
contact zone 198–202
context 32, 36, 73–4, 153, 155–8, 208–9
creative reading 237
Crenshaw, Kimberlé 86–91
Critchley, Simon 94–100
criticism 1–3, 5–6
Culler, Jonathan 34

Davis, Lennard 182–3
de Beauvoir, Simone 231
de Certeau, Michel 102–7
de Man, Paul 94
deconstruction 4, 95; *see also clôtural* reading
defamiliarize 225–8
degradation 41, 43, 45
Deleuze, Gilles and Félix Guattari 110–15
Derrida, Jacques 4, 29, 36, 95; *see also clôtural* reading
desire 43, 214–17, 238–9
deterritorialization 112–14
disability 181–7
discourse 7, 34, 47, 74, 156
discrimination 85–91, 118, 121–2
double-consciousness 119–22
doubting game 12
drag 71, 75–6; *see also* Judith Butler
Du Bois, W.E.B. 118–22

Eagleton, Terry 45
Eco, Umberto 51
ecology 168, 170
Elbow, Peter 11–12
essentialism 63, 65, 89, 100, 230–1, 233
evaluation 2

fantasy 57, 107, 139–42, 238–9
Foer, Jonathan Safran 35, 47
Felski, Rita 4, 124–9
Foucault, Michel 71, 131–5
Freud, Sigmund 79, 138–43
Fuss, Diana 145–50

gender identity 71–3, 230–1
genre 206–07
Girard, René 217
Greenblatt, Stephen 153 8
Griffin, Susan 109, 137–8
grotesque realism 40–3

Harris, Joseph 8
hermeneutics of suspicion 54, 58
homophobia 214–16, 218–19
homosexuality 73–4, 215–19
homosocial 214–19; *see also* Eve Sedgwick
Howe, Susan 35, 46, 109
hybridity 67–8, 121

identity: cultural narratives 22–6; collective 24–8; hybridity 62, 65–8, 121; performing gender 70–3; intersecting identities 84–9; decentralized identities 112–15; human and nonhuman 146–8; disability 183; subverting and conceptualizing 230–6; women vs. woman 232–6; *see also* essentialism
ideology 11, 15–19, 42, 54, 103, 155
indeterminate and interdependencies 66, 98, 109, 141, 163, 168, 171
interpellation 16–19

interpretation 1–2, 4–5, 35, 50–1, 95–6, 105–6, 161–4, 208
intersectional/intersectionality 85–7, 89–91
interstices 63–5
intersubjective 63, 168–71

jargon 10
jouissance 50

Kermode, Frank 161–5
Kristeva, Julia 35, 109
Kroeber, Karl 167–73

Lakoff, George and Mark Johnson 176–80
Leitch, Vincent 11
lesbian 231–2, 234–6
liminality 63, 67
logocentrism 96, 98
Longmore, Paul 186
Lyotard, Jean-François 145

male bonding 215–18
materialist feminism 231–2
memory and antimemory 78, 111, 113–15, 140–1, 209
mimicry 148; *see also* boundaries and borders
Mitchell, David T. and Sharon L. Snyder 183–7
multiculturalism 65
multidimensionality 86, 89–90
multiplicity 47, 49, 110, 113

narrative arc 25, 28
narrative prosthesis 183–6
new historicism 153
nomad 103, 105–6, 113, 115, 237–8

otherness 94–5, 97, 100, 184

Panopticon 131–5
paratexts 192, 194, 206
parody 21, 200, 208, 226

patriarchy 71, 214–17
Percy, Walker 190–5
Perez, Gilberto 5
performative 31–6, 72–4
plaisir 50
poaching reader 103–7
postcolonial 63, 65–7, 115, 142, 148, 199
power 104, 131–5, 156, 187, 193, 200, 209
Pratt, Mary Louise 198–203
presencing 64, 66
psychoanalysis 238

Rabaté, Jean-Michel 50
readerly 47–51, 165
repression 71, 129, 139–43, 145, 216; *see also* uncanny
rhizome 110–15
Rorty, Richard 3
Rubin, Gayle 217

Said, Edward 136
Sanders, Julie 206–11
Scholes, Robert 1–2, 4, 155
scripts 24–7; *see also* identity
Searle, John R. 36
Sedgwick, Eve 214–19
Shklovsky, Viktor 222–7
shock 123–8
simulation 54–5, 57–9; *see also* hyperreality
sovereignty: sovereign individual 190–5; sovereign knower 193–4; sovereign relationship 195
spectacle 132–3
subject position 17, 66, 89, 134, 233–4, 239
subjects/subjectivity: relationship to ideology 14–19; hybridity 63–5; gender 71–2, 74, 231–4; relationship to systems and social structures 110–12; relationship to power 133; relationship to

nonhuman 168–9; fantasy 239;
    see also identity
surveillance 131–3
symbolic packaging 192,
    194–5

theory 3–5, 178–80, 191, 193, 240
transculturation 199–203
trauma 77–83

uncanny 137–43
uncanny valley 147
undecidability 93–4, 141, 235

Wittig, Monique 231–6
writerly 47–51, 165

Žižek, Slavoj 238–9
zombies 93, 147, 235